AMERICA'S
GREATEST
DEPRESSION

AMERICA'S GREATEST DEPRESSION 1929-1941

Lester V. Chandler

ATLANTA UNIVERSITY CENTER

HARPER & ROW, PUBLISHERS
NEW YORK, EVANSTON, AND LONDON

America's Greatest Depression, 1929–1941
Copyright © 1970 by Lester V. Chandler

LIBRARY OF CONGRESS CATALOG CARD NUMBER: 79-108407

Contents

Preface

Three decades have now elapsed since the end of the great depression that swept the Western world during the 1930s and lasted a dozen years in the United States. Some of us still remember the depression vividly; but to the great majority of Americans who were very young at the time or were born later, it is as remote as the Civil War, or perhaps even the Revolutionary War. Some react with disbelief: "It couldn't have happened here!" But it did, and it is one of the great landmarks not only in American history but also in the history of the Western world. After it, things could never again be quite the same, even after the end of the world war that it helped to precipitate.

Volumes would be required to deal adequately with the profound effects of the depression on economic, political, and social thinking; on attitudes, policies, and institutions; and on art and literature. The purpose of this small volume is much more modest. It is to describe, in terms comprehensible to all with even a minimum knowledge of economics, the major economic events during the depression, impacts of the depression on various economic and social groups, major policy responses to the depression, and some of the economic and political ideas that help to explain the policy responses. Although only minimum attention is given to political and intellectual history, it is hoped that the description of the economic aspects of the depression will provide a background that will help in understanding developments in these fields.

To the many who have been helpful, I wish to express my gratitude. I am especially indebted to my research assistants, Katharine Guroff and Dennis Farley. They did so much of the work, and did it so well and so cheerfully, that writing this book was almost fun.

L. V. C.

AMERICA'S GREATEST DEPRESSION

1

Profile of the Depression

In early 1929, as the New Era neared its calamitous end, America was the richest nation in the world; the richest in all history. America's 122 million people had more real wealth and real income, both per person and in total, than the people of any other country. The higher level of real income flowed from the nation's rich endowment of natural resources, its huge stock of capital goods, its advanced technology, the high quality of its work force, and the skill and innovativeness of its entrepreneurs.

Most Americans believed that the future growth potential of the American economy was great indeed. They were right about the potential. Already born were the children who would increase the labor force 12 percent within a decade, and they were healthier and were becoming better educated than their parents and grandparents. Americans had demonstrated repeatedly that with high and rising incomes they would save large amounts and make possible a high rate of capital formation. And there was every reason to expect that the flow of scientific and technological advances would continue and probably accelerate. Most Americans also expected that the growth potential would in fact be achieved without serious interruption. They were disappointed; the future brought economic disaster.

Employment and output began to decline in the summer of 1929, even before the stock market crash in late October. The recession accelerated after the market crash, and by mid-1930 it had become a depression almost worldwide in scope. In the United States, the grinding deflation of employment, output, and prices continued until March 1933, the nadir of the depression. The Roosevelt Administration, which assumed office at that time, made almost frantic efforts to restore prosperity, but the economic recovery was tragically slow, halting, and incomplete. Not until mid-1941, sparked by America's mounting rearmament program, did employment and output again approach full-employment levels. Thus, America's greatest depression lasted about a dozen years, from mid-1929 to mid-1941.

The shrinkage of employment, real output, and real income during the depression did not reflect any decrease in the willingness of workers to supply labor, or in the productive capacity of the economy, or in the desires of the American people for goods and services. Instead, it reflected the failure of the prevailing economic system to translate the wants and desires of the people into a level of spendings, or aggregate money demands for output, sufficiently high to make it profitable for business firms to employ all available labor, to utilize other existing productive resources, and to invest in new capital.

At the center of this system were the business firms, organized primarily for profit. They hired labor and other productive factors only to the extent that their products could be sold at prices sufficient to cover their money costs and contribute to their primary goal of making money profits. Thus, the behavior of the entire system depended on a circular flow of money spendings—on a flow of spending for the output of business firms and on a flow of spending by business firms for labor and other productive inputs. Any significant decrease of spendings for the output of business firms would almost inevitably be reflected in decreased demands for labor and other inputs, reduced output, and lower prices.

The cumulative decline of money demands for output was a highly complex process, involving complicated reverberations and feedback effects among the various sectors of the economy. The process appears to have been initiated by a decline of private investment spending, and especially by declines of demands for new construction and for new productive equipment. This not only reduced employment and output in those capital goods industries, but also lowered the money incomes of workers and owners in those industries. Thus was initiated a downward multiplier process as each decrease of money income induced a decrease of demands for consumption purposes, which decreased still more total demands for output. Moreover, each decrease of consumption and investment spending tended to reduce investment still more by creating excess capacity, by lowering the expected profitability of new capital investment, and by decreasing the creditworthiness of potential borrowers.

This process was intricately related to the financial system. The grinding deflation of money incomes and of prices exerted highly adverse effects on banks and other financial institutions by reducing the flow of savings to them, by reducing their ability to collect quickly and fully on their claims, and by reducing their solvency and liquidity. In turn, financial institutions became less able and willing to lend for consumption and investment purposes, which further depressed the economy. By 1933, the financial structure was in shambles, and the saving-investment process was virtually immobilized.

Later pages will analyze these processes in more detail. In the meantime, it will be useful to outline briefly the behavior of employment, real output or income, and price levels during the depression.

■ **REAL OUTPUT OR INCOME**   As a measure of real output or income, we shall use gross national product (GNP) valued at constant prices—the average level of prices of output in 1929. GNP includes once, and only once, all the goods and services produced by the American economy during the stated period of time. Thus, it includes all currently produced goods and services made available for consumers, for government use, for maintaining and increasing the nation's stock of privately owned capital goods, and for net exports. By pricing output for each year at the level of prices prevailing in 1929, we eliminate the effects of changes in price levels, or in the purchasing power of the dollar, and secure an index of the behavior of real output and income.

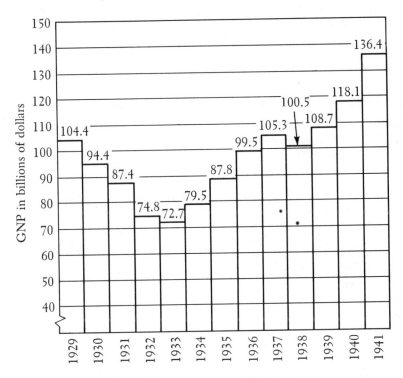

FIG. 1. GNP in Billions of Dollars as Constant (1929) Prices, 1929–1941

Figure 1 portrays the sharp decline of real output and income from 1929 to 1933. By 1932, the decline was nearly 30 percent; by 1933, the decline was slightly larger. However, the figure for 1933 is for the year as a whole, and it reflects some recovery from the lowest point reached early in that year. The decline from 1929 to the bottom of the depression was clearly more than 30 percent. The reduction of real output was not limited to one or only a few sectors of the economy; it pervaded virtually every sector except agriculture. However, as we shall have occasion to emphasize more than once, it hit some sectors much harder than others.

The recovery that began in 1933 was woefully slow and faltering. Not until 1937 did real output reach its 1929 level, and then it fell again in the sharp recession that began in the spring of 1937 and lasted into 1938. Only in 1939 and later years did real output persist above its level in 1929.

The nation lost huge amounts of real output through underutilization of its labor and other productive resources during the years 1930–1941. The losses are staggering even if one measures them as the difference between actual output each year and the level attained in 1929. However, this method would understate the losses, for the productive capacity of the economy was rising. The labor force was increasing, technology was improving, and the stock of capital goods would have grown if the nation's real income had been high enough to permit a high rate of real saving. It is reasonable to assume that the productive potential of the economy should have increased at a compound rate of at least 3 percent per annum after 1929. An average growth rate at least this high had been achieved during most earlier decades and was achieved again after the end of the depression.

In Table 1–1, the column labeled "Potential GNP" reflects a 3 percent

Table 1–1.   GNP at constant (1929) prices
(in billions of dollars)

YEAR	ACTUAL GNP	POTENTIAL GNP	LOST OUTPUT (POTENTIAL GNP MINUS ACTUAL)
1929	$ 104.4	$ 104.4	$ —
1930	94.4	107.5	13.1
1931	87.8	110.7	22.9
1932	74.8	114.0	39.2
1933	72.7	117.4	44.7
1934	79.5	120.9	41.4
1935	87.8	124.5	36.7
1936	99.5	128.2	28.7
1937	105.3	132.0	26.7
1938	100.5	136.0	35.5
1939	108.7	140.1	31.4
1940	118.1	144.3	26.2
1941	136.4	148.6	12.2
Total*	$1,165.5	$1,524.2	$358.7

*Excluding 1929.

Source: Computed from various tables in U. S. Department of Commerce, U. S. Income and Output, 1958.

compound annual growth rate of output for each year from the level actually realized in 1929. In the two most depressed years, 1932 and 1933, real output was more than 35 percent below its potential level. For the years 1930 through 1941, actual GNP was nearly 25 percent below the economy's potential. Lost output during this period aggregated $358.7

billion at 1929 prices. Such magnitudes challenge comprehension and interpretation. However, it may be helpful to note that this amount is more than three times the nation's *total* GNP in 1929. It would have bought 716,000 schools, each costing $500,000; or 35,800,000 homes, each costing $10,000; or 179,000,000 automobiles, each costing $2,000; or 3,580,000 miles of highway at $100,000 a mile. To put it on a more personal level, this sum would support 3,580,000 people for 10 years at an annual consumption level of $10,000.

There is no adequate way of translating these bare statistics into quantitative measures of the frustration, discontent, and suffering during the period. The reduction of real income would have been painful enough if it had been spread evenly over the entire population. However, as will be described later, the impact was highly uneven; for many people, the reduction of real income was at times closer to 100 percent than to 25 percent.

■ EMPLOYMENT AND UNEMPLOYMENT   The actual decline of real output, and the failure of output to achieve its potential levels, reflected widespread underemployment and unemployment of all types of productive factors—of land, mines, factories, commercial establishments, and labor. Table 1–2 presents estimates of the average levels of labor unemployment during the depression years, the figures including only those totally unemployed. In 1929, only 3.2 percent of the labor force was unemployed; in 1930, the unemployment rate had jumped to 8.7 percent.

Table 1–2. Labor force, employment, and unemployment in the United States, 1929–1941 (numbers in millions)

			UNEMPLOYMENT	
YEAR	LABOR FORCE	EMPLOYED	NUMBER	PERCENT OF LABOR FORCE
1929	49,180	47,630	1,550	3.2
1930	49,820	45,480	4,340	8.7
1931	50,420	42,400	8,020	15.9
1932	51,000	38,940	12,060	23.6
1933	51,590	38,760	12,830	24.9
1934	52,230	40,890	11,340	21.7
1935	52,870	42,260	10,610	20.1
1936	53,440	44,410	9,030	16.9
1937	54,000	46,300	7,700	14.3
1938	54,610	44,220	10,390	19.0
1939	55,230	45,750	9,480	17.2
1940	55,640	47,520	8,120	14.6
1941	55,910	50,350	5,560	9.9

Source: U. S. Department of Commerce, *Historical Statistics of the United States*, 1960, p. 70.

During the two worst years, 1932 and 1933, the number of totally un-employed was more than 12 million each year, and the average unem-ployment rate was over 24 percent.

Although the situation improved thereafter, there was no year prior to 1941 in which the number of unemployed fell below 7.7 million, or in which the average unemployment rate declined below 14.3 percent. The average number of unemployed during the eleven years 1930 through 1940 was 9,447,000, and the average unemployment rate was 17.1 per-cent. Even in 1941, when the expanding rearmament program had begun to spark a recovery of economic activity, the average number of unem-ployed was still over 5.5 million and the unemployment rate was almost 10 percent.

It appears that the totally unemployed during the years 1930 through 1941 represented a waste of nearly 104 million man-years of labor. How-ever, this seriously understates the waste of labor, for it leaves out of account the millions who were able and willing to work full-time but could get no more than part-time jobs. It is likely that at the bottom of the depression at least one out of every three employed workers had only part-time jobs. Part-time employment was still common in the latter part of the depression.

Unemployment was pervasive; virtually no geographic area, industry, or skill-group escaped it. However, it was also highly uneven in its impact. The young, the elderly, employees in industries producing capital goods and durable consumer goods, and nonwhites were particularly hard hit. Moreover, while some were unemployed for only short periods, others were without jobs for years on end.

■ **PRICES AND MONEY NATIONAL INCOME**   The same sharp declines of money demands for output that lowered real output also brought painful price deflation. As shown in Table 1–3, average price de-creases from 1929 to 1932 were nearly 22 percent for total output, 31.2 percent for wholesale prices, and 20.6 percent for consumer prices. Prices reached even lower levels in the early part of 1933. Price deflation was per-vasive, but some prices fell much more than others. Thus, the purchasing power of the dollar rose at least 33 percent by 1933. Such price declines were by no means limited to currently produced goods and services; they also extended to almost all types of existing assets, including farms, dwelling units, plants and equipment, and shares of stock. After reaching their low point in early 1933, price levels rose somewhat, but in 1940 they were still at least 15 percent below their 1929 levels.

Reflecting the large decline of prices, the money value of GNP at current prices fell much more than real output. The decrease from 1929 to 1932 was $45.9 billion, or 44.5 percent. (See Table 1–3.) By 1933, the decline had reached $48.4 billion, or nearly 47 percent. This fall of the value of output, or of spendings for output, brought an equal decline of

Table 1–3.   Price indexes and the money value of GNP at
current prices, 1929–1941

| YEAR | GNP AT CURRENT PRICES (IN BILLIONS) | INDEX, 1929=100 | | | |
		INDEX OF GNP AT CURRENT PRICES	INDEX OF PRICES OF TOTAL OUTPUT	WHOLESALE PRICES	CONSUMER PRICES
1929	$104.4	100.0	100.0	100.0	100.0
1930	91.1	86.5	96.4	90.3	97.1
1931	76.3	72.6	86.8	76.3	88.4
1932	58.5	55.5	78.1	67.8	79.4
1933	56.0	53.2	76.9	68.9	75.2
1934	65.0	61.8	81.6	78.4	77.8
1935	72.5	68.9	82.5	83.7	79.8
1936	82.7	78.6	83.0	84.5	80.6
1937	90.8	86.3	86.1	90.3	73.0
1938	85.2	81.6	84.8	82.5	82.2
1939	91.1	86.5	83.7	80.7	80.8
1940	100.6	95.6	85.0	82.3	81.4
1941	125.8	119.5	92.0	91.4	85.5

Sources: U. S. Department of Commerce, *Historical Statistics of the United States*, 1961, pp. 117, 125–126; and various tables in U. S. Department of Commerce, *U. S. Income and Output*, 1958. The Index of prices of total output is the GNP price deflator. The wholesale and consumer price indexes are those of the Bureau of Labor Statistics. All indexes have been converted by the author to a 1929 base.

gross national income, for each decline of spendings by one group inevitably decreased receipts of money income by others. Almost all forms of money income fell, some much more than others. For example, total gross national income decreased by $45.9 billion, or 44.5 percent, between 1929 and 1932.

Table 1–4 shows how this decrease in gross national income was divided among the various types of income shares. Total compensation of employees fell 39.1 percent. Net incomes of business firms fell even more. In 1929, corporations as a group enjoyed net profits of about $10 billion; in 1932, they suffered net losses of $2 billion. Losses were especially large for medium-sized and small corporations. Total incomes of the proprietors of unincorporated business firms fell from $14.8 billion to only $5.3 billion, a decrease of 64.1 percent. Since this measure of income includes salaries and other payments for the labor of owners, it is almost certain that unincorporated firms as a group received no net return on their property in 1932 and 1933; they probably suffered large net losses. While their profits turned into losses, most business firms also incurred large losses in the value of their inventories and of their other assets.

These drastic declines of money income and of prices of output and assets were accompanied by serious disruptions of creditor-debtor relationships, widespread defaults, and reduction of new credit flows to a mere

Table 1–4.   Gross national income at current prices, 1929 and 1932 (in billions of dollars)

	1929	1932	AMOUNT OF DECLINE 1929–1932	PERCENTAGE DECLINE 1929–1932
Total gross national income	$104.4	$58.5	−$45.9	44.5
Claims against gross national income				
Indirect business taxes	7.0	6.8	− 0.2	3.0
Capital consumption allowances	8.6	7.6	− 1.0	11.6
Compensation of employees	51.1	31.1	− 20.0	39.1
Net interest	6.4	5.4	− 1.0	15.6
Rental income of persons	5.4	2.7	− 2.7	50.0
Corporate profits	10.1	− 2.0	− 12.1	—
Income of proprietors of unincorporated businesses	14.8	5.3	− 9.5	64.1

Source: Various tables in U. S. Department of Commerce, *U. S. Income and Output*, 1958. Because of ommission of minor items, the items shown may not add to the total shown. Corporate profits as shown do not include profits or losses resulting from changes in the prices of inventory stocks. Such inventory losses were huge between 1929 and 1932.

trickle. As is always true, but especially so after a long period of prosperity characterized by high rates of saving and investment, large amounts of debt were outstanding at the end of 1929. (See Table 1–5.)

Table 1–5.   Net public and private debt in the United States, end of 1929 (in billions of dollars)

TYPE OF DEBT		TOTAL
Federal government		$ 16.5
State and local government		13.2
Corporations		
Long-term	$47.3	
Short-term	41.6	
Total		88.9
Farm		12.2
Nonfarm, noncorporate		
Mortgage		31.2
Commercial and financial		22.4
Consumer		6.4
Total		$190.9

Source: Economic Report of the President, 1964, p. 270. Net public and private debt outstanding is a comprehensive aggregate of the indebtedness of borrowers after elimination of certain types of duplicating governmental and corporate debt.

These debt contracts typically obligated debtors to pay fixed numbers of dollars for interest and principal regardless of what might happen to the purchasing power of the dollar or to money incomes. Some of these debts would undoubtedly have fallen into default even if prosperity had continued. However, the great bulk of them would have been serviced fully and promptly if prices and money incomes had remained near their 1929 levels. It was the grinding deflation of incomes and prices that increased the burden of debt, brought widespread defaults, and accelerated bankruptcies.

The ability and willingness of the federal government to meet its debt obligations was never seriously threatened, although irrational fears that its mounting deficits, reflecting decreased tax collections, would threaten its creditworthiness led to tax increases and to decreases of federal expenditures in 1932, which further depressed the economy. State and local governments, faced with declining revenues and rising needs for relief, were less fortunate. Three states and some 1,300 municipalities actually defaulted, and many more escaped only narrowly. Bankruptcies, defaults, and near-defaults were widespread in the private sectors. Millions of business firms, farmers, and households met their obligations in full, although many lost everything in the process. Other millions defaulted. As farms, homes, and other assets were thrown on the market because of delinquencies in taxes, debt payments, or both, prices were depressed even more.

Well before the spring of 1933, the grinding deflation had created conditions highly unfavorable to business recovery. For one tning, excess capacity was pervasive, which seriously discouraged new investment spending. There was little prospect for recovery of residential construction while vacancies were widespread and old houses could be bought for a fraction of the cost of building new ones. Excess capacity in industry was almost endemic. Few firms were likely to rush into building new factories or buying new equipment while so much of their existing capacity lay idle. However, many could not have commanded the necessary funds even if they had wished to spend large amounts for capital formation. Those that had defaulted and accumulated large unsatisfied liabilities could neither sell new shares of stock nor borrow on acceptable terms. Even among those that did not default, many had suffered such large losses of net worth and liquidity that their creditworthiness was at best doubtful. Such conditions, generated during the decline, help to explain why the recovery of capital formation was so delayed and faltering after 1933.

The deflation of income and prices, together with the deteriorating quality of debts, virtually assured distress for the financial system, and especially for financial intermediaries.

■ **THE FINANCIAL SYSTEM**   The distress of the financial system was dramatized by the collapse of the commercial banking system at the beginning of March 1933. Virtually every bank in the nation was closed when Roosevelt became President. This dramatic event did not come suddenly and without warning. Between 1929 and the end of 1932, nearly 5,100 banks had failed—more than one out of every five. Only the best, or most fortunate, would have been solvent if their assets had been valued at current market prices. There were also many failures and near-failures among other types of financial intermediaries, such as savings and loan associations, mutual savings banks, insurance companies, and mortgage companies.

Many factors contributed to the vulnerability and distress of financial intermediaries. Among these were the prevalence of small banks excessively dependent on only one or a few local industries, inexpert management, lack of deposit insurance, and lack of adequate facilities for borrowing to meet drains. However, the prime source of their distress was the deflation of incomes and prices and the accompanying deterioration of debt claims.

The intermediaries were literally "caught in the middle." Their essential function is to gather funds from others by issuing claims against themselves. These claims, such as deposits, are typically stated in fixed numbers of dollars and are payable on demand or short notice. The funds thus amassed are then invested in financial claims against others, such as government and private bonds, mortgages, and other debt claims. To meet withdrawals by those to whom it has issued claims against itself, a financial intermediary has four principal sources of funds: (1) inflows of savings, (2) receipts of interest and promised repayments of principal on its investments, (3) sales of assets from its portfolio, and (4) borrowings from others.

In periods of prosperity, when national income is close to full-employment levels, the first two sources alone are normally sufficient, or nearly sufficient, to meet withdrawals from an intermediary. Inflows of savings are large, and most debtors make their interest and principal payments promptly and fully. If the intermediary needs to sell assets to cover net withdrawals, it can usually do so at little loss of value. Also, it can normally borrow from other intermediaries that are not suffering drains. All these sources of funds deteriorated as the depression deepened.

As incomes fell, saving fell even more sharply. From a positive level of $4.2 billion in 1929, personal saving fell to a negative $646 million in 1932. More and more people became net withdrawers of funds from financial intermediaries, rather than net suppliers. Debtors became delinquent on their promises to pay interest and principal to the intermediaries. Financial assets could be sold in the depressed market only at large losses. With financial distress so widespread, an intermediary found no adequate and reliable source of borrowing. Some could and did borrow from institutions sponsored by the government, such as the Federal Reserve and the Federal Intermediate Credit banks. However, many intermediaries had no access to such institutions, and the assistance provided by the latter was woefully inadequate.

Thus, thousands of financial intermediaries became unable to meet their obligations and to meet them promptly. Many failed and closed their doors, with large losses to their depositors and deprivation for those who had formerly relied on them for credit. Of those that remained open, many restricted withdrawals or paid off claims at only a fraction of their face value. Most of them failed to perform their economic function of gathering funds in large amounts and making them available to finance economic activity. They could attract only a trickle of funds, partly because total saving was so low and partly because people had lost confidence in the safety and liquidity of the claims that they offered. However, they were unwilling to lend even the trickle of funds that they received. Managers knew that their institutions were illiquid, that they would be insolvent if their assets were valued at market prices, and that new waves of withdrawals might occur at any time. Moreover, fewer and fewer borrowers remained creditworthy.

We shall later describe the government actions that began in 1932 and were then broadened in an effort to rehabilitate financial institutions by lending to them, by relieving them of illiquid and depreciated assets, and by insuring claims against them. However, the damage had been too great for recovery to be rapid and complete. The plight of financial institutions prolonged the depression.

■ **THE INTERNATIONAL SYSTEM**   By mid-1930 the depression was virtually worldwide in scope. Almost the only economically important country to escape was the Soviet Union, with its autarkic policies and its reliance on centralized physical planning. Elsewhere, the general pattern was similar to that in the United States, although in most countries the depression was less deep and prolonged. Unemployment was widespread; in 1932, the total number of unemployed in the world was at least 30 million. Output, and especially industrial output, declined sharply. Price declines for both output and assets were endemic. As in the United States, price decreases were especially large for agricultural and other raw materials. Nor were the effects limited to the economic sphere. Governments toppled in country after country. In Germany, where the effects were especially severe until 1933, the depression played an important and perhaps crucial role in enabling the Nazis to rise to power.

While the depression was lowering employment, real incomes, prices, and money incomes in the various nations, it virtually destroyed the financial and trading mechanisms that had interconnected their economies. International trade in goods and services fell sharply. In large part, this reflected the effects of decreases of incomes in the various countries, which reduced their demands for the exports of other nations. In addition, the fall was exacerbated by increased tariffs and other official restrictions on trade. International lending and investing came to a virtual standstill. For this there was a complex of reasons: decreased desires to borrow and spend for investment in the face of depressed conditions, decreased flows of savings in nations that normally lent abroad, decreased creditworthiness of borrowers, and increased official restrictions on international transfers of funds.

These drastic decreases of internationl flows of trade and capital funds deranged balances of payments and destroyed the international monetary system. By 1929, almost all countries had recovered from the monetary and fiscal disorders generated during and immediately following World War I and had stabilized their currencies. Almost all had adopted some form of gold standard as a means of stabilizing exchange rates on their currencies, and they held their international reserves in the form of gold and foreign moneys, the latter consisting principally of American dollars and British pounds sterling.

Cracks in this structure began to appear as early as 1930. First to be hit were countries relying heavily on exports of agricultural products and raw materials, whose prices declined early and sharply. Suffering large decreases in their export earnings, these countries found it difficult to reduce their international payments correspondingly and to protect their gold and others international reserves. To make matters worse, international capital flows reversed. In the 1920s many of these countries received foreign loans; now they were asked to repay. By the end of 1930, four countries had abandoned gold. In 1931, the retreat from gold became a rout. Starting in Austria in the spring of that year, the storm spread to Germany, the United Kingdom and most members of the British Empire, and many other countries. By the spring of 1932, only the United States and a mere handful of other countries remained on gold standards with relatively free international payments. The United States suspended its gold standard in March 1933 and initiated a series of monetary experiments.

The downfall of gold standards need not have led to tragic consequences for world trade. Nations might have devised other monetary mechanisms to promote relatively free and efficient international flows of trade and capital funds. But they did not. Instead, they retreated into nationalism, restrictionism, and autarky. New arguments for restricting imports and increasing exports became persuasive in many countries: keep home markets for home producers, provide employment for our own people and and not for foreigners, increase exports to increase jobs for our own workers, and so on.

Many restrictive devices were used. Import tariffs were increased. The United States was early in the procession; the Smoot-Hawley Act of 1930 raised tariff rates on imports to the highest levels in the nation's history. Other nations rapidly followed suit. Many also resorted to quantitative limitations on imports; to various types of subsidies on exports; to restriction, and even prohibition, of capital exports; and to exchange control systems, under which no payments to other nations could be made without permission of the government.

By the mid-1930s, world trade and capital movements were strangling in this network of restrictions. There were many critics of this system in the United States and elsewhere. Economists and others argued that reductions of restrictions through international agreements would not only increase the efficiency of the world's economy but would also promote economic recovery by expanding total exports and trade. Some efforts in this direction were made, and limited progress was achieved. However, restrictions were still widespread when World War II erupted. Not until the 1950s, more than 20 years after restrictions began to be increased so rapidly in the early 1930s, did world trade and capital movements again become relatively free.

■ **CONCLUSIONS**   Such, in broad profile, was America's greatest depression, which began in the summer of 1929 and dragged on for a dozen years. The following pages will describe more fully both the painful descent of the economy until the nadir of the depression was reached in the spring of 1933, and also the numerous, often frenetic, and only partially successful efforts to achieve recovery.

2

The Depression Begins

■ THE ECONOMY IN THE 1920s   During the depression many contended that not only the onset of the depression but also its severity and long duration resulted inexorably from imbalances and strains built up in the economy during the 1920s. Among the allegations were that the prosperity of the period was more apparent than real, consisting largely of paper profits; that the productive capacity of the economy was under such serious strain that a fall of output was inevitable; that the nation was "living beyond its means"; and that the economy was "permeated by inflation." None of these allegations appears valid.

The prosperity of the 1920s was indeed "real," in the sense that it reflected high and rising rates of real output. The nation's real GNP in 1929 was 22 percent above its level in 1923, about 62 percent higher than in 1914 when World War I began, and 75 percent above its level two decades earlier in 1909. Although the real growth rate in the 1920s was gratifying, it was not extraordinarily high by American historical standards. At a compound annual rate of 3 percent, it was approximately the same as the average growth rate during the decades immediately preceding World War I and slightly below that experienced after World War II.

The economy achieved this growth rate without any signs of unusual strain. Only 3.2 percent of the labor force was unemployed in 1929, but there was not such an excess demand for labor as to raise wage rates faster than productivity, increase labor costs, and lower business profits. Plant capacity was not being strained, and there was excess capacity in many lines. The behavior of prices of output indicated no signs of strains on productive capacity; in fact, prices drifted gently downward after 1926. The economy was clearly capable not only of maintaining the rate of output achieved in 1929 but also of increasing it with the passage of time.

The allegation that "the nation was living beyond its means" fares no better. Households did use a major part of the increase of their incomes to increase their consumption. As evidence of this, one had only to note their purchases of more than 3 million new automobiles a year, which raised total registrations from less than 11 million in 1921 to more than 26 million in 1929; purchases of radios, electric refrigerators, and other electrical appliances never before available; the increased attendance at the movies, especially after the advent of the talkies; more frequent vacations at home and abroad; and many other goods and services. However, both households and business firms also used a considerable part of their rising incomes to raise their rate of savings.

A large part of these business and personal savings was used to create and purchase new capital goods for private ownership. During the years 1921–1929, a total of nearly $35 billion was invested in over 6.7 million new dwelling units, and at least $55 billion was spent for new plants and equipment for agriculture, commerce, and industry. Investment in capital goods for government ownership was also large. Most conspicuous were over 275,000 miles of new surfaced roads and streets to accommodate the motor age; new and expanded water, light, and sewage systems in the growing cities; and new schools and other public buildings. Public investments in durable projects of these types amounted to at least $10 billion, and probably considerably more. While all this capital was being accumulated at home, American net investments abroad rose more than $4 billion. This is hardly the picture of a profligate society intent on consuming today without thought of tomorrow.

It is more to the point to argue that the high rate of personal and business saving increased the economy's vulnerability to depression. Full employment could be achieved and maintained only if the high rate of saving out of full-employment levels of income was fully offset and reinjected into the spending stream for output through private expenditures for capital formation, government spending in excess of its current income, and net loans to foreigners who would use the proceeds to buy American exports. Any decline of the total of these "offsets" below the amounts that households and business elected to save out of their full-employment levels of income would decrease total money demands for output.

This began to happen in 1929. The very high rate of net investment during the preceding years had raised the stock of private capital to such high levels that the expected profitability of further investment probably declined somewhat, although it is not certain that this occurred. Even such an event would not necessarily have lowered investment spending if interest rates and other costs of capital funds had declined. But interest rates did not decline; instead, they rose sharply, primarily because of restrictive policies by the Federal Reserve System. Dismayed by an increase of speculation in the stock markets and by the use of increasing amounts of credit for speculation, the Federal Reserve had instituted a restrictive policy early in 1928 and continued it to the time of the stock market crash. By selling most of its holdings of government securities, reducing its holdings of acceptances, and raising its discount rates, the Federal Reserve increased the cost and reduced the availability of bank reserves. This resulted in sharp increases in interest rates and in increasing difficulties in selling mortgages and bonds.

These conditions discouraged all the major types of spending that served as offsets to saving. Reflecting the rising cost of mortgage financing, new construction was the first to fall. Investment in business plants and equipment was discouraged by the rise of interest rates and fall of bond prices, although many firms were able to finance cheaply by issuing common stocks before the stock market crash. State and local governments, especially the latter, encountered increasing difficulty in financing their public works programs. Foreign borrowings in the American market began to decline in the latter half of 1928, and they fell very sharply in 1929.

Such were some of the major developments that precipitated the initial decline of aggregate demands for output in 1929, a decline that later became cumulative.

■ THE STOCK MARKET   Every major period of strong prosperity in American history has been accompanied by speculative activity in some sector, such as land, canals, railroads, urban real estate, public utilities, or the stock market. The 1920s were no exception. One area of speculation was real estate. Interruption of building during the the war, together with rising incomes and a rapid growth of the urban population, had brought a building boom, which culminated in 1926. The nation seemed temporarily oversupplied with housing relative to demand, and residential construction declined in the last years of the 1920s. There had also been highly speculative activities in some other lines of construction, such as apartments, hotels, and office buildings, which were financed by the issue of securities of low and even fraudulent quality. Some readjustments in this area would have to occur, but it was believed that these could be made without far-reaching repercussions.

More widespread and persistent was speculation in the stock market. Many accounts of stock market behavior in the 1920s are overly dramatic and sensational. There were certainly sensational events—many get-rich schemes, dramatic confrontations of bulls and bears, pool operations and manipulations, buying on slim margins, circulation of false rumors, and so on. No one can deny that excesses did occur, with serious consequences, or that prices of many stocks reached unsustainable levels. Yet a large part of the rise of stock prices during the 1920s was justified. Most leading stocks were underpriced during the first years of that decade. Even as late as 1924, when some alarmists were already saying that stock prices had risen too much, the average dividend yield on stocks was still above its level during the years immediately preceding World War I. Also, average dividends per share rose about 38 percent from 1923 to 1927, and 61 percent from 1923 to 1929. Even with the benefit of hindsight, it is impossible to say when stock prices reached levels that could not have been maintained if full employment and economic growth had continued. An estimate would be no earlier than mid-1928, and probably later. Yet by the autumn of 1929 the prices of many speculative stocks had reached levels that could not be justified by any reasonable forecast of future earnings.

At their peak in September 1929, the average price of stocks, as measured by the Standard Statistics index of 421 common stocks, was 128 percent higher than in 1926. (See Figure 2.) By this time the market had become

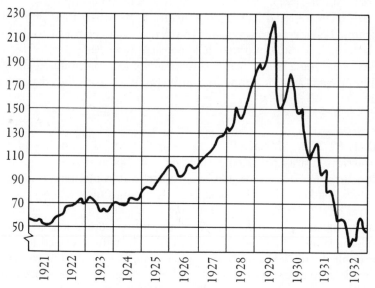

FIG. 2. Standard Statistics Index of Prices of 421 Common Stocks, Monthly Averages (1926 = 100)

jittery, as evidenced by erratic price movements and an increase in the volume of shares traded on the New York Stock Exchange. Continued increases in the prices of some stocks during September 1929 were more than offset by declines in others. In early October the market became even more jittery. There were still strong bullish sentiments, but more caution began to appear. The high prices and low current yields on stocks caused second thoughts. The rise of loans to brokers and dealers to more than $8,500 million to enable their customers to purchase and carry securities on margin was considered a source of weakness, as were the widely publicized bull and bear raids. Also, people had begun to note the reports of declining economic activity, especially in the durable goods industries.

On October 1, with 4,525,000 shares traded on the New York Stock Exchange, the prices of many stocks fell 5 to 10 points. October 3 brought another break, larger than that of two days earlier, with a volume of 4,747,-000 shares. The decline continued the next day. An experienced judge of the market observed, "Fear is in the saddle." For the next two weeks prices fluctuated erratically but with some downward trend, and with the daily volume of trading rarely exceeding 4 million shares. Prices declined again on Friday and Saturday, October 18 and 19, with volume relatively low. Nearly 6.1 million shares were traded on Monday, with significant price declines. Prices moved erratically on Tuesday.

On Wednesday, October 23, trading opened quietly with many prices higher. The pace began to increase about 10 o'clock and then accelerated; about 2.6 million shares were traded in the last hour. When the exchange closed for the day, 6,374,960 shares had changed hands and the value of shares listed on the exchange had fallen $4 billion. Then came an avalanche on Thursday, October 24. Some 12,894,650 shares were traded, the ticker lagged four hours behind, and prices dropped sharply. A similar avalanche overwhelmed the New York Curb Exchange, where 6,337,415 shares were traded.

Business and political leaders intervened desperately to stop the decline. They assured the nation that the worst was over and that the economy was fundamentally sound. Some observed optimistically that weak spots had been eliminated and a solid base established for further progress. Leaders in banking and finance formed a pool to support prices. For a few days the market was steady. But on Monday, October 28, came what one reporter called "a nationwide stampede to unload." On sales of 9,212,800 shares, of which one-third occurred in the last hour of trading, the value of shares listed on the exchange fell $14 billion. The next day was no happier: 16,410,030 shares were traded with widespread losses.

Business and political leaders renewed their efforts. Banks lowered margin requirements and stood ready to lend to those who could still provide margins. Wealthy individuals announced their intention to buy, and groups of banks and others formed pools for the same purpose. The public was assured again that business was fundamentally sound, that liquidation had now run its course, and that "now is the time to buy stocks." Rallies did follow, but they were more than offset by declines, so that stock prices reached their temporary low point only in the second week of November.

At the end of this decline the Standard Statistics index of common stock prices was 39 percent below its peak in September. The value of all shares listed on the New York Stock Exchange, which had been about $90 billion in September, declined nearly $26 billion. Stocks listed on the Curb Exchange and other exchanges, as well as those traded over the counter, also suffered large declines. These were indeed large price decreases. But it is equally important to note that even at this low point stock prices were still as high as they had been in mid-1928. The worst was yet to come.

Stock prices rallied somewhat in the first months of 1930; in April, they reached a level 20 percent above their low point of the preceding November. Then the rally ended and gave way to a calamitous fall. By the summer of 1932, when stock prices reached their trough, they were 83 percent below their peak in September 1929 and 72 percent below the lowest levels reached in November 1929.

It is still impossible to appraise precisely the effects of the stock market crash of October 1929 on the course of the depression. It did not initiate the decline of economic activity, for that had already begun during the preceding summer. However, the rate of decline increased after the crash. For example, industrial production in September 1929 was only 1 percent below its peak in June; by the end of the year it had fallen 12 percent.

The sharp fall of stock prices probably contributed to the decline of business activity in at least three ways. (1) By reducing the wealth of households as measured in terms of money. Feeling poorer on capital account, many households may have reduced their consumption expenditures relative to their current incomes, and especially their expenditures for luxuries and other items whose purchase could be easily postponed. (2) By depriving business firms of a cheap source of finance. Before the crash, firms could issue new shares on very favorable terms; now this was impossible. (3) By adversely affecting expectations concerning the profitability of new investment. Their expectations concerning stock market prices having proved to be so wrong, many businessmen probably became more cautious about capital spending. Thus, the stock market crash was undoubtedly a depressive force on the economy. Yet the severity and duration of the depression were not inevitable results of the crash. Developments within the depression itself and mistaken public policies played important roles.

We turn now to a brief description of the behavior of real output and the money value of output during the great slide from 1929 to 1933. There are two recurrent themes: the pervasiveness of the declines, and the widely differing impacts on the various sectors of the economy.

■ **REAL OUTPUT AND INCOME**   The data in Table 2–1 indicate that the declines of real GNP—of GNP at constant prices—from the levels prevailing in 1929 were 10 percent for 1930, 16 percent for 1931, 29 percent for 1932, and 30 percent for 1933. Declines to the lowest points in the summer of 1932 and in the spring of 1933 were greater than those shown by the annual totals.

Although declines of real output were pervasive, some types of output fell much more than others. (See Table 2–2.) For example, while total GNP declined about 30 percent from 1929 to 1933, gross private domestic investment—the amount of output used to maintain and increase private stocks of capital goods—fell nearly 89 percent. This reflected declines of approximately 82 percent in residential construction, 75 percent in other construction, and 67 percent in producers' durable equipment. In 1929, business firms purchased output to make net additions to their inventories; in the early years of the depression, they reduced their inventories sharply. Sales of consumer durable goods also declined markedly—nearly 50 percent. On the other hand, nondurable consumer goods and consumer services declined only about 15 percent.

Wide differences in the extent of declines also become apparent when we

Table 2–1.   The gross national product of the United States
in constant (1954) dollars, 1929–1933 (in billions of dollars)

	1929	1930	1931	1932	1933
GNP—Total	$181.8	$164.5	$153.0	$130.1	$126.6
Personal consumption	128.1	120.3	116.6	106.0	103.5
Durable goods	14.9	11.8	10.3	7.8	7.5
Nondurable goods	65.3	62.1	61.8	56.9	55.2
Services	48.0	46.4	44.6	41.4	40.8
Gross private domestic					
investment—Total	35.0	23.6	15.0	3.9	4.0
New construction—Total	20.9	15.4	10.9	6.0	4.6
Residential—nonfarm	8.7	5.1	4.2	2.1	1.6
Other	12.2	10.4	6.6	3.9	3.0
Producers' durable equipment	11.1	8.8	5.9	3.5	3.7
Change in business inventories	3.0	− 0.7	− 1.8	− 5.6	− 4.2
Government purchases of goods					
and services—Total	18.5	20.5	21.6	20.5	19.9
Federal	2.9	3.4	3.7	3.9	5.3
State and local	15.6	17.1	17.9	16.6	14.6
Net exports of goods and services	0.2	0.2	− 0.3	− 0.3	− 0.8
Exports	11.1	9.9	8.4	6.8	6.8
Imports	10.9	9.7	8.7	7.1	7.7

Source: U. S. Department of Commerce, U. S. Income and Output, 1958, p. 118.

examine another measure of real output—indexes of industrial production by industry classification. (See Table 2–3 for a sample of industries.) Several of these industries experienced declines of 50 percent or more. All had at least this in common: They produced durable goods. And most of them relied heavily on demands for purposes of capital formation. At the other extreme, several industries experienced declines of less than 10 percent. All of these were producers of nondurable consumer goods.

These facts should be borne in mind when we later examine the widely differing impacts of unemployment in various industries and geographic areas and local problems of unemployment relief. For example, imagine the implications of the 82 percent decline of residential construction and the 75 percent decline of other construction for architects, structural engineers, construction workers, the lumber industry, and other industries heavily dependent on construction. Consider the impact of the 59 percent decline of iron and steel production on such places as Birmingham, Bethlehem, Pittsburgh, Gary, and the Mesabi Range. Or the effect of the 65 percent decrease in automobile production on Detroit, Toledo, Akron, and other cities heavily dependent on the manufacturing of cars and their components. Or the impact of the 79 percent decline of copper production on

Table 2–2.   Changes in the real gross national product of the
United States, 1929–1933

	CHANGE, 1929–1933 (IN BILLIONS OF 1954 DOLLARS)	PERCENT- AGE CHANGE	PERCENT OF THE TOTAL DECLINE OF GNP
GNP—Total	−$55.2	−30.4	100.0
Personal Consumption	−24.6	−19.3	44.6
Durable goods	− 7.4	−49.7	13.3
Nondurable goods	−10.1	−15.5	18.3
Services	− 7.2	−15.0	13.0
Gross private domestic investment—Total	−31.0	−88.6	56.2
New construction—Total	−16.3	−78.0	29.5
Residential—nonfarm	− 7.1	−81.6	12.9
Other	− 9.2	−75.4	16.7
Producers' durable equipment	− 7.4	−66.7	13.4
Change in business inventories	− 7.2		13.0
Government purchases of goods and services—Total	+ 1.4	+ 7.6	2.5
Federal	+ 2.4	+82.8	4.3
State and local	− 1.0	− 6.4	1.8
Net exports of goods and services	− 1.0	—	1.8
Exports	− 4.3	−38.7	7.8
Imports	− 3.2	−29.4	

Source: U. S. Department of Commerce, U. S. Income and Output, 1958, p. 118.

mining areas and on Bridgeport and other copper-fabricating centers.
Similar examples could be multiplied. Such direct losses of employment
and income would have been serious enough for the communities, but
they were often magnified by a sort of local multiplier effect as those whose
incomes dropped decreased their demands from local merchants, service
industries, builders, and others. Many whole communities were impoverished and unable to support their unemployed.

■ PRICE LEVELS AND THE MONEY VALUE OF OUTPUT AND
INCOME   The same sweeping decreases of demand that lowered real
output and employment also brought price deflation throughout the
economy. Price declines were pervasive, but they were much greater for
some things than for others. Discussion here shall be confined to the behavior of the prices of output, measured by an index of the prices of
items included in GNP. As indicated in Table 2–4, the average price level

Table 2–3.   Changes in real output in the United States,
1929–1933, by industrial classification

INDUSTRY	1929–1933 PERCENTAGE DECLINE
Shoe production	3.4
Textiles and products	6.4
Cigarette production	6.6
Leather and products	7.4
Gasoline production	7.4
Woolen and worsted cloth production	7.7
Cotton consumption	11.4
Tobacco products	16.7
Manufactured food products	17.8
Cigar production	34.4
Tire and tube production	34.8
Polished plate glass production	42.7
Ship building	53.1
Furniture production	55.6
Nonferrous metals and products	55.9
Lumber production	57.9
Iron and steel	59.3
Machinery	61.6
Cement production	63.1
Nonferrous metal smelting	63.5
Transportation equipment	64.2
Automobile production	65.0
Railroad car production	73.6
Copper production	78.9
Common and face brick production	83.3
Locomotive production	86.4

Source: Computed from Federal Reserve indexes of industrial production.

of total output had fallen 23 percent by 1933, and the average prices of all goods bought for consumption had fallen 27 percent. Thus, the dollar had risen about 37 percent in its power to purchase consumer goods and services.

This fall of prices, together with the fall of real output, reduced sharply the money value of GNP, which is the same as the nation's gross money income. Table 2–5 shows that from 1929 to 1933 the money value of the nation's output fell 46 percent. By the latter year the nation had only 54 percent as much gross money income with which to pay taxes, consume, meet debt obligations, and save in other ways.

How was this drastic drop of money income shared among the various industries? We shall use as a measure not GNP but *national income*. This is simply the money value of GNP minus depreciation allowances and all taxes on business except income taxes. (A few minor adjustments need

Table 2–4. Price indexes for the U. S. gross national product and its components, 1929–1933 (1929=100)

	1929	1930	1931	1932	1933
GNP—Total	100.0	96.5	86.9	78.2	77.0
Personal consumption—Total	100.0	95.8	85.4	75.5	72.7
Durable goods	100.0	97.6	86.3	75.8	74.4
Nondurable goods	100.0	95.0	81.3	69.3	69.8
Services	100.0	96.1	90.3	82.8	75.9
Gross private domestic investment—Total					
New construction—total	100.0	95.9	87.5	74.6	74.8
Residential—nonfarm	100.0	97.6	88.8	72.0	71.3
Other	100.0	95.4	87.0	76.2	76.7
Producers' durable equipment	100.0	96.2	91.2	86.7	82.1
Government purchases of goods and services—Total	100.0	98.0	93.2	86.0	88.0
Federal	100.0	93.9	93.7	85.8	86.1
State and local	100.0	98.7	93.3	86.1	89.2
Net exports of goods and services					
Exports	100.0	87.2	68.5	57.4	55.8
Imports	100.0	85.3	69.3	56.4	51.1

Source: U. S. Department of Commerce, *U. S. Income and Output*, 1959, p. 220. The indexes presented here are the "implicit price deflators" converted to a 1929 base.

not concern us here.) In effect, this measures the net money income of the nation—all the value of output accruing as net income to the owners of businesses and to labor and other factors of production working for businesses and for the government. National income can also be viewed as the sum of *values added* by all the individual industries. The value added by an individual industry is simply the value of the output sold by that industry minus the value of the components and services included in the

Table 2–5. Gross national product of the United States at current prices, 1929–1933

YEAR	GNP (IN BILLIONS)	GNP AS PERCENT OF 1929 LEVEL
1929	$104.4	100.0
1930	91.1	87.3
1931	76.3	73.1
1932	58.5	56.0
1933	56.0	53.6

Source: U. S. Department of Commerce, *U. S. Income and Output*, 1959, p. 220.

output that were purchased from other industries. This difference, or value added by the industry, measures the amount of net money income available to it to pay wages, salaries, rentals, and interest, and to provide profits, if any, to firms in the industry. Table 2–6 shows the behavior of total na-

Table 2–6.   U. S. national income by industrial origin

	MONEY INCOME IN 1929 (IN MILLIONS OF DOLLARS)	MONEY INCOME IN 1932 AS PERCENT OF 1929	MONEY INCOME IN 1933 AS PERCENT OF 1929
All Industries—Total	$87,814	48.5	45.7
Government and government enterprises	5,093	101.1	104.6
Communications and public utilities	2,864	79.8	69.8
Agricultural services, forestry, and fisheries	195	68.2	63.1
Services	10,338	59.3	53.8
Transportation	6,636	48.4	45.8
Finance, insurance, real estate	12,693	53.2	45.3
Farms	8,083	39.6	44.4
Wholesale and retail trade	13,358	47.6	41.1
Rest of world	810	48.5	39.9
Manufacturing	21,888	32.9	34.5
Mining	2,048	32.9	31.6
Contract construction	3,808	27.7	19.8

Source: U. S. Department of Commerce, *U. S. Income and Output,* 1959, p. 130. This source provides a much more detailed breakdown.

tional income and of the value added, or money incomes, of all industries (classified into broad categories).

The 54 percent decline of total national income between 1929 and 1933 was shared quite unequally among the various categories of industries. Most fortunate was "government and government enterprises," in which money income actually rose. This income was mostly in the form of wages and salaries paid to government employees. In communications and public utilities, total money income declined only 30 percent from 1929 to 1933. At the other extreme, declines of money income in this period were 80 percent in contract construction, 68 percent in mining, and 65 percent in manufacturing as a whole. These statistics reemphasize a point already made: the tremendous differences in the impacts of the depression on the various sectors of the economy. More detailed breakdowns by industries and regions reveal even greater disparities.

Table 2–7 shows how the declining national money income was shared by employees and other participants in the productive process. While

Table 2–7.   U. S. national income by type of income share,
1929–1933

TYPE OF INCOME	MONEY INCOME IN 1929 (IN MILLIONS OF DOLLARS)	MONEY INCOME IN 1932 AS PERCENT OF 1929	MONEY INCOME IN 1933 AS PERCENT OF 1929
National income—Total	$87,814	48.5	45.7
Compensation of employers	51,085	60.8	57.8
Rental incomes of persons	5,425	50.0	35.3
Net interest	6,445	84.3	78.2
Proprietors' Incomes—Total	14,759	36.0	37.9
Of farms	5,968	32.4	40.8
Of other business and professional	8,791	38.5	36.0
Corporate profits before income taxes	10,100	Negative	Negative

Source: U. S. Department of Commerce, U. S. Income and Output, 1959, p. 126.

total national income fell by 54 percent from 1929 to 1933, compensation of employees, mostly wages and salaries, fell less than proportionally— only 42 percent. Later pages will describe the extreme diversity of impacts on various types of workers.

Two items call for more extended comment—proprietors' incomes and corporate profits. The former includes all the income earned by owners of unincorporated businesses. Because so many of these owners also supply labor or other services to their firms and can increase or decrease their own compensation, it is impossible to isolate any meaningful figure comparable to corporate profits.

Proprietors' incomes and corporate profits play several very important roles in the economy. (1) As determinants of owners' money and real incomes, and therefore of their living standards. (2) As incentives to produce and to invest in capital formation to maintain and expand capacity. It is true, of course, that a wholly rational profit-maximizing firm would base its investment decisions not upon present or past profit experience but rather upon expectations as to whether or not the contemplated new investment will improve its profit position. But there can be little doubt that current profits and their recent trends exert a powerful influence on expectations as to the profitability of new investment. For example, a firm already suffering losses is unlikely to be optimistic concerning the profitability of new investment. (3) As an internal source of funds to finance production and investment. Many firms prefer to finance all or most of their investment from internal sources, some solely from preference, others because they could command funds from others only at high cost. For this reason, low and falling proprietors' incomes and corporate profits tend to impede investment. (4) As determinants of the availability and cost of external financing. A firm with high and rising profits may be able to sell new stock or other ownership shares on favorable terms, it can comfortably meet its outstanding debt obligations, and it is likely to be considered so creditworthy that it can borrow on favorable terms. However, it is in a far less favorable position if its net income falls sharply, and especially if it incurs large losses. New issues of stock or other ownership shares become infeasible, the firm faces increasing difficulty in meeting its outstanding debt obligations, and its creditworthiness falls. If the firm suffers large and protracted losses or if its owners withdraw from it more than its net income, its assets will be drawn down, its net worth decreased, and its liquidity impaired. It will be able to borrow, if at all, only by paying high interest rates to compensate for the high risk. For all these reasons, except possibly the first, falling business profits, and especially losses, discourage business investment and even the maintenance of production within existing capacity.

With these points in mind, let us return to Table 2–7. Net incomes of farm proprietors fell 67.6 percent, and those of proprietors of other unincorporated firms 61.5 percent. Declines in some industries were greater— 89 percent in mining, 83 percent in contract construction, and 65 percent in manufacturing. Thousands of firms in almost all industries suffered losses. The business failure rate rose 50 percent. The total number of firms, which had increased steadily during the 1920s, actually declined 252,000, or about 11 percent, from 1929 to 1933, partly because of an increased rate of business closings and partly because of a decreased rate of formation of new firms. Many proprietors must have felt like the disgusted Brooklyn merchant who locked the front door of his store and hung on its doorknob a sign reading, "Opened by mistake."

Corporate profits before taxes, which had totaled $9,628 million in 1929, declined by two-thirds in 1930 and turned into losses of $780 million in 1931 and $3,017 million in 1932. (See Table 2–8.) At least two things

Table 2–8.   Corporate profits in the United States, 1929–1933
(in millions of dollars)

	1929	1930	1931	1932	1933
Corporate profits before tax	$9,628	$3,322	−$ 780	−$3,017	$ 151
Less: tax liability	1,369	842	498	385	521
Equals: profits after tax	8,259	2,480	− 1,278	− 3,402	− 370
Less: dividends paid	5,813	5,490	4,088	2,565	2,056
Equals: undistributed profits	2,446	− 3,010	− 5,366	− 5,967	− 2,426

Source: U. S. Department of Commerce, U. S. Income and Output, 1959, p. 126.
The profit figures are adjusted to eliminate profits and losses on inventories.

stand out. One is the sharp decline of profits in 1930, the large losses in 1931 and 1932, and the very small profits in 1933. Another striking fact is the extent to which corporations maintained dividend payments despite falling net profits after tax or actual net losses. Total dividend payments did fall 65 percent between 1929 and 1933, but net income available for dividend payments fell much more. As a result, in the four years 1930–1933, corporations paid out as dividends $16,769 million more than their profits after taxes. This was a drain on corporate assets, and especially on their more liquid assets, which served not only to reduce corporate working capital but also to reduce creditworthiness, seriously in many cases. Large numbers of corporations faced difficult problems of financial rehabilitation.

Corporate profit experience varied greatly from industry to industry. In some industries, total corporate profits remained positive even in the worst year, 1932. These included most public utilities—electric, gas, telephone and telegraph, and pipeline transportation—plus tobacco manufacturing, food manufacturing, producers of petroleum and natural gas, and chemicals. In a year when corporations as a whole had net losses of $3,017 million, corporations in these industries had net profits of $897 million. This means that all other corporations suffered net losses of nearly $4 billion. Among the industries whose corporations had the largest net losses during 1932 were iron and steel, other metals and metal products, railroads, machinery, retail trade and automotive services, wholesale trade, and real estate.

Profit and loss experience also varied greatly by asset size of corporations, with smaller corporations generally suffering more than larger ones. This was confirmed in an interesting study by Solomon Fabricant covering the experience of 381,000 corporations in 1931, and 392,000 in 1932.[1] He found that in both 1931 and 1932, corporations with net assets of $50 million or more still enjoyed net profits as a group, while all smaller-size categories suffered net losses as groups. The rate of loss, measured by the percentage of loss to total capitalization, increased with each decrease in asset size. For example, in 1932, the percentages of losses to total capitalization were 2.7 percent for corporations with assets of $10–$50 million, 6.3 percent for those with assets of $500,000–$1 million, 14.0 percent for those with assets of $50,000–$100,000, and 33 percent for those with assets below $50,000.

The same general pattern was found in almost every industry. Even in those industries in which all corporations as a group had net profits in 1932, the smaller corporations had losses. In 1932, about 323,800 corporations, or 83 percent of all those studied, were in the smaller-size classes whose average loss rates as percentages of total capitalization were 9.9 percent or greater.

The purpose here is not to argue that large corporations and their owners did not suffer in the depression. Most of them did. Large corpora-

[1] *Profits, Losses and Business Assets, 1929–1934*, Bulletin 55, National Bureau of Economic Research, April 11, 1935, pp. 1–12.

tions suffered at least declines in their net incomes, many had net losses, and many suffered further from deflation of the values of their assets. Their shareholders suffered from sharp decreases in the prices of their shares as well as from decreases, if not cessation, of their dividends. In general, however, the impact on hundreds of thousands of small to medium-size corporations and on unincorporated businesses was even more severe. While the unemployed, the partially employed, and farmers were suffering, thousands upon thousands of businessmen were not unscathed. One unemployed man commented: "I'd rather be me than the boss. I may not have any income, but at least I'm not making losses."

■ CONCLUSIONS   This chapter has had two main themes—the pervasiveness and the great unevenness of impact of the losses during the great slide from 1929 to 1933. This applies to employment opportunities; real output; the real and money incomes of various industries; and the real and money incomes of workers, employers, and others. Both the pervasiveness of the losses and the great unevenness of their distribution are pertinent to problems and policies considered in the following pages.

3

The Unemployed

America was totally unprepared philosophically, politically, financially, and administratively to cope with the massive unemployment, loss of incomes, and poverty that came with the great depression. There was no federal program to assist the unemployed. Not one state had an unemployment insurance system, and existing private plans, instituted by a few progressive companies, covered only 150,000 workers. Nor were there any specialized organizations or plans to provide relief to the unemployed; there were only the more general arrangements for relief of those who were destitute for whatever reason, whether because of broken families, physical or mental illness, age, unemployment, or depravity. In 1929, these agencies had only limited financial and administrative resources, at best barely enough to meet the minimum needs of those who remained destitute under conditions of general prosperity.

Prevailing attitudes toward the pauper who sought relief and toward the provision of relief had developed out of the poor laws of Elizabethan England. To be so poor was in itself a stigma, suggesting shiftlessness or worse.[1] To discourage such conduct, relief should be given only to those truly destitute, and then only in minimum amounts.

Almost sole responsibility for caring for the destitute was believed to lie in the local community. First in line of responsibility came family and relatives. Then came various types of private charity, organized and unorganized. Such government relief as might be given should come, it was believed, almost solely from local government—from town, city, or county units. Most of these units provided two types of relief, "indoor relief" and "outdoor relief." The first refers to care of the destitute in government institutions, mostly in almshouses. In 1929, this was still the basic method of providing for paupers of all types. The second method provided care for the needy in their own homes, a practice considered by many to be especially questionable, not only because of difficulties of supervision and administration but also because it was costly and likely to encourage

[1] For an excellent history of the development of American attitudes and relief policies, see Josephine Chapin Brown, *Public Relief, 1929–1939*, Holt, Rinehart and Winston, New York, 1940.

idleness. Moreover, no one was legally eligible for relief of either kind until he had exhausted all of his resources and could come completely empty-handed.

State governments did provide some specialized types of aid, such as care for the insane, the tubercular, and "the unsettled poor," but in 1929 they were providing no relief for the unemployed. They entered this field only belatedly and reluctantly after the burden in many communities had proved to be too heavy for private charity and local government. In some cases, existing laws and even constitutional provisions prohibited state governments from financing outdoor relief.

In 1929, the federal government was providing no funds for direct relief of the unemployed, and the Administration was determined that it should not enter this field. President Hoover did increase federal expenditures somewhat for public works to support the level of employment, provided very limited amounts of loans to lower levels of government in 1932 for the same purpose, and repeatedly called upon communities to meet their responsibilities. But he was adamantly opposed to "taking the federal government into the relief business." There were several reasons for this. For one thing, he seriously underestimated the depth and duration of the depression and the burden it would impose on private charities and local governments, just as he overestimated the financial ability of these agencies to provide relief to the mounting numbers of unemployed who were exhausting their own resources. He also worried about the effects of expenditures for relief on the federal budget, which was already showing increasing deficits, and on the state of the federal government's credit. In addition, he had basic philosophical objections to a federal "dole." As he put it, "The money involved is indeed the least of the costs to American ideals and American institutions." He wished to preserve individual self-respect and "the principles of individual and local responsibility and mutual self-help."[2] Thus, the federal government provided no funds for direct relief of the unemployed before July 1932, and then only as loans to states.

One manifestation of the federal government's refusal to accept responsibility for relief of the unemployed was its failure to gather reliable, comprehensive information concerning both the total amount of unemployment and its distribution among industries, localities, and types of workers. The federal government made no monthly surveys, such as now exist, nor even annual ones; its first comprehensive survey came only in 1937. A few states did conduct investigations as the depression deepened, as did some local governments. But for the most part, estimates of current unemployment and its incidence came from private sources, and these were incomplete and differed widely. For example, private estimates of unemployment in March 1933 ranged from 13.5 million to 15.7 million. This paucity of reliable, comprehensive information probably inhibited and delayed

[2] William Starr Myers, ed., *The State Papers and Other Public Writings of Herbert Hoover*, Vol. I, Doubleday, New York, 1934, pp. 496–499.

development of effective programs for dealing with the situation. It also makes more difficult the task of presenting a relatively full and accurate description of events during the period. Many of the statistics that we shall use were developed after 1933 and are believed to be fairly accurate, but it is necessary to rely heavily on many fragments of evidence and on statistics that in some cases are imprecise and not fully compatible with each other. However, the resulting errors will be only in detail, not in the faithfulness of the overall picture.

■ **UNEMPLOYMENT AND LABOR INCOMES**   Let us now examine the behavior of employment, unemployment, and the money and real incomes of workers, centering attention on the period of the great slide from 1929 to 1933, but commenting also on some developments in the following period. As before, there will be two main themes: the pervasiveness of losses to workers and the highly uneven impacts on various classes of workers.

The real income of any worker or group of workers depends, of course, on both size of money income and the purchasing power of each dollar of that income. As noted earlier, the purchasing power of a dollar over consumer goods and services rose significantly between 1929 and 1933. The average prices of these things fell about 25 percent; the purchasing power of each dollar in these terms rose about 33 percent.[3] Thus, workers whose money incomes fell less than 25 percent actually gained real income. Only a minority were so fortunate; most suffered much larger losses. These losses came in two forms—in decreases in money wage rates, measured by average hourly earnings, and in decreases in hours of employment.

During the first year of the depression, decreases of money wage rates were quite limited in both numbers and amounts. Wage cuts in a depression usually come only after a delay, but this time President Hoover launched a campaign to prevent them. Summoning to the White House representatives of both employers and labor, he extracted promises from employers that they would not initiate wage reductions, and promises from labor leaders that there would be no moves for wage increases beyond those already in process. He emphasized the desirability of maintaining wage rates because of the human considerations involved and also as a means of maintaining the consuming power of the country. He seems to have paid little attention to wage rates as a determinant of costs of production, and to the possibility that the rise of real wage rates accompanying decreases in the prices of output might actually decrease total employment.

Although wage lines held during most of 1930, they gave way as unemployment mounted, prices of output fell, and more and more businesses saw their profits turn into larger and larger losses. Wage cuts became widespread in 1931 and even more widespread and larger in 1932. One study

---

[3] See Table 2–4, p. 24.

covering a large number of concerns in many industries revealed that as of the end of 1932 or early 1933, about 87 percent of the firms had lowered wage rates at least once and some several times, for an average reduction of 18 percent; 89 percent had lowered executive salaries an average of 22 percent; and 90 percent had lowered other salaries an average of 18 percent.[4] Thus, on the average, reductions in wage and salary rates were not as large as the 25 percent decline in the cost of living.

Here again the averages conceal wide differences in the behavior of individual types of wages and salaries. For example, at least 10 percent of the firms covered in the study just cited did not cut wage and salary rates at all. Among those that either did not reduce wage rates or reduced them by less than the average were the organized building trades and some others with powerful labor unions; the public utilities, in which production declined less than in most industries; and many, but not all, governmental units. At the other end of the scale, agricultural wage rates fell sharply. One measure puts the average decline at 50 percent, but many farm workers received little more than "board and keep" plus a little spending money occasionally. Reductions were also large in many branches of the highly competitive cotton textile industry, in the manufacture of inexpensive apparel for women and children, in many service industries, and in several other lines that were highly competitive and in which labor unions either did not exist or were ineffective. By 1933, "sweatshops" were certainly numerous, but not pervasive.

The other, and larger contributor to the loss of both money and real income by workers was, of course, the decrease of employment. We have already noted the great increase in the number totally unemployed.[5] In 1929, only 3.2 percent of the labor force was totally unemployed; this rose to 8.7 percent in 1930, 15.9 percent in 1931, 23.6 percent in 1932, and 24.9 percent in 1933. The number of unemployed was over 12 million in 1932 and 12.8 million in 1933. We do not know how many people were in the families of those totally unemployed in 1933, but they must have numbered well over 30 million. It will also be recalled that the unemployment rate remained above 20 percent in both 1934 and 1935, and that in no year before 1941 did it fall below 14.3 percent.

While increasing numbers were becoming totally unemployed, a rising number of other workers had only part-time employment. A large part of this rise of part-time unemployment resulted almost automatically as more and more plants came to operate on less than a full-time basis. For instance, a survey in March 1932 of more than 6,500 companies in all branches of industry revealed that less than 26 percent of the firms were operating full-time, and only 28 percent were operating five days or more per week.[6] There were wide differences among industries; for example,

[4] National Industrial Conference Board, *Salary and Wage Policy, 1933–34*, New York, 1935, pp. 2–3.
[5] See Table 1-1, p. 4.
[6] U. S. Department of Labor, *Monthly Labor Review*, September 1932.

the percentages operating at or near full time were 70 percent for commercial establishments and only 14 percent in the machinery group. Of all employed workers, 56 percent were part-time, working an average of 59 percent of normal full time.

Another reason for the widespread prevalence of part-time work was the share-the-work philosophy of the period. Many employers would have adopted such policies without urging in order to support more of their employees, to keep a labor force together and preserve its skills, or for other reasons. However, assisted by the blessings and urging of President Hoover, "share-the-work" became a nationwide movement, using advertising and other mass media of persuasion. Although dubbed by critics as "share-the-poverty," the movement was beneficial on the whole, especially in view of the meager relief provided for the unemployed. However, the movement and the prevalence of only part-time work did have unfavorable implications for the totally unemployed. Employers could easily meet even sizable increases of demands for their products by using part-time employees more hours and without new hirings. This helps explain why the number of totally unemployed declined so slowly when output began to rise again.

The extent of both total unemployment and partial unemployment differed greatly from industry to industry. In general, these differences were in line with the differences in the behavior of real output in the various industries, described in the preceding chapter.

Table 3–1, showing total wage and salary payments, reflects the behavior of all the direct determinants of the money incomes of workers—reductions in wage and salary rates and reductions in time worked because of total or partial unemployment. The total money income of all workers in the form of wages and salaries fell 42.5 percent from 1929 to 1933, but the losses varied greatly from industry to industry. For example, the total wages and salaries of government employees actually rose slightly, and losses to employees in communications and public utilities were only about 30 percent. Note, however, the huge losses at the other end of the scale. Decreases were 75 percent in contract construction, nearly 55 percent in mining, and more than 51 percent in manufacturing as a whole and in agriculture, forestry, and fisheries. The addendum to Table 3–1 presents information about some industries, more narrowly defined, in which losses were especially large. In every case, the decrease of employees' money incomes was at least 60 percent, and in metal mining it was 74 percent.

Even within each industry the impacts of total and partial unemployment on various classes of workers differed greatly. For one thing, the unemployment rate varied with the age of the worker, being highest for the very young, lower for the middle-aged, and higher again for elderly workers. Although comprehensive statistical date on this point for the early years of the depression is lacking, current reports stressed widespread unemployment among the young and the special problems of the elderly. These general conclusions are supported by the few available case studies

Table 3–1.   Total wages and salaries by industry, 1929–1933

	WAGES AND SALARIES IN 1929 (IN MILLIONS)	WAGES AND SALARIES IN 1932 AS PERCENT OF 1929	WAGES AND SALARIES IN 1933 AS PERCENT OF 1929
All Industries—Total	$ 50,423	60.4	57.5
Government and government enterprises	4,937	100.6	104.1
Communications and public utilities	1,520	78.4	69.7
Finance, insurance, and real estate	2,918	71.7	65.0
Services	5,517	67.7	60.7
Wholesale and retail trade	9,319	63.4	56.8
Transportation	4,719	56.3	52.0
Agriculture, forestry, and fisheries	1,401	53.0	48.8
Manufacturing	16,092	47.7	48.6
Mining	1,515	45.1	45.3
Contract Construction	2,484	33.1	24.6
Addendum: Selected industries with largest decreases of total wages and salaries			
Metals, metal products, and miscellaneous	3,105	36.8	39.5
Nonferrous metals and their products	541	38.1	38.1
Iron and steel and their products, including ordinance	2,117	33.9	38.0
Nonmetallic mining and quarrying	124	41.9	37.1
Stone, clay, and glass products	618	38.5	36.7
Services allied to transportation	245	42.4	36.3
Automobiles and automobile equipment	979	37.7	35.9
Transportation equipment, except automobiles	262	44.7	35.5
Machinery, except electrical	1,396	35.0	35.4
Lumber and furniture products	1,319	32.4	34.1
Lumber and timber basic products	708	25.0	28.1
Metal Mining	200	26.5	26.0

Source: U. S. Department of Commerce, *National Income*, 1954, p. 180.

in the period. For example, a study of employment conditions in Philadelphia in April 1931, almost two years before the depression reached its bottom, revealed that 25.5 percent of all workers were totally unemployed and 13.8 percent were employed only part-time. (See Table 3–2.) The percentages totally unemployed were 34.4 for those 66 years and over, 34.7 for those in the 16–25 age group, and 21.8 in the age group 36–45.

Table 3–2.   Percent of gainful workers in Philadelphia totally
unemployed and employed part-time in April 1931, by age groups

AGE GROUP	PERCENT TOTALLY UNEMPLOYED	PERCENT EMPLOYED PART-TIME
Average for all ages	25.5	13.8
16–25	34.7	13.9
26–35	24.0	15.9
36–45	21.8	14.9
46–55	23.0	14.2
56–65	26.6	10.9
66 and over	34.4	9.2
Age not reported	16.3	13.8

Source: Industrial Research Department, Wharton School of Finance and Commerce,
Unemployment in Philadelphia Families, April 1931. Philadelphia, 1931, p. 20. "Gainful
workers" include all adults willing and able to work.

In Massachusetts in January 1934, when the overall unemployment
rate in that state was 24.9 percent, the rate was 47.6 percent for the 14–20
age group and 22.7 percent for those 21 and over.[7] Table 3–3 shows that
when the average unemployment rate was 18.8 percent in Michigan in
January 1935, the rates were 34.3 percent for those in the 15–19 age group

Table 3–3.   Unemployment by age groups in Michigan on
Jan. 14, 1935

AGE GROUP	PERCENT UNEMPLOYED
Average for all ages	18.8
15–19	34.3
20–24	24.0
25–29	15.1
30–34	13.0
35–39	13.2
40–44	14.2
45–49	16.8
50–54	19.7
55–59	23.0
60–64	27.3
65 and over	24.5

Source: U. S. Department of Labor, *Monthly Labor Review,* November 1936, pp.
1157–1161.

[7] U. S. Department of Labor, *Monthly Labor Review,* December 1934, p. 1335.

and above 25 percent for those 60 and over. Comprehensive surveys in 1937 and 1940 revealed much the same pattern. (See Table 3–4.)

In November 1937, about 16.4 percent of the labor force was totally unemployed, but the unemployment rate for the 15–19 age group was 36.5 percent and for the 20–24 age group it was 21.3 percent. The unem-

Table 3–4.   Percentages of labor force unemployed and in public emergency work, 1937 and 1940

	1937		1940	
AGE GROUP	PERCENT TOTALLY UNEMPLOYED	PERCENT IN PUBLIC EMER- GENCY WORK	PERCENT TOTALLY UNEMPLOYED	PERCENT IN PUBLIC EMER- GENCY WORK
Average for all ages	16.4	3.6	9.6	4.8
15–19	36.5	4.7	24.1	7.6
20–24	21.3	3.0	13.5	4.9
25–34	13.6	2.7	7.7	3.9
35–44	12.4	3.6	6.7	4.5
45–54	13.0	4.3	7.5	5.2
55–64	15.1	4.8	9.9	5.6
65–74	16.2	2.7	7.7	2.5
Age not reported	4.9	1.9		

Sources: Data for 1937 are for the period Nov. 14–20, 1937, and come from *Census of Partial Employment, Unemployment, and Occupations,* Vol. IV, The Enumerative Check Census, 1937. They are based on an extensive house-to-house canvass covering about 1,950,000 people. Data for 1940 refer to April and come from the regular census of that year.

ployment rate was lowest for the 35–44 age group at 12.4 percent, and then rose to 16.2 percent for those aged 65–74. In April 1940, the general level of employment was lower but the pattern similar. While the overall unemployment rate was 9.6 percent, it was 24.1 percent for those in the 15–19 group and 13.5 percent for the 20–24 group. It was lowest at 6.7 percent for those aged 35–44.

It will be noted that statistics for the later period do not support our earlier statement that the unemployment rate of the oldest workers was considerably above the overall average. In 1937, it was about equal to the average and in 1940 it was below the average. However, this should not cast doubt on our assertion relating to the pre-New Deal period. The later decline was not due to the fact that so many more of the elderly became employed; rather, it reflected the fact that so many who would otherwise have been unemployed withdrew from the labor force, and the principal reason for withdrawal from the labor force was to qualify for the more generous old-age relief payments made available under the New Deal. No such acceptable alternative was available earlier. In fact, it was the widespread unemployment and suffering among the elderly, and the burdens imposed on their families, that lent power to the radical Townsend Movement and several others and culminated in the establishment of old-age insurance and more liberal old-age relief.

How many young members of the labor force were unemployed at the bottom of the depression when the overall unemployment rate was at least 25 percent and the total number of unemployed was at least 12.8 million? We have no direct evidence on this point, but we can make some rough guesses. We do know that in 1937, when the overall unemployment rate was at the lower level of 16.4 percent, there were 1.7 million totally unemployed in the 15–19 age group and another 1.7 million in the 20–24 group. Another half million were in effect receiving relief by working on government emergency projects of types not available before 1933. Thus, in 1937, when the overall unemployment rate was only two-thirds as high as it was at the bottom of the depression, a total of 3.9 million members of the labor force in the 15–24 age group were either totally unemployed or working only on government emergency projects. It is surely safe, therefore, to estimate that the number of young people unemployed at the bottom of the depression was at least 4 million, and probably was considerably higher. This helps explain current reports about rising discontent among the young, angry young men and women, increasing juvenile delinquency and minor crime, and over a million young people wandering about the country. They were frustrated by many things—lack of income, postponed marriages, loss of purpose and prospects, sheer boredom, and a weakening or loss of confidence in the values and institutions they had been taught to respect. This also helps explain why the New Deal quickly instituted the Civilian Conservation Corps and other plans to "get the young people off the streets and highways" and to restore their health, self-respect, morale, and purpose.

It is easy to see why unemployment among the young became so severe. The young who actually found employment were often the first to be laid off because of their lack of seniority, relative inexperience, or the desire of employers to favor men with families. New entrants to the labor force were in an even worse position. Many who poured out of schools and colleges in the spring of 1930, before unemployment became widespread, were told, "Sorry, we're not in a position to hire anyone this year." Those who entered the labor force in 1931 and in later years of the decline received even more discouraging replies: "Sorry, we're firing, not hiring. And when things do get better, our first responsibility will be to give more employment to our people who are working only part-time and to rehire some of our old employees that we had to lay off." Even after overall conditions had improved considerably, many young entrants to the labor force found employers giving preference to old employees who had been laid off and to those already working short-time. Thus, by the end of the decade, great numbers of young people who had come out of schools and colleges in the preceding years had never had a steady job, and even more had never had a steady job worthy of their ability and education.

Unemployment was also more severe for those with less education and skills, from less privileged social and economic classes, and in nonwhite groups. There was plenty of unemployment among the educated and skilled—among architects, engineers, mathematicians, bond salesmen, teachers, musicians, artists, writers, and others ordinarily in the higher income and social groups. The situation was even worse at lower levels. This was partly because most of those in higher positions could, if they wished, take positions at lower levels—even positions that they would scorn in normal times—while those ordinarily in the lower positions could not move upward under existing conditions. There was a kind of "pecking hierarchy" or "bumping system," which often operated despite efforts to be "fair" in the allocation of available work. In some industries, there was literally a bumping system: A man in a higher position could bump a man below him. In numerous other cases the results were similar, although the power to bump might come from different sources. For example, the number of hired farm workers decreased by 514,000 between 1929 and 1933, while the number of family workers on farms increased by about the same number. Many of the latter were probably the farmers' sons and daughters who in ordinary times would have migrated to the city, or returning children who had gone to the city and lost their jobs. The boss hires his son, a relative, or the son of friends rathers than someone from a family that he does not know socially. College graduates take jobs at filling stations or as taxi drivers. Engineers become willing to take jobs as draftsmen or clerks. Professional women become secretaries or waitresses. In these and many other ways, the people who would normally have had the jobs lost them or failed to get them.

Most severe of all was unemployment among Negroes and other nonwhites. The study of conditions in Philadelphia in April 1931 revealed unemployment rates of 23.9 percent for whites and 34.8 percent for Negroes. Surveys in several cities in early 1931 found that the incidence of unemployment of Negroes was far above that for whites. (See Table 3–5.)

Table 3–5. Incidence of unemployment of Negroes and whites in selected cities, early 1931

CITY	NEGROES AS PERCENT OF POPULATION	NEGROES AS PERCENT OF TOTAL NUMBER OF UNEMPLOYED
Baltimore	17	32
Charleston	49	70
Chicago	4	16
Memphis	38	75
Philadelphia	7	25
Pittsburgh	8	38

Source: U. S. Department of Labor, Monthly Labor Review, June 1931, pp. 60–62.

Another survey relating to the same period revealed appallingly high unemployment rates among Negro women in cities with generally high unemployment rates. Some of the reported rates are hardly credible. (See Table 3–6.) Unemployment rates in Massachusetts in January 1934 were 32

Table 3–6.   Unemployment rates of women in selected cities, January 1931

CITY	PERCENT NATIVE WHITE WOMEN	PERCENT NEGRO WOMEN
Chicago	20	58
Cleveland	18	55
Detroit	19	75
Houston	14	46
Pittsburgh	17	51
St. Louis	16	48

Source: U. S. Department of Labor, Monthly Labor Review, April 1934, pp. 790–795.

percent for Negroes and 19 percent for whites. These include only those totally unemployed. When the partially unemployed and those with only temporary employment on government projects are included, the rates become 50 percent for Negroes and 34 percent for whites.[8] In 1937, unemployment rates were 23.2 percent for Negroes and 15.7 percent for whites.

Among those who were unemployed one or more times during the depression, there were wide differences in degree of privation because of differences in the total duration of unemployment. For many in low-income groups, even a month or two of unemployment was a hardship, but hardship turned into suffering as the period of unemployment dragged on or as the worker became unemployed several times with only brief spans of work in between. As the executive director of the Welfare Council of New York City told a Congressional committee early in 1932:

. . . when the breadwinner is out of a job he usually exhausts his savings if he has any. Then, if he has an insurance policy, he probably borrows to the limit of its cash value. He borrows from his friends and from his relatives until they can stand the burden no longer. He gets credit from the corner grocery store and the butcher shop, and the landlord foregoes collecting the rent until interest and taxes have to be paid and something has to be done. All of these resources are finally exhausted over a period of time, and it becomes necessary for these people, who have never before been in want, to ask for assistance.

The specter of starvation faces millions of people who have never before known what it was to be out of a job for any considerable period of time

8 U. S. Department of Labor, Monthly Labor Review, December 1934, p. 1335.

and who certainly have never known what it was to be absolutely up against it.[9]

This helps explain why the relief burden increased so much as the depression dragged on. In 1930, demands for relief were relatively small, partly because of the number of unemployed, but also because so many of the unemployed could still manage somehow on their own. Then requests for relief grew enormously, in part because of the growth of unemployment, but also because more and more of the unemployed had exhausted their resources.

The Philadelphia survey in April 1931 indicated that 20 percent of the unemployed had been without work more than a year, and 49 percent for more than six months. A study two years later would undoubtedly have revealed a larger fraction suffering long-run unemployment. Of those unemployed in Massachusetts in January 1934, nearly 62 percent of the males and 54 percent of the females had been unemployed for a year or more. (See Table 3–7.) Nearly one-quarter of the men and over 17 percent of the women had been unemployed three years or more.

Table 3–7.   Duration of unemployment of those totally unemployed in Massachusetts on Jan. 2, 1934 (percent of total unemployed)

DURATION OF UNEMPLOYMENT	MALES	FEMALES
1 year or more	61.9	54.2
2 years or more	44.5	34.5
3 years or more	24.6	17.5
4 years or more	11.0	8.4

Source: U. S. Department of Labor, Monthly Labor Review, December 1934, pp. 1332–1337.

Of the unemployed registering with the U. S. Employment Service in the period July 1936–March 1937, 9.5 percent had been unemployed more than four years, 15.7 percent more than two years, and 22.6 percent more than a year.[10] In April 1940, 15.5 percent of unemployed males had been out of work at least two years and 29.4 percent at least one year.[11] Among unemployed women, 11.8 percent had been without jobs at least two years and 26 percent more than a year. The picture emerging from these bare statistics is black enough, but it fails to reveal how many of the unemployed lost jobs more than once and were out of work during a major part of the depression.

[9] U. S. Senate Hearings before a subcommittee of the Committee on Manufactures on S. 174 and 262 (Unemployment Relief), 72nd Congress, 1st Session, p. 13.
[10] U. S. Government Employment Service, Survey of Employment Service Information, U. S. Government Printing Office, 1938.
[11] U. S. Decennial Census, 1940.

■ **SOME DISTRESSED AREAS**   Earlier pages have stressed the uneven impact of unemployment on various industries and on various cities and regions. It was noted that some communities, heavily dependent on one or more industries that closed down or operated at only a fraction of normal levels, were virtually impoverished. This was due not only to these primary losses of employment and income, but also to the downward multiplier effects as the totally and partially unemployed decreased their demands for locally produced goods and services. Yet under the prevailing philosophy, these communities that had suffered the largest losses of income were expected to carry their huge unemployment burdens through local taxes and donations to charity. A few examples will suggest the plight of some of these communities. Most of those cited will be large cities, but some smaller communities, more heavily dependent on only one or a few highly unstable industries, suffered even more.

Jefferson County, Alabama, which includes Birmingham, relies heavily on iron, steel, and soft coal. The county was hit hard. George Huddleston, Congressman from that district, told a Congressional committee in January 1932:

> . . . we have about 108,000 wage and salary workers in my district. Of that number, it is my belief that not exceeding 8,000 have their normal incomes. At least 25,000 men are altogether without work. Some of them have not had a stroke of work for more than 12 months, maybe 60,000 or 75,000 are working from one to five days a week, and practically all have had serious cuts in their wages and many of them do not average over $1.50 a day.[12]

Both the city and county governments were in financial difficulty; many banks had failed, with losses to depositors. A bond issue for road construction, which would have provided some employment, was voted down.

The city manager of Cincinnati reported that at the end of 1931, when the city's labor force was a little over 200,000, about 48,000 were wholly unemployed and some 40,000 were on short time. Relief payments to needy families averaged $7 to $8 a week.

> Relief is given to a family one week and then they are pushed off for a week in the hope that somehow or other the breadwinner may find some kind of work. . . . We are paying no rent at all. That, of course, is a very difficult problem because we are continually having evictions, and social workers . . . are hard put to find places for people whose furniture has been put out on the street.[13]

Many lumbering areas were deeply distressed. In several counties in Oregon, all lumber mills were closed, with obvious implications for Portland and other cities. The County Commissioners of Spokane and the City Council of Spokane wired their Congressmen, "The local communities

---

[12] U. S. Senate Hearings before a subcommittee of the Committee on Manufactures, 72nd Congress, 1st Session p. 239. (Hereafter cited as Hearings on S. 174.)
[13] Ibid., pp. 251–253.

have now carried on the work for two years and have about exhausted their ability."[14] People in Tacoma were collecting pennies, nickels, and dimes to help meet relief costs. Widespread distress was also reported from other lumbering areas, such as those in Arkansas, the upper peninsula of Michigan, and northern Wisconsin.

Detroit was virtually impoverished. In November 1931 it had 223,000 jobless; by early 1933 about 350,000 of its 689,000 potential wage earners were totally unemployed and many others were working only short time. As relief costs rose and tax delinquencies mounted, both the city and the county fell into serious financial difficulties. The Vice Chairman of the Mayor's Unemployment Committee of Detroit described the situation in June 1932:

> Many essential public services have been reduced beyond the minimum point absolutely essential to the health and safety of the city, such as public health nurses for school children and other medical and hospital services for adults. Other indispensable provisions for the health of the city, such as dental clinics in the schools, have been eliminated entirely.
>
> Recreation and library facilities, never more urgently needed, have been drastically curtailed. The salaries of city employees have been twice reduced amounting to a one-fifth cut, and hundreds of faithful employees of long years of service to the city have been furloughed. Thus has the city borrowed from its own future welfare to keep its unemployed on the barest subsistence levels. During the past year, the food costs for unemployment relief have been successively reduced out of proportion to falling food prices, until today thousands are fed in Detroit's city cafeterias at less than 10 cents a day.
>
> A wage work plan which had supported 11,000 families collapsed last month because the city was unable to find funds to pay these unemployed —men who wished to earn their own support.
>
> For the coming year, Detroit can see no possibility of preventing widespread hunger and slow starvation through its own unaided resources. The increased amount of fixed charges necessary to meet the municipal obligations incurred in other years has limited the amount of money available for welfare aid to less than one-half of the year's expenditures. The anticipated tax delinquencies have already reduced this amount to one-third of the 1931–32 expenditures in face of the certainty that the imperative needs of next year will be greater than those of the fiscal year just ending— now that the long awaited seasonal upturn in Detroit's basic industry has been postponed for another year.
>
> A very well-organized and manned drive for private funds to supplement city welfare resources failed to raise more than a quarter of its original goal. . . . The large amount of personal charity, that is, that given by poor neighbor to poor neighbor, which has until now cushioned the burdens of the public welfare agencies by caring for at least one-half of the unemployment burden, is being rapidly made smaller and smaller by wage reductions and short time among those who are still employed.[15]

Similar stories came from many other cities.

[14] *Ibid.*, p. 247.

[15] U. S. Senate Hearings before a subcommittee of the Senate Committee on Manufactures on S. 4076, pp. 14–15. (Hereafter cited as Hearings on S. 4076.)

By October 1931, Chicago already had 624,000 unemployed, or 40 percent of its labor force. The unemployed had lost $2 million of wages a day, but only $100,000 a day was available for relief. Help was being given only to the totally destitute. As a public welfare officer testified, ". . . we insist that the people who come to our private and public agencies . . . shall use up, absolutely and completely use up and come to us empty handed, all their available resources."[16] No aid was given for rent or to help the unemployed keep their homes. Conditions became even worse. By early 1933, more than 800,000 were unemployed in Cook County, equal to more than half the total labor force in 1930. Never celebrated for their proficiency in fiscal management, both Chicago and Cook County became unable to meet their bills as relief burdens grew and tax delinquencies rose. Relief was woefully inadequate in many cases. By mid-1932, some families were being separated, men to the men's shelter and women to the women's shelter. One official reported:

> In the city of Chicago, there are 1,000 men eating in the bread lines food that costs 4½ cents a day, and these men are from the so-called gold coast of Chicago. These resources are about to end, and they are confronted with one meal a day within, say, 30 days after the city funds will become exhausted.[17]

Chicago school officials, pleading in early 1933 for food for their schools, cited deterioration in the children's health.

> Every day we find children who come to school without breakfast and who state that they have nothing to eat in their homes. . . . Many of our children are anemic through lack of proper nourishment. In this neighborhood, there are homes where the father has not worked for three years. And in some of the homes we have families of 10 to 13, and no wage earner. Milk is a luxury in most of the homes where black coffee and bread is a large part of the diet. We have 240 children in school who have been examined by a doctor and declared clear cases of malnutrition anaemia. . . . The number of underfed children is alarming and seems to be growing. . . .[18]

Nor was all the industrial distress in Illinois confined to the Chicago area. It was also widespread in the southern coal-mining counties, where only a few of the mines were running even part-time; in such manufacturing cities as Moline, Peoria, and Rockford; and in Centralia, where the railroad shops were closed. And one can imagine the suffering in nearby Gary, Indiana, so dependent on the steel industry.

In New York City, 250,000 were in need by the end of 1931 and 100,000 were receiving aid. In the summer of 1932, the head of the Emergency Conference on Unemployment of New York testified:

---

[16] Hearings on S. 174, p. 31.

[17] Hearings on S. 4076 (June 20, 1932), p. 15.

[18] U. S. Senate Hearings before a subcommittee of the Senate Committee on Manufactures on S. 5125, 72nd Congress, 2nd Session (January 1933), p. 267. (Hereafter cited as Hearings on S. 5125.)

Here on the starving front families are breaking up and homes are being destroyed. More than 20,000 children have passed into institutions and boarding houses because parents can not provide for them. Aid for soldiers has increased 600 per cent in the past two years. Jobless men and women advertise in local papers of their willingness to work for a room and meals. The depression has swallowed up working girls and is now reaching teachers, college graduates, and trained office women who have been accustomed to good incomes and comfortable homes.

Even the measure of relief that has been extended to the jobless and the hungry is short of that standard that is required to maintain human beings in moderate comfort and decency.

It is impossible to adequately describe the economic tragedy that has overwhelmed hundreds of thousands of men, women, and children in New York City. When many thousands of breadwinners are locked out of industry through no fault of their own, then industry has failed in its primary duty of providing employment. There is no tribunal in industry to which discharged men and women can appeal. The decree of discharge is final.[19]

One West Virginia coal-mining county with 1,500 totally unemployed and less than half a dozen mines working over two days a week had only $9,000 to meet relief needs for a year. Another rural mining county with over 300 unemployed had only $300 for aid. An administrator of food relief stated, "It is no longer a question of providing even the most minimum dietary standard, but purely of keeping body and soul together."[20]

Distress was widespread in Pennsylvania in both urban and rural areas. In 27 counties, 47 percent of the coal mines normally employing 10 or more men had closed by mid-1931. In five anthracite counties, 40,000 miners and many others were unemployed. Many families in the state were getting only $8 to $12 a month for food.[21]

Unemployed transients posed special problems for some communities, especially in warm areas such as Florida, Arizona, New Mexico, and California. As more and more of the unemployed despaired of finding work in their own communities, great numbers wandered about the country, walking, hitchhiking, riding freight trains, and driving old jalopies. One estimate, believed to be conservative, placed the number at 1,250,000. At the end of 1931, even before the influx of refugees from droughts in the Midwest, there were 100,000 nonresident jobless, homeless, and penniless men in California, with perhaps 70,000 in Los Angeles alone; new arrivals numbered about 1,200 a day.[22]

Railroad officials in Kansas City reported that 1,500 a day were passing through on freight trains, and small towns in Texas, Arizona, and New Mexico reported arrivals of as many as 200 a day. Most numerous among the wanderers were boys and young men, but there were also many girls and even entire families. Nor were all of them from social and economic

[19] Hearings on S. 4076, pp. 17–18.
[20] Hearings on S. 174, pp. 94–95.
[21] Ibid., pp. 48–50.
[22] Hearings on S. 5125 (January 1932), p. 2.

classes that might be expected to "bum around." The chairman of the California Labor Camp Committee stated in January 1932:

> Many of them were laborers, but there were also businessmen and tradesmen. There were many professional men and many high-school and college graduates. In one camp we had 18 college graduates and 33 high-school graduates, which is a very high percentage. We have graduates of some of the largest colleges in the United States. As I say, we have quite a number of small tradesmen and businessmen who have gone broke. We have a doctor and a dentist. . . . We have men who had been bankers and brokers. They listed themselves as clerks, and after that they came in to get a job, many of them giving a false name, as a matter of pride.[23]

Most communities were both unwilling and unable to provide relief for large numbers of the transient unemployed. Many were already in financial distress and unable to care adequately for their own unemployed. A common rule was, "One night in the jail, breakfast, and on your way." Other communities did more, but were overburdened in the process. State governments, most of which were reluctant to provide relief for their own people, were even less inclined to help the unemployed from other states. About 39 states had residence requirements for relief, some running as high as 5 or even 10 years. Several imposed or increased this requirement after the onset of the depression.

■ SOURCES OF AID TO THE UNEMPLOYED   The examples cited, which could be multiplied many times, suggest why it was virtually impossible for private charity and local governmental units to provide adequate relief in those communities hit hardest by unemployment. They simply lacked the resources. For one thing, they lacked adequate administrative machinery. The staffs of both private and public welfare agencies were adjusted to case loads in a period of general prosperity and could not cope with the huge amount of interviewing and investigating that became necessary as unemployment and requests for relief mounted. Most of all, they lacked money. The contributions of organized private charity were large and commendable. Community chests, churches, other religious organizations, fraternal societies, labor unions, chambers of commerce, and many others collected money, food, and clothing. They also organized "give-a-job" campaigns and promoted community gardens and arrangements through which the unemployed could barter their services among themselves and for products of nearby farms. But these private sources, commendable as they were, became utterly inadequate by 1931.

Most local governments tried to provide relief, but those in communities hit hardest by unemployment and loss of incomes found their resources inadequate. They found it politically difficult to levy additional local taxes on people whose incomes were declining; and they also discovered that to levy taxes was one thing, to collect them from the unemployed and from

[23] *Ibid.*, p. 4.

others with decreased incomes was quite another. Most of these local governments depended largely, many almost exclusively, on property taxes, primarily taxes on real estate. The great virtue of this tax was believed to be its stability of yield. This proved illusory as incomes fell. Great numbers of homeowners became delinquent on their taxes, and many on their mortgages as well; many landlords, unable to collect rents from either tenants or relief agencies, did the same. By 1932, the average percent of taxes delinquent in a sample of 145 cities was found to be 22 percent; by 1933, it had risen to 26 percent.[24] In many places it was much higher. For example, it was 69 percent for Hamtramck, Michigan, and 40 percent for that state as a whole. Efforts to increase tax levies were also thwarted in some areas by statutory ceilings on property tax rates. In many cases, these ceilings became effective as assessed values were lowered in recognition of the decline of real estate values. In others, new ceilings were imposed or old ones lowered.

An alternative way of financing relief and other local government expenditures was, of course, to borrow. Many did just that. However, as the depression wore on, this source of finance became increasingly costly to an increasingly large number of local governments, and for many it became virtually unavailable. One reason for this was the general deterioration of financial markets, especially after mid-1931. Even more important was the deterioration of the creditworthiness of municipalities as an increasing number became unable to service their existing debts, to say nothing of new ones, and still more were expected to slide into the same condition. To make matters worse, many local governments entered the depression with large debts incurred during the 1920s to finance local improvements. Some would probably have fallen into financial difficulties even if the depression had not occurred. Much worse was the plight of those that entered the depression with large outstanding debts and then suffered serious tax delinquencies and extraordinarily large relief costs. Some were stopped by statutory debt limitations from issuing new debt; others found no purchasers, or purchasers only on very unfavorable terms.

Most local governments did meet all their debt obligations, although many succeeded only by cutting relief and other social services. But increasing numbers defaulted; by early 1933, nearly 1,000 had defaulted on their bonds, and by the end of the year the number was 1,300.[25] These included 303 counties, 644 cities and towns, 300 school districts, and 60 other districts. Under such conditions, new borrowing became very difficult, even for some local governments that were meeting all their debt obligations. In 1932, 697 issues totalling $260 million could not find a market; of those actually sold, 38 percent bore interest rates above 5 percent. In 1933, some 528 issues totaling $212 million found no purchasers. Among the thwarted issuers were such cities as Buffalo, Philadelphia,

[24] Hearings before the House Banking and Currency Committee on H. R. 3082, February–March 1934, p. 584.
[25] Ibid., pp. 584–588.

Cleveland, and Toledo.[26] It was under these conditions of mounting relief costs, delinquent taxes, and deteriorating creditworthiness that increasing numbers of local governments came to demand state or federal assistance.

A basic reason for the reluctance of state governments to respond was, of course, the tradition that provision of relief, and especially outdoor relief, was a local responsibility. To break quickly such a long tradition would have been difficult even under favorable conditions, but some conditions were unfavorable. One was the combination of the strong influence of farmers in state legislatures and the current economic distress of farmers. Representatives of farmers were normally opposed to burdening their constituents for the benefit of cities; their opposition became even greater as farm incomes fell and as increasing numbers of farmers found it difficult, if not impossible, to pay their taxes and to meet their debt obligations. Another influential force was the financial plight of state governments themselves, even without large relief responsibilities. Their incomes fell with the decline of incomes within their states. Delinquencies on state property taxes became widespread in rural as well as urban areas, and revenues from some types of taxes declined automatically. Among these were taxes on corporate profits, personal incomes, and sales. Many states did impose new taxes, such as selective or general sales taxes, or raised rates of existing taxes, but the opposition was very strong.

In general, the creditworthiness of state governments suffered less than that of municipalities. Only three states actually defaulted on their debts—Arkansas, Louisiana, and South Carolina. Several others escaped only narrowly, and still more could borrow only at high rates, if at all. For example, Mississippi and Montana could find no purchasers of proposed new issues in 1933.

State government assistance for relief was extremely small before September 1931; only five states had appropriated a few millions each. Then in September, New York State appropriated $10 million to last through the coming winter. By April 1932, six other states had followed suit—Illinois, New Jersey, Ohio, Pennsylvania, Rhode Island, and Wisconsin. Most other states followed in the remaining months of 1932 and in 1933. Two points about state aid for relief before 1933 should be noted. First, it was in all cases pitifully small relative to current needs. Second, such grants for relief were in many cases offset at least in part by decreases in aid for other purposes, such as education.

As one surveys the behavior of state and local expenditures in this period, two facts stand out. One is the smallness of total expenditures for direct relief of all kinds. In 1932, these were $317 million, which would have provided less than $27 for each of the 12 million unemployed.[27] The other striking fact is the extent to which net decreases in total state and local

---

[26] Alvin H. Hansen and Harvey S. Perloff, *State and Local Finance in the National Economy*, Norton, New York, 1944, p. 57.

[27] U. S. Department of Commerce, *National Income*, 1954, p. 212.

spending in the latter part of the great slide contributed to declines of demand, business activity, and total money incomes. These units actually tended to support demand and business activity in the earlier stages by increasing their total spending $749 million, or 9.7 percent, between 1929 and 1931. Then their total spending fell sharply from 1931 to 1932, and still further in 1933. While total expenditures for direct relief rose $71 million from 1931 to 1932, other spending fell $966 million. In 1933, when their expenditures for direct relief were $382 million above the 1931 level, their expenditures for everything else had fallen $1,638 million. Hardest hit was construction, which fell $1,356 million. In many areas, state and local government construction of public buildings, streets, highways, sewer systems, and other facilities came to a virtual standstill, with obvious implications for employment. Mounting relief burdens were only partially responsible for these declines; other powerful influences were declining revenues, deteriorating abilities to borrow, and pervasive fear and caution. Thus, while state and local governments were providing so inadequately for the unemployed, their general fiscal policies were creating still more unemployment in 1932 and 1933.

By October 1931, pressure for federal relief assistance was mounting. To many it was becoming increasingly evident that distress was widespread and would increase during the coming winter, that the relief being provided by private charity and local government was inadequate, that many municipalities were heading into financial difficulties, and that help from state governments would be belated and small. In December, Senator Costigan of Michigan and Senator La Follette of Wisconsin introduced similar bills in Congress, which were later consolidated. This bill proposed $375 million in outright grants to the states for the period ending June 30, 1933, of which 40 percent was to be allocated among states on the basis of population and the remainder on the basis of need. Hearings on the bill produced voluminous evidence confirming the seriousness of the situation.[28] Opposition remained so strong, however, that the bill was defeated in the Senate in February 1932. Several other bills to provide federal grants suffered similar fates, dying in committee or on the floor of Congress. Only one such measure passed—one to transfer some government-owned wheat and cotton to the American Red Cross and other organizations for distribution in distressed rural areas.

Thwarted in their efforts to get outright federal grants to states, proponents of federal assistance turned to the possibility of federal loans. The outcome was the Emergency Relief and Construction Act of 1932. President Hoover vetoed the first version on July 11, but signed one only slightly revised on July 21. He signed with obvious reluctance, stating later that "this expenditure has been forced upon the Government by the Democratic leaders."[29] Title I of this Act empowered the Reconstruction Finance

---

[28] See Hearings before a subcommittee of the Committee on Manufactures on S. 174 and S. 262, 72nd Congress, 1st Session (December 1931–January 1932).

[29] Myers, *op. cit.*, Vol. 2, p. 372.

Corporation to lend $300 million to the states and territories for relief and work relief. The principle of primary responsibility of local and state governments had been retained; the funds were not grants but were loans to be repaid in full with interest at 3 percent, repayments to be made through deductions from future federal aid to states for construction of highways and rural post roads. (The repayment provision was repealed before it became operative.) Moreover, a state became eligible for loans only when its governor certified the state's necessity and the inadequacy of its own resources. Applications began to pour in even before the Act became effective. However, only $30 million had actually been disbursed by the end of 1932.

There were several reasons for this slowness. At least some officials of the Reconstruction Finance Coporation seem to have been quite severe in their interpretation of "need" and in extracting the required certifications from governors. But the states themselves were responsible for a large part of the delay. For example, some had to await sessions of their legislatures, some had to amend laws prohibiting the use of state funds for relief, some were still opposed to state aid, some objected to certification of their inability to cope with the problem. Not until 1933 did large amounts of federal funds begin to flow to states and local governments for relief. The major point here is that at the end of 1932, when the depression was already more than three years old, only $30 million of federal funds had been supplied for relief.

This story of mass unemployment and inadequate relief leads inevitably to the question, "How did they manage to survive, especially those who were without jobs for long periods?" Some did not; they died of starvation, exposure, and lack of medical care. Some others would have met the same end if they had been too proud to paw through garbage for scraps of food. Many more suffered from serious malnutrition and impairment of health. But we are still left with the question, "Why weren't more people reduced to such states?" The answer is far too complex to be known with accuracy, but it is a compound of the strength of the survival instinct, human ingenuity in time of crisis, and many warm examples of human kindness. We shall mention only a few of the sources resorted to, other than aid from government and organized charity.

One method has already been noted: Use up any resources that you may have. Use up your savings, sell your house and realize any equity that may remain, sell anything you have that is not necessary for survival. Borrow on anything that you have—your house, your life insurance policy, your good name. Borrow from anyone who will lend to you—from banks and other institutions, your relatives, your friends, your grocer, just anyone. At the end of this process you may be penniless and so deeply in debt that it will take years to repay, but at least you may survive.

If your assets and borrowing power became exhausted, you hoped for some kind of "invisible relief"—help not from government or organized charity, but from relatives, friends, neighbors, and others. The role of invisible relief in the depression can hardly be overstated. It took many forms. For example, one relative helped another and even whole families by giving money, food, clothing, or by taking them into the home. In fortunate situations, the giver could well afford it. Perhaps more often, the giver was himself in need, or close to it. In case after case, elderly parents helped their children, grandchildren, or other relatives at the sacrifice of their own security in old age. Children helped their parents while their own children were in need. Also, friend helped friend and neighbor helped neighbor. In many cases the help was small—a little money, a bit of food, some old clothing. There were many stories of poor families living in only a few rooms taking in other whole families for long periods of time, and of poor families caring for the children of others who were destitute. "Huddling" became common, and among the families huddled together were many who could not pay their share. Then there was the neighborhood store and shoe repair shop that often extended credit, knowing full well that payment would be long delayed, if it came at all. No one knows how many shopkeepers were bankrupted in the process and themselves made destitute.

The story would not be complete without a tribute to one of the least-loved economic classes in America—the landlords. Unable to collect rents from unemployed tenants or from relief agencies, great numbers of landlords postponed evictions until taxes, mortgage payments, or both were long delinquent. Many saw their properties sold because of these delinquencies. Cynics may say that early evictions would have been of no advantage to landlords; they could not have rented their properties to anyone else. But whatever their motives, tolerant landlords saved thousands upon thousands of families from becoming homeless.

■ CONCLUSIONS   Thus, invisible relief was the principle of mutual self-help in operation at the local level. It was heartwarming to behold, and it helped greatly in ameliorating suffering. But in the end it was a failure. It was highly inequitable in distributing the costs of providing relief and, above all, it was utterly inadequate. By 1933, millions were demanding something better. Within a few years they would have unemployment insurance, old-age insurance, and more adequate relief of the unemployed and the aged. Such measures might well have come anyway at some later date, but there can be little doubt that their coming was hastened by the widespread suffering during the great slide.

4

Farmers in the Depression

Even before the depression, great numbers of farmers were complaining loudly about their economic status. They lamented that they had not shared fairly in the general prosperity of the 1920s; that the prices they received for their products were too low relative to their prices they had to pay for the things they bought; that their prices fluctuated too widely; that farm incomes were too low relative to those of urban dwellers; that their debt burdens were too heavy and that credit for farmers was both too limited in amount and too costly; and that their burdens of taxes, especially of property taxes, were inequitably heavy. Although many farmers, particularly those operating large farms and using efficient production methods, were hardly in the dire condition suggested by the loudness of the laments, it cannot be denied that real farm problems existed. Some of these were legacies from the war and the sharp postwar depression. Others were generated, or at least magnified, by developments during the decade of the 1920s.

World War I had brought increasing prices for farm products and great prosperity for farmers. Even as early as 1915, rising foreign demands began to raise the prices of farm products, and the rise continued as America first initiated its rearmament program and then became an active participant in the war. During the period of America's participation in the war and up to the time when prices reached their peaks in May 1920, prices of farm products were more than twice their average levels in the prewar period, 1910–1914. Farmers would not soon forget the wonderful price increases they enjoyed during this period. For example, cotton rose from about 12 cents to 35 cents a pound, wheat from about 90 cents to $2.16 a bushel, and corn from about 65 cents to $1.52 a bushel. Of course, the farmers' costs of production and the prices of other things that they bought also rose, but the increases in prices of farm products were great enough to bring a marked rise of farmers' real incomes. This is shown in Table 4–1.

Since the *parity ratio* came to play such an important role in farm policy, its meaning should be noted carefully. The parity ratio for any period is computed by dividing the index of prices received by farmers by the index of prices paid by farmers, and then multiplying the result by 100 to put

Table 4–1.   Indexes of prices received by farmers, prices paid by farmers, and parity, 1915–1929 (1910–1914=100)

YEAR	PRICES RECEIVED BY FARMERS	PRICES PAID BY FARMERS	PARITY RATIO
1915	99	105	94
1916	119	116	103
1917	178	148	120
1918	206	173	119
1919	217	197	110
1920	211	214	99
1921	124	155	80
1922	131	151	87
1923	142	159	89
1924	143	160	89
1925	156	164	95
1926	145	160	91
1927	140	159	88
1928	148	162	91
1929	148	160	92

Source: U. S. Bureau of the Census, Historical Statistics of the United States, Colonial Times to 1957, 1960, p. 282.

it in percentage terms. Thus, the parity ratio for any stated period is an index of the ability of a unit of a farm product, or of a stated collection of farm products, to purchase things bought by farmers, this being stated as a percentage of the amount of the other things that unit of farm products would have bought in the 1910–1914 period. For example, the parity ratio of 119 for 1918 indicates that in that year a unit of farm products would buy 119 percent as much of other things as it would have commanded in 1910–1914.

Largely in response to these highly profitable conditions in the war period, but perhaps also in part because of nationwide campaigns for "food to win the war," farmers stepped up production. They brought under cultivation several million acres of land formerly used for grazing or other purposes, competed vigorously for other land, and stepped up purchases of equipment. The period also brought a sharp inflation of land values. The average increase between 1914 and 1920 appears to have been about 70 percent, although it was greater for land well-suited to such important cash crops as cotton, wheat, and corn. Much farmland changed hands at such values, and many mortgages were created on this basis. Farm debts rose sharply. In 1914, total farm debt was about $6.3 billion, with $4.7 billion in mortgages and $1.6 billion in other forms. By 1921, the total had risen to $14.1 billion, of which $10.2 billion was in mortgages and $3.9 billion in other forms.[1]

[1] U. S. Bureau of the Census, Historical Statistics of the United States, Colonial Times to 1957, 1960, pp. 286–287.

Then came the sharp decline of prices during the postwar depression that began in May 1920 and culminated in 1921. In this short period, prices received by farmers dropped at least 43 percent below their peak. (See Table 4-1.) Corn fell from $1.52 to 52 cents a bushel, wheat from $2.16 to $1.03 a bushel, and cotton from 35 to 16 cents a pound. Net incomes of farm proprietors fell from a peak of $9.5 billion in 1919 to $3.9 billion in 1921. Land values, as well as values of livestock and other types of farm inventories, also dropped sharply. Thousands of farmers went into bankruptcy quickly, but most did not. With the tolerance of their creditors, some of whom knew that to foreclose would be ruinous to themselves as well as the debtors, they hoped to recover and to be able to service their debts.

Prices received by farmers recovered somewhat in 1922, and then in the 1923–1929 period tended to stabilize around levels about 40–50 percent above the average in 1910–1914 but about one-third below the level in 1919. Prices of things purchased by farmers also stabilized, but at a level about 60 percent above their 1910–1914 average. Thus, the parity ratio averaged about 90 in the latter part of the 1920s. Prices of farmland had by this time drifted down to a level about 20 percent above their average in 1914, but 30 percent below their peak.

This behavior of the prices of farm products reflected, of course, both supply and demand conditions. On the supply side, the dominant trend was one with which we have since become so familiar—rising output despite net decreases of labor on farms, due to increased inputs of other types, especially of technology and capital. Land brought under cultivation for the first time during the war remained in use, but little more was added between 1920 and 1929. The number of people employed in farm work actually fell 669,000 during this period, while the total farm population decreased 1,394,000. These net changes fail to reveal the widespread migration from farms. In this period, the net excess of births over death on farms was 4,425,000; this was more than offset by the net migration of 5,819,000 people away from farms.

Continued advances in technology were a major force tending to increase total farm output. These took many forms: improvements in methods of farm management, better adaptation of crops to soils, development of more efficient plants and animals, and so on. The increase of capital in agriculture also took many forms, but most spectacular were the increases in automobiles, trucks, tractors, and other power-operated equipment. Farm automobiles and trucks, together with improvement of roads, increased the efficiency of transportation to and from markets, and the use of these and other types of power equipment decreased the need for horses and mules. As the number of draft animals declined sharply, about 23 million acres of land formerly used to produce feed for them was made available to produce output for the market, thus accentuating oversupply.

While farm output was rising, demand schedules for farm products were not increasing as fast. One reason for this was the depressed level of foreign demand for American farm products. In the early part of the decade, this was due in part to economic dislocations abroad, evidenced in low incomes there, disturbances in exchange markets, and so on. But a more basic reason was the increase of farm production abroad and the rise of protectionism against agricultural imports, especially in countries that had suffered from food shortages during the war. The decrease of exports freed about 16 million acres of land from production for this purpose and made it available to produce for the domestic market.

Domestic demands did tend to rise as both population and average income per capita grew. But they did not rise enough to support the level of farm prices in the face of increasing total output, decreased exports, and shifts of land away from producing feed for draft animals and toward production for the market. The income-elasticity of demand for food was rather low, partly because the majority of Americans were already fairly well fed. There were also important shifts in taste. A nation becoming increasingly one of white-collar rather than manual workers and paying homage to the svelte, if not skinny, female figure reduced its caloric intake. This was evidenced by shifts of demand from such things as wheat, corn, and potatoes and toward fruits, fruit juices, and vegetables. In the area of fibers, cotton was beginning to feel the competition of rayon.

It was not true, as some members of the farm bloc implied, that all American farmers were in distress even before the onset of the great depression. Many were prospering, especially the larger farmers employing the most efficient methods of production. Most of these would have been able to solve their debt problems and make a good living if the period of prosperity had continued. However, great numbers of farmers were already in difficult economic positions. Among these were most small farmers, those using backward farming methods, and those heavily in debt. Not only these but many others as well proved to be highly vulnerable in face of the depression.

One point of vulnerability was the size and distribution of farm debt. In 1929, total farm debt was about $12.4 billion, with $9.8 billion in mortgages and $2.6 billion in other forms. Mortgage debt was equal to about 20 percent of the total value of farm real estate. This debt was quite unevenly distributed among farming regions and among farmers within each region. For example, in 1930, about 39 percent of all owner-operated farms were encumbered with mortgages averaging 40 percent of their value.[2] Seven states accounted for more than half of the total value of all farm mortgages—California, Illinois, Iowa, Minnesota, Nebraska, Texas, and Wisconsin.[3] States in which more than half of all farms were mortgaged included Iowa, Nebraska, South Dakota, and Wisconsin. These and many

[2] John D. Black, "The Agricultural Situation, January 1933," *Review of Economics and Statistics*, Feb. 15, 1933, p. 35.

[3] Robert F. Martin, *Income in Agriculture, 1929–1935*, National Industrial Conference Board, New York, 1936, p. 55.

other areas proved vulnerable when prices of farm products and farmland fell.

Even in 1929, farmers were complaining about the scarcity and high cost of agricultural credit. The Federal Land Bank system, established in 1916, provided a source of long-term loans. The Federal Intermediate Credit Banks, established in 1923, encouraged intermediate-term loans to farmers by standing ready to rediscount such paper offered by lenders. Farmers were still dissatisfied. They felt that for long-term loans they were too dependent on distant insurance companies and local lenders, and for short-term and intermediate-term loans too dependent on local commercial banks. It was quite true that many local banks had not been generous sources of credit. Many were unable to increase their loans very much, partly because the limited rise of farm incomes limited the rise of total deposits and lending power in farming areas. And many banks failed during the 1920s. Within a few years, farmers were to have even more reason to complain as thousands of country banks closed. Farmers not only lost their deposits and a major source of credit but sure also called upon by receivers of the closed banks to pay their debts.

■ **FARM INCOMES IN THE GREAT SLIDE**   Then came the great depression, which made farmers long for the conditions of the 1920s about which they had complained so loudly. Table 4–2 tells the story of farm

Table 4–2.   Farm incomes, 1929–1933 (in millions of dollars)

	1929	1930	1931	1932	1933	1932 AS PERCENT OF 1929
Realized gross farm income	$13,985	$11,432	$8,385	$6,371	$7,081	45.9
Less: total farm production expenses	7,631	6,909	5,499	4,443	4,314	58.2
Equals: realized net income of farm operators	6,264	4,523	2,886	1,928	2,767	30.8
Addendum Net incomes to persons on farms from farming	7,024	5,060	3,981	2,510	3,012	35.7

Source: U. S. Bureau of the Census, *Historical Statistics of the United States, Colonial Times to 1957*, 1960, p. 283. "Realized gross farm income" includes not only cash income but also value of farm output consumed on farms and the rental value of farm dwellings. In 1932, these amounted to about $1.6 billion. "Net incomes to persons on farms from farming" includes net incomes of farm operators and wages of farm laborers living on farms.

incomes in cold statistics. Here we shall deal with changes from 1929 to 1932, because the figures for 1933 reflect some of the effects of New Deal farm policies. By 1932, realized gross farm incomes, including the value of farm products consumed on farms and the rental value of farm dwellings, had fallen 54 percent. Because costs of production did not decline in proportion, net incomes of farm operators fell nearly 70 percent. Net cash income fell even more because the figure for net income shown in the table includes the value of farm output consumed on farms and the rental value of farm dwellings. But think of the impact on farmers with large property tax and debt liabilities even if the decline of their net cash incomes was only 70 percent! The addendum shows that the net incomes from farming of farmers and of hired workers living on farms declined over 64 percent, and was only $2,510 million in 1932. This was equal to an average of $80 for each of the 31,388,000 people living on farms in that year. This figure is difficult to interpret meaningfully. A number of the people living on farms had income from other sources, but most probably did not and many had incomes below the average.

In contrast to behavior in most other industries, real output in agriculture did not fall. In fact, as shown in Table 4–3, total farm output in

Table 4–3.   Indexes of real farm output, 1929–1933

	1929	1930	1931	1932	1933
Total farm output	100.0	98.4	106.4	103.2	95.2
Total crops	100.0	94.5	105.5	100.0	89.0
Feed grains	100.0	90.3	101.6	117.7	90.3
Hay and forage	100.0	83.5	91.1	93.7	87.3
Food grains	100.0	108.8	116.2	92.6	69.1
Vegetables	100.0	101.4	102.7	104.1	100.0
Fruits and nuts	100.0	97.3	122.7	100.0	101.3
Cotton	100.0	94.2	115.0	87.5	87.5
Tobacco	100.0	108.0	101.1	65.9	90.9
Oil-bearing crops	100.0	107.7	107.7	100.0	161.5
Total livestock and products	100.0	101.6	103.2	104.8	106.3
Meat animals	100.0	101.6	106.5	108.1	112.9
Dairy products	100.0	101.3	104.0	105.3	105.3
Poultry and eggs	100.0	102.3	100.0	100.0	100.0

Source: Economic Report of the President, January 1963, pp. 258–260. The indexes have been converted from a 1957–1959 base to a 1929 base.

1931 and 1932 was slightly higher than in 1929. The most important reasons for this maintenance of output were the recognition by each individual farmer that he could not raise prices by reducing his output, and the absence of any way of getting effective cooperative action to this end; the high ratio of fixed costs to total costs, especially on family farms; and probably also the continuing hope of farmers that "prices will get better soon." Although the consequences for farmers were ruinous, urban dwellers could be thankful that farmers did not follow the output patterns of most other industries.

While farmers maintained their rates of output, both domestic and foreign demands for agricultural products declined sharply. That domestic demands should decline is easily understood in view of the sharp decreases of American money incomes. For cotton, the situation was worsened by the rapid rise of rayon fibers. The even sharper decrease of foreign demands for American farm products reflected not only the decrease of money incomes abroad but also the fall in the prices of farm products of other countries and growing protectionism against imports.

Thus, the entire decrease in the money incomes of farmers resulted from declines in the prices of farm products. The first part of Table 4–4 shows

Table 4–4. Indexes of prices received by farmers, prices paid by farmers, and parity, 1929–1933

	1929	1930	1931	1932	1933
Part I.					
Index: 1929 = 100					
Prices received by farmers	100.0	84.5	58.8	43.9	47.3
Prices paid by farmers	100.0	94.4	81.3	70.0	68.1
Part II.					
Index: 1910–1914 = 100					
Prices received by farmers	148	125	87	65	70
Prices paid by farmers	160	151	130	112	109
Parity ratio	92	83	67	58	64
Part III. Prices received by farmers for selected farm products (prices in dollars)					
Corn (bu.)	$0.80	$0.60	$0.32	$0.32	$0.52
Wheat (bu.)	1.04	0.67	0.39	0.38	0.74
Cotton (lb.)	0.17	0.09	0.06	0.07	0.10
Tobacco (lb.)	0.18	0.13	0.08	0.10	0.13
Potatoes (cwt.)	2.18	1.52	0.76	0.63	1.37
Oranges (box)	3.59	1.35	1.22	0.88	1.39
Whole milk (cwt.)	2.53	2.21	1.69	1.28	1.30

Source: U. S. Bureau of the Census, *Historical Statistics of the United States, Colonial Times to 1957*, 1960. The price indices are from p. 283, the other data from various tables.

that by 1932, prices received by farmers had fallen 56 percent below their levels in 1929, while prices paid by farmers had declined only 32 percent. The second part of the table indicates that by 1932, prices received by farmers had fallen 35 percent below their average levels in the prewar period, 1910–1914, and that on the average a unit of farm products would buy only 58 percent as much of other things as in the earlier period. The capacity of each unit of farm products to meet taxes, debt obligations, and other fixed dollar commitments had fallen even more. Consider this question: "Suppose that a farmer was under obligation to pay $100 a year in taxes or debt service. How many units of his output would be required for this in 1932 as compared with 1929?" Data for computing this answer appear in Part III of Table 4–4. These are the results. To meet obligations fixed in terms of dollars required, in 1932, 2.5 times as much corn as in 1929, 2.7 times as much wheat, 2.4 times as much cotton, 1.8 times as much tobacco, 3.5 times as many potatoes, 4.1 times as many oranges, and 1.9 times as much whole milk. When one keeps in mind these facts and the 70 percent decrease in the net incomes of farm proprietors, it becomes easy to

FARM PRODUCT	AMOUNT REQUIRED TO MEET A $100 OBLIGATION IN 1929	AMOUNT REQUIRED TO MEET A $100 OBLIGATION IN 1932	AMOUNT REQUIRED IN 1932 AS A MULTIPLE OF AMOUNT REQUIRED IN 1929
Corn	125 bushels	313 bushels	2.5
Wheat	96 bushels	263 bushels	2.7
Cotton	588 pounds	1,429 pounds	2.4
Tobacco	556 pounds	1,000 pounds	1.8
Potatoes	46 cwt.	159 cwt.	3.5
Oranges	28 boxes	114 boxes	4.1
Whole milk	40 cwt.	78 cwt.	1.9

understand why delinquencies on farm taxes and farm debts became so widespread. For this purpose, also bear in mind the sharp deflation of farmland values. One index indicates that by March 1932, months before they reached their lowest levels, prices of farmland had fallen 23 percent below 1929 levels, 47 percent below their levels in 1920, and 11 percent below their prewar levels.[4] In many communities, such statistics had little meaning because it was almost impossible to find anyone both able and willing to buy a farm.

How did farmers adjust to such great losses of income? For one thing, they cut sharply their consumption expenditures. Most were able to get enough food, but many had little beyond that and the use of a farm dwelling. Great numbers allowed their farms to deteriorate, failing to spend enough for maintenance, repair, and new capital goods to offset current depreciation and depletion. Observers frequently commented on the deterioration of farm buildings and, in many areas, the abandonment of soil conservation measures. Purchases of new capital goods fell sharply, as indicated by Table 4–5.

Expenditures for lime and fertilizers declined 60 percent by 1933,

[4] Black, *op. cit.*, p. 32.

Table 4–5.   Farmer expenditures for selected types of
investment goods, 1929–1933 (in millions of dollars)

TYPE OF PURCHASE	1929	1930	1931	1932	1933	1933 AS PER-CENT OF 1929
Fertilizer and lime	$ 300	$297	$202	$118	$120	40.0
Private farm construction	307	193	97	37	49	16.0
Tractors	186	174	112	56	30	16.1
Other farm machinery	265	252	114	62	49	18.5
Total	$1,058	$916	$525	$273	$248	23.4

Sources: Various tables in U. S. Department of Commerce, National Income, 1954, and U. S. Bureau of the Census, Historical Statistics of the United States, Colonial Times to 1957.

which is not irrelevant to the widespread deterioration of soils, discussed so much in later years. Expenditures for farm construction, tractors, and other farm machinery all declined more than 80 percent. It was certainly true, as many pointed out at the time, that impoverished farmers are not good customers of other industries. However, it does not necessarily follow, as many argued, that the most strategic method of increasing industrial activity would be to supply farmers with more income.

Some trends in the 1929–1933 period are in striking contrast to those of the preceding decade. In the earlier period, farm output increased despite decreases in the farm population and labor force, primarily because farmers increased greatly their inputs in the form of technology and capital goods. Now the trends were reversed. It is doubtful that farmers' expenditures for capital goods in the 1929–1933 period were more than enough to offset current depreciation. But the farm population, which had declined 1,394,000 between 1920 and 1929, actually rose more than one million from the latter year to 1933. This reflected a continued excess of births over deaths on farms, and a sharp decrease of net migration from farms. The latter, in turn, reflected both a smaller flow of people away from farms and a larger flow to farms. As indicated earlier, the total amount of labor employed on farms remained about constant, as the 500,000 decrease of hired workers was offset by an approximately equal rise in the number of family workers.

Like their urban counterparts, many farmers and farm workers also tried to adjust to decreases of their incomes by spending away any liquid assets that they might own and by borrowing. Most found that any money and other liquid assets that they may have had did not last long. Additional borrowing was a real alternative for some who remained creditworthy, but this source became decreasingly available as the depression wore on. One reason was the deteriorating creditworthiness of farmers. Also important was the deteriorating condition of the country banks on whom the farmers depended so heavily. This was especially true of independent unit banks whose deposits, and therefore lending power, came mostly from farmers in their areas or from businesses heavily dependent on local farmers.

Very early in the depression these banks began to suffer net losses of deposits, reserves, and lending power to banks in larger centers. There were two principal reasons for this. One was the decline in the incomes of the banks' depositors. As their incomes declined, farmers made net transfers of deposits to suppliers and creditors in cities, many of which were some distance away. The other reason was the cessation of capital flows from financial centers to farmers, and then a reversal of these flows. In the earlier period, both farmers and their banks received a flow of funds from insurance companies, Federal Land Banks, and other lenders in financial centers. Now the flow stopped and farmers were requested to make net payments on outstanding debts. Many country banks also suffered drains as depositors lost confidence in their safety. Banks suffering such drains of deposits, reserves, and lending power were in no position to make large additional loans, and most were under strong pressure to reduce outstanding loans. Thousands of them failed. In the three years 1930–1932, 5,096 banks failed in the United States; 3,448 of these, or nearly 77 percent, were in places with populations below 2,500. Farmers whose banks failed not only had their deposits frozen and lost their principal source of credit, but also faced the probability that bank receivers would press for repayment of outstanding debts. Many had no alternative source of credit under the circumstances. Even the decreasing number that remained creditworthy often found that other banks in the area, if any remained, had their hands full in trying to accommodate their old customers.

Another way of adjusting to decreased income was, of course, to become delinquent on taxes and debt service, and this farmers did in swelling numbers. Most farmers appear to have made strong efforts to meet their obligations. It is true, of course, that farmers are notorious grumblers about taxes, and that even the most conservative Republicans among them have not historically been great admirers of financial institutions, especially not those in the "East." Increasing numbers sat before their radios and listened to Father Coughlin, speaking from the Church of the Little Flower in Detroit, as he denounced the nefarious practices of "the money changers." More and more turned bitter and came to believe that equity was on their side and took precedence over legal obligations. However, farmers knew that delinquency on taxes or debts could well lead to loss of their farms and other property, which represented all their savings and their source of livelihood. Only great strain could bring widespread delinquency.

■ **DELINQUENCIES ON TAXES AND DEBTS**   In 1929, there were 19.5 forced sales because of delinquent taxes and debt payments for every 1,000 farms in the United States. By 1932, this figure had risen to

41.7.[5] Tax sales alone rose from 4.7 per 1,000 farms in 1929 to 15.3 in 1933. These figures grossly understate the increase of delinquency because it became decreasingly common for delinquencies to lead to forced sales. It is easy to see why local tax officials became increasingly tolerant of delinquencies on farm taxes, and even more reluctant to force sales of farms, especially when delinquency became almost community-wide. As elective or appointive officials, they knew that to press too hard was to be out of a job. Also, many of them were farmers, or friends or relatives of farmers, and quite sympathetic. However, even an official determined to do his job without fear, sympathy, or favor had good reason to avoid forced sales if he could. By 1932, it became virtually impossible to find buyers in some areas, and in other cases sales prices were too low to cover the total of delinquent taxes even though in normal times a large equity would have remained for the farmer. By the end of 1932, many sheriffs would have encountered violence if they had tried to conduct a forced sale.

For somewhat similar reasons, holders of mortgages and other farm debts also came to foreclose in only a decreasing fraction of the cases of delinquency. Some followed this policy out of sympathy for the farmer and a hope that he would be able to pay soon. Even the coldly calculating creditor realized that he faced only three alternatives, none very attractive. The first was to tolerate delinquencies, encouraging the farmer-debtor to stay on the land, keep up with his taxes, maintain buildings and land in good condition, and pay what he could when he could. The second was to foreclose on the mortgage and buy the land, or agree to take it over without formal foreclosure proceedings, and become a landlord. He would then face all the problems of a landlord—of finding an efficient and reliable tenant, of protecting the condition of the farm, of paying taxes, and perhaps of seeing the value of the land fall still more. The third alternative was to foreclose on the mortgage and let the farm be sold to someone else. By 1932, farmers were becoming increasingly effective in making this and the second alternative unavailable to creditors. However, even this course of action had serious disadvantages for creditors, even when it was available. Foreclosure preceedings in many states were time-consuming and costly, buyers were difficult to find, and the proceeds from farm sales were in many cases below the face value of the mortgage. The foreclosing creditor therefore had to write down the values of his assets and net worth, an ordeal that many financial institutions were not prepared to face in the later stages of the great slide.

It was for reasons such as these that foreclosures on farms and other farm properties rose far less than delinquencies on farm taxes and debts.

One study, whose results are summarized in Table 4–6, found that by the beginning of 1933, delinquency rates on farm mortgages in the country as a whole were 45 percent if related to the number of mortgaged farms and

[5] U. S. Bureau of Agricultural Economics, *The Agricultural Situation*, April 1933, p. 12.

Table 4–6.   Farm mortgage delinquency at the beginning of 1933

U. S. AREA	PERCENT OF MORTGAGED FARMS REPORTED DELINQUENT	PERCENT OF MORTGAGED DEBT REPORTED DELINQUENT
New England	25.3	21.9
Middle Atlantic	29.8	35.6
East North Central	35.0	42.1
West North Central	49.2	56.3
South Atlantic	48.6	60.1
East South Central	43.5	49.0
West South Central	49.8	56.9
Mountain	49.9	56.8
Pacific	40.0	43.6
United States as a whole	45.1	52.2

Source: U. S. Bureau of Agricultural Economics, *The Agricultural Situation,* December 1934, p. 4. These results are based on study of a sample of 12,000 farmers.

52 percent if related to the value of mortgages. A closer study of the figures reveals that delinquency occurred all over the country; it was no localized thing. Even in New England, with the best record, one-fourth of all farm mortgages, representing nearly 22 percent of the total value of mortgages, were delinquent. Worst of all by a narrow margin was the South Atlantic region, with nearly 49 percent of the number of farm mortgages and 60 percent of their value in delinquency. Not far behind were the West South Central, Mountain, and West North Central regions. One observer commented that early in the depression delinquency was largely limited to "poor mortgages"—to those issued by inefficient farmers. By 1932, even "good" mortgages were becoming delinquent in increasing numbers. The endemic nature of this delinquency helps explain farmer reactions in 1932 and 1933. If delinquency had been rare and largely limited to inefficient farms, there would probably have been little protest. But when a large fraction of all mortgaged farms in an area became delinquent, including those of many of the most respected farmers, the stage was set for direct action, political action, or both to prevent creditors from exercising their legal rights.

■ **DIRECT AND POLITICAL ACTION BY FARMERS**   As already indicated, most farmers made every effort to pay their debts, many deeded their farms to creditors when they were no longer able to make payments, and most conducted themselves in a peaceful manner. However, by 1932, frustration and bitterness had grown to such a point that a minority of farmers resorted to violence and many more were determined to get favorable political action. Much of the violence started in efforts to raise prices of farm products by withholding supplies from markets. Groups of farmers stopped market-bound trucks and poured cans of milk into the ditch; loads of fruit, vegetables, or eggs were overturned; and farmers were threatened with injury if they did not return supplies to their farms. Most active was the Farmers' Holiday Association, which had spread rapidly in the early years of the depression.[6] Most of the violence was in Iowa, Minnesota, and Wisconsin, but there were also disorders in Nebraska, South Dakota, and several other states.

By late 1932, violence was directed primarily at foreclosure sales. On December 28, a group of about 75 farmers tried to prevent an eviction in Ashland County, Wisconsin, but were thwarted by deputy sheriffs. On Jan. 4, 1933, farmers in LeMars, Iowa, were more successful: They over-powered the judge and sheriff and threatened the life of the attorney of the insurance company. Half a dozen sales were broken up during the next week. Another favorite device of farmers was "to keep order" and bid in properties at very low prices. For example, in Shelby, Nebraska, a farm mortgaged to a bank for $4,100 was bid in by friendly neighbors for $49.50 and turned back to the owner. In another case, the price was $25. A horse and an automobile were purchased for a total of 20 cents.

While farmers were slowing foreclosures by direct action, they were also busy on the political front, demanding state laws providing moratoria on farm mortgages and in some cases home mortgages as well. Minnesota was the first state to pass such a law in early 1933. By the end of the year, most other important agricultural states had followed suit. In various ways, these laws prevented foreclosures, or at least inhibited them: they introduced more complex and time-consuming foreclosure procedures; provided arrangements for scaling down principal, or interest, or both; outrightly suspended foreclosures for stated periods, usually at least two years; and prohibited deficiency judgments against farmers. Somewhat similar provisions were included in the Frazier-Lemke Amendment to the National Bankruptcy Act. This Act was later declared unconstitutional, but was soon replaced by another that was upheld by the courts.

■ CONCLUSIONS   Thus, by the spring of 1933 the legal rights of holders of farm mortgages had been sharply modified and limited, and there were heated debates about the legitimacy and equity of the new federal and state laws. However useful this legislation may have been in delaying foreclosures, it solved none of the basic problems. Farmers' money incomes were still abysmally low. In many case, the current values of farms were less than the face values of the mortgages on them. Insurance companies, other financial institutions, and other holders of farm mortgages found that this type of asset was frozen; they could not collect currently, and the amount of ultimate recovery was doubtful. Savers with claims on

[6] This section draws heavily on Archibald M. Woodruff, Jr., *Farm Mortgage Loans of Life Insurance Companies*, Yale University Press, New Haven, Conn., 1937, pp. 101–182.

these financial institutions had still another reason to worry about the liquidity and safety of their claims. Farmers were desperate, but the position of their creditors was unenviable. Major rehabilitation was clearly required. A basic need was to raise farm incomes, but to accomplish this would require time. In the meantime, steps would have to be taken to solve, or at least to alleviate, farm debt problems, not only to help farmer-debtors and their creditors but also to revive a flow of credit to farmers so that they could again live better, accumulate capital, increase productivity in agriculture, and become buyers of industrial products.

5

The Distressed Financial System

The grinding deflation of employment, output, prices, and money incomes was accompanied by a breakdown of the financial system. We have already noted that between 1929 and the end of 1932, nearly 5,100 commercial banks failed, more than one out of every five. Failure rates increased in late 1932, a banking panic developed in February, and virtually every bank in the country had closed by the time Franklin Roosevelt was inaugurated. Closings of other types of financial institutions were widespread but not so endemic. In another sense, most of the financial institutions that remained open were failing: They were failing to provide the flows of credit that are the lifeblood of a modern economy. They were almost literally frozen; they were receiving only a trickle of new funds from savers, and most of them were trying to reduce outstanding loans rather than increase them, even though this served to accentuate the depression. Few were free from fear of failure.

■ **FINANCIAL INTERMEDIARIES**   To describe the plight of the financial system, and the reasons for this plight, we shall concentrate on financial intermediaries, and especially on four principal types: commercial banks, mutual savings banks, savings and loan associations (or building and loan associations, as they were commonly called at that time), and life insurance companies.

As noted earlier, the essential function of a financial intermediary is to gather funds by issuing claims against itself and to use the funds thus gathered to acquire financial claims against others. The claims issued by an intermediary against itself typically have two characteristics: They are payable in stated numbers of dollars and they are payable on demand or short notice. For example, commercial banks gather most of their funds by issuing deposit claims. Checking deposits are payable on demand; time and savings deposits are legally payable only after a period of notice, but in fact people expect to be permitted to withdraw on demand. Claims issued by mutual savings banks are quite similar to time and savings deposit claims against commercial banks. Claims against savings and loan associations were often called "shares," but their holders expected them to be payable at face value and on demand. Claims against life insurance companies, mostly insurance and annuity policies, were somewhat longer term in nature, but their holders could withdraw funds by surrendering their policies or by borrowing against them.

On the other hand, the financial claims acquired by financial intermediaries and held as assets are typically of longer maturity and subject to wider fluctuations in value. For example, as shown in Table 5–1, the

Table 5–1. Selected assets and liabilities of certain financial intermediaries in 1929[a] (in billions of dollars)

	COMMER-CIAL BANKS	MUTUAL SAVINGS BANKS	SAVINGS AND LOAN ASSOCIA-TIONS	PRIVATE LIFE INSURANCE COMPANIES	TOTAL
Number of institutions	25,113	609	12,342	438	38,502
Total assets	$66.2	$9.9	$8.7	$17.5	$102.3
Principal types of assets					
Stocks				0.4	0.4
Bonds	13.7	3.6		6.0	23.3
Mortgages	6.3		6.5	7.3	20.1
Loans	29.4	5.8[b]			35.2
Principal claims issued to savers					
Demand deposits	22.5				22.5
Time deposits	19.6	8.9			28.5
Savings and loan shares			6.2		6.2
Life insurance and annuities				[c]	
Total of claims issued	$42.1	$8.9	$6.2		

[a] Data only approximate because they come from various sources and apply to different dates in 1929.
[b] Mortgages included in loans.
[c] Current value not available.

principal assets of these institutions were bonds issued by corporations and all levels of governmental units; mortgages on farms, urban dwellings, and other real estate; and various other types of loans with a wide range of maturities.

The quantity of financial claims that financial intermediaries can acquire and hold is, of course, limited by the amount of claims against the intermediaries that the public is willing to hold. To meet any withdrawals by holders of claims against them, intermediaries have four principal sources of funds: (1) receipts of new savings, (2) receipts of interest and principal repayments on their portfolios, (3) sales of assets from their portfolios, and (4) borrowing from others. We shall find that all these sources of liquidity deteriorated as the depression deepened.

■ SOURCES OF FINANCIAL DISTRESS   Why did the financial system fall into such distress? Some of the oversimplified answers popular at the time or later must be discounted as general explanations. (1) Banks and other financial institutions became distressed because during the 1920s they loaded up with foreign bonds that later lost most of their value. It is true that the values of many of these issues fell sharply, although some performed as well as many domestic issues, and that a few institutions may have been seriously damaged by this alone. However, since these securities constituted less than 2 percent of the total assets of financial intermediaries, they could not account for more than a tiny fraction of total losses. (2) Financial institutions were in distress because their owners or managers were dishonest, or at the very least had betrayed their trust in managing other people's money. It is true that some did engage in speculation and peculation, and perhaps more were imprudent in taking loans for themselves, friends, and associates. In individual cases, institutions suffered acutely because of such practices, but it seems highly unlikely that this was a major source of the general distress of financial institutions. (3) They were in distress because in the 1920s they loaded up with domestic loans and securities that would have proved unsound even if prosperous conditions had continued, and that certainly could not weather even a mild depression. Such allegations are difficult to appraise.

It was certainly true that in 1929, as in any other period of high prosperity, some securities had been purchased and loans made on the basis of highly optimistic assumptions about the future. There were indeed many risky mortgages, mortgage bonds, other bonds, and loans. Even a mild depression would have brought some losses, but not widespread and large ones. It must be conceded, therefore, that the lending and investment policies of some of these institutions in the 1920s did increase their vulnerability to depression, but there is no need to agree with those who argue that these policies brought on the depression and were the major cause of later financial distress. And there is certainly no need to agree with those who imply that lending and investing policies in the 1920s should have been so conservative that financial institutions would be safe and sound even after years of grinding depression. Under such policies, there would be no periods of prosperity. The major sources of widespread distress among financial institutions were generated in the course of the depression itself.

The vulnerability of financial intermediaries was enhanced by the absence of protective governmental programs that we take for granted today. There were no agencies, such as the Federal Deposit Insurance Corporation and the Federal Savings and Loan Insurance Corporation, to insure the safety of depositors' claims and to reduce the probability of withdrawals. There was no Federal Housing Administration or any similar agency to insure the safety of home mortgages or of other assets acquired by financial intermediaries. There was only one set of federal institutions to lend to ultimate borrowers—the Federal Land Banks. There were only two federal agencies to rediscount for or lend to financial institutions— the Federal Intermediate Credit Banks and the Federal Reserve Banks. And their direct assistance was quite restricted; they lent on only a few types of assets and to only a fraction of all financial intermediaries. The Federal Intermediate Credit Banks lent on only one type of asset—intermediate-term loans to farmers. The Federal Reserve lent to only one class of financial institutions—commercial banks that were members of the Federal Reserve System. Thus, the 15,500 nonmember commercial banks that proved to be so vulnerable had no direct access to Federal Reserve credit. Neither did the mutual savings banks, savings and loan associations, and life insurance companies. Moreover, Federal Reserve loans to member banks were restricted to only two types of assets: United States government securities and short-term commercial paper. These were only a fraction of member bank assets. In short, only a small number of the financial intermediaries had direct access to assistance from any government agency during the early years of the depression, and those that did have direct access could borrow on only a few types of their assets. The private system was largely on its own, and it was expected to solve its problems through mutual self-help.

As we shall see, Federal Reserve policies during much of this period were ineffective, if not wrongly conceived. This was partly due to legal limitations on its powers. Senator Glass of Virginia and some other Congressional leaders in this field were wedded to the commerical loan theory of banking and were reluctant to permit the Federal Reserve to lend on a wider range of assets. However, it was in larger part because the Federal Reserve did not use forcefully the powers that it had. The Federal Reserve clearly did not want a decrease in bank credit and the money supply, and it took some steps to maintain them. But the outcome was a decrease of almost 25 percent in the money supply between 1929 and the end of 1932.

Thus, both past policies and deficient institutional arrangements enhanced the vulnerability of financial institutions. However, the increasing stress on the financial system was generated as a part of the deflationary process—the process that reduced sharply money incomes, flows of saving, the ability of debtors of almost all classes to service their outstanding debts, and the creditworthiness of potential borrowers.

■ SAVING AND FINANCIAL INTERMEDIARIES   A major direct contributor to the growing distress of financial intermediaries was the sharp decline of total saving as the nation's money income fell. As the depression wore on, loss of confidence in the ability of these institutions to pay promptly and in full became increasingly important in explaining withdrawals and the dwindling of their cash receipts. But the decline of total savings would have lowered cash receipts and increased withdrawals even if full confidence in the institutions had been maintained. This applies especially to personal savings.

In the 1920s, when their incomes were high, households saved large amounts. They used some of this current saving to buy tangible assets, such as houses, and some to buy direct securities, such as stocks and bonds. But a large part of personal savings flowed to financial intermediaries, some to increase deposits there and some to reduce mortgages and other debts owed to the intermediaries. While such large cash receipts continued, the intermediaries could easily maintain their liquidity. The stock market crash and the subsequent fall of national money income tended in two ways to maintain the cash flow to intermediaries. (1) Disenchanted with the stock market, people tended to entrust a larger part of their savings to these institutions. (2) Also, with the decline of national money income, payrolls, and trade, households and business firms needed less currency to carry on their transactions, and some of the excess currency was exchanged for deposits or used to pay debts to these institutions.

However, these effects were swamped by the sharp decline of savings as money incomes fell. The estimates in Table 5–2 indicate that personal

Table 5–2.   Gross private savings in the United States,
1929–1933 (in millions of dollars)

YEAR	PERSONAL SAVINGS	CORPORATE NET SAVINGS[a]	CAPITAL CONSUMPTION ALLOWANCES, ETC.	TOTAL PRIVATE GROSS SAVINGS
1929	$4,168	$2,918	$8,617	$15,703
1930	3,406	250	8,541	12,197
1931	2,507	− 2,952	8,166	7,721
1932	− 646	− 4,920	7,615	2,049
1933	− 648	− 4,569	7,161	1,944

[a] Corporate net savings is undistributed corporate profits after inventory valuation adjustment.

Source: U. S. Department of Commerce, National Income, 1954, p. 164.

savings were below 1929 levels by 19 percent in 1930 and by 40 percent in 1931. In both 1932 and 1933, it was negative by nearly $650 million. Those who were spending beyond their current incomes outweighed those who were still positive savers. With such great declines in the flow of savings, it was inevitable that financial intermediaries as a group would suffer a decline in their cash receipts, and that at least some would suffer net with-drawals as depositors used their accumulated savings to finance consumption in excess of their current incomes.

These impacts differed greatly by type of institution, by location, and by type of depositor. Hit hardest were those most heavily dependent on deposi-tors whose incomes declined most sharply.

■ **THE DEBT SITUATION**   We turn now to the assets of these institutions, which were mostly debt claims issued by governmental units, business firms, farmers, and households. The story is gloomy; it could hardly be otherwise in view of the sharp deflation of money incomes and asset values. It is a story of spreading delinquencies on interest and principal payments, of rising business failures and near failures, and of deteriorating creditworthiness. Because the story is so gloomy, it is well to remember that great numbers of debtors met all their obligations promptly and in full. The creditworthiness of the federal government was never seriously questioned despite dire predictions concerning the ruinous effects of deficits. Millions of households, business firms, and governmental units were never delinquent, but the number of millions of whom this could be said declined sharply as the depression deepened and lengthened.

We shall be especially interested in two aspects of these debts. (1) The value and liquidity of these debts as assets of the financial intermediaries. The value of outstanding debt obligations fell for two reasons. Prices of even the best bonds fell during the credit stringency from August 1931 to June 1932, when all interest rates rose. Far greater, however, were the price declines resulting from actual delinquencies or failures of debtors and from rising fears that debtors would be unable to pay. Many securities became virtually unsalable at any price. These developments obviously decreased the ability of the intermediaries to attract new funds, to retain those already on hand, and to meet demands for withdrawals. They also damaged the solvency and liquidity positions of the intermediaries so much that the latter became reluctant to increase their risk exposure by making new loans. (2) The relationship of these debts to the creditworthiness of debtors, to the willingness of debtors to incur further risks by borrowing, and to the interest rates and other terms on which they could get credit, if at all. As increasing numbers became unable to service their existing debts or could do so only with increasing strain, they became reluctant to increase their risk exposure through additional borrowing. And increasing numbers could not borrow further on reasonable terms even if they wanted to, partly because lenders had become so fearful and partly because their creditworthiness deteriorated so badly as their incomes and asset values fell.

We shall consider here only four types of debts—those of state and local governments, farmers, homeowners, and business firms. The first two, already discussed, can be disposed of quickly. As noted earlier, most state and local governments did meet all their debt obligations, but increasing numbers did not. Three states and more than 1,300 municipalities actually defaulted on their bonds, others averted default only narrowly, and even more serviced their debt only by reducing drastically their public services. Many issues depreciated sharply as the creditworthiness of their issuers deteriorated.

The story of farm mortgages has already been told—spreading delinquencies, rising foreclosures, and increasingly effective action to prevent creditors from exercising their legal rights. The story of shorter term farm debts was much the same. Farmers who could not pay their property taxes or service their long-term debts were hardly in a position to pay their short-term debts promptly and in full.

In 1929, about half of all urban homes were mortgaged for a total of approximately $19 billion. The status of many of these mortgages came to resemble that of farm mortgages as the industrial depression deepened. Owners became delinquent on taxes, mortgage payments, or both; foreclosures soared; and in some areas it became difficult to find buyers of houses at any price. As might be expected, the situation was worst in the most depressed cities. There are no reliable statistics on the extent of defaults on home mortgages in the early years of the depression. However, a survey of 22 cities as of Jan. 1, 1934, found that the lowest rate of default on mortgages on owner-occupied houses was 21 percent.[1] The rate was above 38 percent in half the cities, between 50 and 60 percent in Indianapolis and Birmingham, and 62 percent in Cleveland. Default rates on rented properties were slightly higher. The lowest rate found was 22 percent. It was at least 40 percent in half the cities and 69 percent in Indianapolis.

Many lenders on home mortgages suffered large losses when they foreclosed, and a large part of their remaining holdings were frozen assets of highly uncertain value. Only when this situation was somehow remedied could a flow of new funds for home financing be restored. At stake was the welfare of the homeowners, the lenders, the construction industry, and the entire economy that ordinarily relies so heavily on home construction for investment spending.

Chapter 2 noted the sharp decline in the net incomes of business firms as the depression deepened. The net incomes of unincorporated businesses dropped sharply; and for corporations as a group, profits turned into large losses. Losses were especially large for small corporations. Fewer firms wanted to spend much for investment purposes, but those that did encountered increasing difficulties in financing. They could no longer rely on a large amount of internally generated funds in the form of retained net earnings and depreciation allowances. As shown in Table 5–2 (page 27), corporate net savings fell from $2.9 billion in 1929 to negative figures of $2.9 billion in 1931, $4.9 billion in 1932, and $4.6 billion in 1933. Gross

---

[1] The Twentieth Century Fund, *Debts and Recovery, 1929–1937*, The Twentieth Century Fund, New York, 1938, p. 164.

business savings, including both retained net earnings and depreciation and other similar alowances, fell from $11.5 billion in 1929 to $5.2 billion in 1931, $2.7 billion in 1932, and $2.6 billion in 1933. This was for the group as a whole; for those with the largest losses, even gross savings were negative. Businesses were depleting their liquidity and working capital by these large net outpayments. To issue new stock under existing conditions was infeasible for all but a very few. More and more found it increasingly difficult to borrow, partly because their creditworthiness was deteriorating. Increasing numbers failed, and more became delinquent on their existing debts. Only the most fortunate escaped some reduction in their credit ratings. This meant higher costs of borrowing, if they could borrow at all.

The data in Table 5–3 indicate the extent to which market prices of outstanding corporate bonds fell between 1928 and 1932. In the former

Table 5–3.   Corporate bonds in all industries classified by their prices as percentages of par value, 1928 and 1932

	1928		1932	
	NUMBER OF OUTSTANDING ISSUES	PAR AMOUNT OUTSTANDING	NUMBER OF OUTSTANDING ISSUES	PAR AMOUNT OUTSTANDING
Total number of issues	3,854		3,783	
Total outstanding par amounts (in millions)		$24,586		$27,369

PRICE CLASSES AS PERCENT OF PAR	PERCENT OF TOTAL			
Under 20	1.0	0.4	5.4	3.6
20–39	0.3	0.1	12.9	9.3
40–49	0.4	0.2	8.1	7.8
50–59	0.7	0.3	7.9	7.3
60–69	2.8	1.3	9.7	11.0
70–79	3.2	3.3	12.5	17.0
80–89	6.9	5.7	15.4	19.0
90–99	31.6	30.5	24.0	19.1
100–109	49.3	51.1	4.0	5.8
110–119	2.4	6.4	a	0.1
129 and over	1.4	0.7	a	—
Total	100.0	100.0	100.0	100.0

a Less than 0.1.

Source: W. Braddock Hickman, *Statistical Measures of Corporate Bond Financing Since 1900* (Copyright © 1960 by Princeton University Press), published for the National Bureau of Economic Research, Table 46, p. 71. Reprinted by permission of Princeton University Press. This includes only bonds for which there were market quotations and for which other relevant information was available.

year, 53 percent of the number of outstanding issues and 58 percent of
the par amount of these issues were selling at par or above. The prices of
85 percent of the number and 89 percent of the amount outstanding were
at least 90 percent of par. Note the great decline that had occurred by
1932. In that year, only 4 percent of the number of outstanding issues
was at par or above, and only 28 percent at 90 or better. About 44 percent
had depreciated 30 percent or more, and 26 percent had fallen by more than
half. In terms of par amounts outstanding, only 6 percent were at par or
above and only 25 percent at 90 or better. About 39 percent had depreciated
30 percent or more and 31 percent had fallen more than half. These data
suggest both the great losses incurred by holders of corporate bonds and
the difficult problems that many corporations would have faced if they
had tried to market new issues.

Let us now examine the impacts on selected classes of financial intermediaries.

■ SAVINGS AND LOAN ASSOCIATIONS   In 1929, there were
21,342 savings and loan associations in the United States, with total assets
of $8,695 million. Thus, the "typical" association was relatively small,
with assets averaging about $705,000. Most of them were also predominantly
local institutions, gathering funds from local people and lending most of
their funds locally. As already indicated, they accumulated assets almost
exclusively by issuing shares. These were purchased primarily by people of
modest means. For example, the average claim of each of the 12,351,000
members of the associations was only $700. Funds gathered in this way
were used almost exclusively to buy one type of asset—mortgages on one-
to four-family houses, almost all of which were located in the local area.
Thus, each association was dependent on the prosperity of its area for its
funds and for the safety and liquidity of its mortgage holdings.

During 1929, these associations as a group were able to increase their
outstanding shares by $480,000; in 1930, the increase was only $60,000.
Then there were net withdrawals of $380,000 in 1931, $590,000 in 1932,
and $580,000 in 1933.[2] Thus, during the four years 1930–1933, net with-
drawals were about $1,500 million, equal to 17 percent of the total assets
of the associations in 1929. They would have been much larger if the associations had met all requests for withdrawals.

By 1931, increasing numbers of the associations were in distress. Some
escaped; among these were associations that had been very conservative in
their lending and were fortunate in having depositors whose incomes had
fallen least. At the other extreme, some of those in greatest distress had
been guilty of reckless lending. But of overriding importance were declines
in incomes of depositors and debtors and, as the depression wore on, loss
of confidence in the ability of associations to pay. Testifying before a Con-

[2] U. S. Bureau of the Census, *Historical Statistics of the United States, Colonial
Times to 1957*, pp. 153–154.

gressional committee in January 1932, representatives of the industry cited waiting lists of shareholders wishing to withdraw, widespread delinquencies on home mortgages, unavailability of further loans from banks to the associations, and unavailability of mortgage money.[3]

For example, a witness from South Bend, Indiana, testified that every association in his city was restricting withdrawals and had waiting lists, that delinquencies on home mortgages were widespread and foreclosures common, and that "it is impossible to get money in South Bend to take care of these people who want to pay for their homes."[4] A witness from Cleveland asserted that every savings and loan association in his city required notices for withdrawal, that most had waiting lines, that the same was true in Youngstown and other large cities in the state, and that

> . . . the banks are not making loans now as formerly to the building and loan associations, because they have their hands full to protect their own deposit liabilities and are striving for liquidity, so no relief is afforded in that direction.[5]

Another witness from Cleveland agreed, stating that many associations were at least 60 days behind in meeting requests for withdrawal and some were four, five, or even six months behind. An official from Houston testified that his own association had cash receipts of $3,750,000 in 1931 but could lend only $350,000 because the remainder was withdrawn by members to meet their own needs.

> Private investors have had their minds so disturbed about mortgage loans as investments under present conditions that they are in the same mad dash for liquidity that seems to be abroad generally in the United States, evidenced in the attempt to reduce everything to cash. . . . They cannot come to us or to anyone else at this time and get money for refinancing. . . . In the small towns you will find no credit facilities at all under present conditions open to the prospective home owner.[6]

A building and loan association officer from Topeka, Kansas, stated:

> The people have been pulling out their savings, and using them, and for that reason they are not full handed in the way of cash as they have been for some time. They have not been able to make any loans, I would say, for a year. . . . We have not had the money to make loans and meet the demands for withdrawals. . . . I should say that 80 percent of the institutions in Kansas, and I think in Oklahoma, are not able to pay out now, because they cannot borrow the money as they did from banks. They say to the building and loan associations, as they do to the farmers, "We have not the money to pay. Even if we have it, we do not know what is going to happen. The people who own it may call on us any time."[7]

Similar testimony came from many other areas, including Florida, Louisiana, Massachusetts, Michigan, Missouri, New Jersey, and Pennsylvania.

[3] U. S. Senate Hearings before a subcommittee of the Senate Banking and Currency Committee on S. 2959, 72nd Congress, 1st session, January 1932.
[4] *Ibid.*, p. 406.
[5] *Ibid.*, p. 63.
[6] *Ibid.*, pp. 181–190.
[7] *Ibid.*, pp. 399–402.

One after another, witnesses pointed to the adverse consequences of the situation. (1) Disappointment and even suffering of savers who had accumulated for a rainy day and now were denied use of their funds. (2) Widespread foreclosures on home mortgages, which wiped out the savings of many homeowners. (3) A "slaughtering of urban real estate values." The process described by a witness from Philadelphia was not unique to his city:

> There will be this situation: There will be three mortgages in a block, on all equally valued property. One mortgage may be for $3,000 on a house, another for $4,000 and another one for $5,000, on houses that sold originally for $7,500, which are cut down in value now to $4,500. The holders of the mortgages buy the properties in. The man who holds the $3,000 mortgage on the first property wants to get his money. Someone comes along and says, "I will give you $2,500 for it." He replies, "Make it $2,750," and the deal is closed on that basis. That fixes the value for the whole row. . . .[8]

(4) Strangling of the home construction industry. No witness contended that shortage of mortgage funds was the only reason for the low levels of new construction, repairing, and remodeling; they also stressed, of course, the fall of incomes and the fear of going into debt. However, many noted that a man who wished to go into debt for this purpose was unlikely to be able to do so under current conditions:

> Very often he is absolutely prohibited today from going into debt, because the banks, speaking generally, will not give him any mortgage accommodation under any circumstances—not even a 20 percent mortgage on his proposed house. That means, to my mind, a throttling of the building trades, the building industry, labor, and everything else that goes into the building game. They are strangling today.[9]

It was for these reasons that attempts began to be made in 1932 to provide assistance to savings and loan associations and other lenders on urban homes.

■ **COMMERCIAL BANKS**   The commercial banks, of which there were about 25,000 in 1929, are of special interest here for several reasons. (1) Because of their size. (See Table 5–1, page 68.) Their assets in 1929 made up 65 percent of all the assets of the four types of financial institutions we are considering. The volume of time and savings deposits at these institutions, at $19.6 billion, exceeded all the claims issued by savings and loan associations and mutual savings banks. (2) Because of their power to create and destroy money in the form of demand deposits. A reduction of the money supply would inevitably bring deflationary pressures throughout the economy. (3) Because of their importance as sources of loan funds throughout the country and to almost every major type of borrower. For business firms of all sorts they were the principal source of short-term

8 *Ibid.*, p. 151.
9 *Ibid.*, p. 221.

credit; and for small and medium-size firms without access to the capital markets, they were the principal source of intermediate-term funds as well. They were also a major source of funds for households, governmental units, and occasionally for other financial institutions. Thus, the performance of these institutions was of special importance to depositors, to those seeking funds, and to the economy as a whole.

American commercial banks had long been noted for their high failure rates. In the nine years 1921–1929, bank failures totaled 5,712, equal to nearly 20 percent of all commercial banks in existence at the beginning of the period. These failures were heavily concentrated on small banks, and especially on those located in farming areas. For example, assets per failed bank averaged well below $300,000, and a large proportion of these banks were in the South Atlantic and West North Central regions. With the onset of the depression, failures began to rise, reaching 1,350 in 1930, 2,293 in 1931, and 1,453 in 1932—a total of 5,096 in three years. At first, the pattern was much like that of the preceding decade; failures were largely small banks in rural areas. But by 1931, larger banks in larger cities began to fall. Here again there are two main themes: the pervasiveness of banking distress and the highly uneven impacts on the various classes of banks.

There were, of course, many reasons for these differences in impact and performance. For example, there were differences in quality of bank management and in the extent to which local boom conditions or speculative activity in the 1920s had led banks to make risky loans or to purchase risky securities. However, we shall concentrate on two variables that appear to have been highly important in determining not only differences in failure rates but also differences in the degree of credit contraction by banks: differences in the extent to which a bank depended on its own local area for its deposits, and differences in the extent to which money incomes declined in the various areas.

Most unfortunate was the bank whose deposits came almost exclusively from an area in which incomes fell most and which made most of its loans in the same area. Such a situation could not arise in a nation whose banking system was composed of a few large banks, each operating a nationwide system of branch offices. In such a system, each bank could in effect pool the deposits gathered by its many branch offices and lend in each area without regard to the volume of deposits gathered there. Moreover, its loan portfolio would almost automatically be highly diversified, both by industry and by region.

However, many banks in the United States could and did find themselves in such a dangerous position because of the preponderance of unit banking—of banks operating only a single office. Of the 23,251 commercial banks in 1930, nearly 97 percent were in this category. In the following 18 states, there was not a single bank with a branch:

Colorado   Nevada
Connecticut   North Dakota

Florida	Oklahoma
Idaho	South Dakota
Illinois	Texas
Iowa	Utah
Kansas	Vermont
Missouri	West Virginia
Montana	Wyoming

Note that these include some of the most important farming states. Also, many of the banks were small and heavily dependent on farming and on local towns closely linked to farming. There were 751 branch banks operating a total of 3,522 banking offices, but most of these were largely confined to a single town or city. For example, 2,391 of the offices were in the head-office city, and only 1,131 outside. In the following states, there were either no branches at all outside the head-office city, or at most a total of three:

Indiana	New York
Michigan	Oregon
New Hampshire	Washington
New Mexico	Wisconsin

Of the 1,131 branches outside head-office cities, 552 were in California, leaving only 579 for all other states. Thus, most American banks operated either only a single office or had branches only within their own cities.

It does not necessarily follow that a bank confined to a single office or to branching within a city must draw most of its deposits from the locality and make most of its loans there. Very large banks, such as those in New York, Chicago, and other major centers, can draw deposits from many individuals and business firms located in many parts of the country, and even abroad. Their lending can be similarly diversified. But small banks are in a far different position. The fortunes of many of these banks depended largely on the status of the local economy.

With these facts in mind, we can now examine the performance of the various classes of commercial banks, noting not only their failure rates but also their differing degrees of credit contraction. We shall not at any point minimize the importance of the quality of bank management. However, we shall contend that the fate of a bank and of its customers depended heavily on factors beyond the control of the management of the individual bank, and especially on the flow of funds between that locality and other areas.

As noted in Chapter 4, the money incomes of farmers fell more rapidly than those of urban dwellers in the early part of the depression, declining 28 percent from 1929 to 1930 and then continuing downward. Also, as the creditworthiness of farmers deteriorated, flows of loans from financial centers dwindled, and farmers were called upon to repay some of their debts. But farmers did not decrease their payments to other areas as fast as their receipts from other areas fell. The result was a net shift of deposits, reserves, and lending power away from country banks to other areas. This early drain of deposits, reserves, and other liquid assets from the country banks did not depend on any loss of confidence in these banks. It was the earlier drains owing to the sharp fall of farm incomes and to reversals of capital flows that made loss of confidence in these banks more likely and that reduced their capacity to withstand runs.

The data in Table 5–4 do not prove this hypothesis, partly because they do not explain why total deposits behaved as they did, but they are consistent with it. In June 1931, total deposits at all commercial banks were 4 percent below their level two years earlier. But note the great differences

Table 5–4.   Indexes of total deposits at commercial banks, by classes (June 1929 = 100)

	JUNE 1929	DECEMBER 1930	JUNE 1931	JUNE 1932	DECEMBER 1932	JUNE 1933
All commercial banks	100	99	96	72	73	65
Nonmember banks	100	88	82	58	55	41
Member banks total	100	103	101	78	80	74
In New York City	100	114	110	82	91	92
In Chicago	100	106	95	65	73	79
In other cities, 500,000 and over	100	108	108	84	86	76
In cities 100,000– 500,000	100	99	85	80	73	77
In cities under 100,000	100	93	90	70	68	57
All country banks	100	94	92	72	69	59
Country member banks in Federal Reserve districts of						
Atlanta	100	86	81	66	55	60
Boston	100	97	94	73	75	70
Chicago	100	90	83	57	52	33
Cleveland	100	90	85	63	60	46
Dallas	100	87	91	61	62	59
Kansas City	100	93	88	69	66	62
Minneapolis	100	93	89	72	66	60
New York	100	101	102	83	80	72
Philadelphia	100	100	99	85	84	72
Richmond	100	87	85	65	66	57
St. Louis	100	84	85	66	62	51
San Francisco	100	92	87	64	59*	49

Source: Computed from data in various tables in Board of Governors of the Federal Reserve System, *Banking and Monetary Statistics*, Washington, D.C., 1941. The data cited are for operating banks only. Thus, their behavior through time is affected by bank failures. Allowance for this does not invalidate the general conclusions reached, but it does, of course, counsel cautious interpretation of the figures.

in their behavior at the various classes of banks. Deposits at member banks in New York City actually rose 10 percent compared with June 1929; at member banks in all other cities of 500,000 or more, except in Chicago, they were up 8 percent. These banks had obviously received net transfers of deposits and lending power from other banks in the system. Pressure on them to liquidate loans should have been at a minimum. All other classes of banks suffered net losses of total deposits, and these losses, as a percentage of deposits in June 1929, tended to be larger for smaller cities. Moreover, they tended to be larger in predominantly agricultural areas. At nonmember banks, mostly located in smaller places, deposits had declined 18 percent by mid-1931. Some of the other largest losers of deposits are shown in Table 5–5. Note the very large losses by country banks in the South, Midwest, and West.

Table 5–5. Classes of banks losing largest percentages of deposits, June 1929–June 1931

CLASS OF BANK	PERCENTAGE CHANGE OF TOTAL DEPOSITS, JUNE 1929–JUNE 1931
All nonmember banks	−18
Country member banks in Federal Reserve District of	
Dallas	−19
Atlanta	−19
Chicago	−17
Cleveland	−15
Richmond	−15
St. Louis	−15
San Francisco	−13
Kansas City	−12
Minneapolis	−11
Boston	− 6
Philadelphia	− 1
New York	+ 2

Source: Data based on Table 5–4.

Imagine how a loss of 15 to 20 percent of deposits within a two-year period, with prospects of more losses to come, would drain a bank's reserves and other liquid assets, put it under pressure to contract loans, and reduce its ability to withstand runs. It was in this period that country banks were finding more and more of their loans uncollectable, or at best slow. It may be true, as often alleged, that country banks were so much more distressed than city banks in this period partly because country bankers were poorer managers than their big-city counterparts, but they were also under much more pressure.

The behavior pattern of deposits from June 1931 to December 1932 differed significantly from that of the two preceding years. For one thing, total deposits fell more rapidly, declining 24 percent in 19 months. This was the period of most rapid liquidation, especially during the year following June 1931. Also, declines occurred in all major classes of banks. It is true that there were similarities to the earlier patterns. Declines of deposits tended to be smaller for member banks in larger cities and larger for nonmember banks and for country member banks. For example, the decline was 33 percent in all nonmember banks. For country member banks, it was 37 percent for those in the Chicago Federal Reserve district, 32 percent in the San Francisco district, 29 percent in the Cleveland district, and 27 percent in the St. Louis district. However, the pattern now became less clear and exhibited many more exceptions. Many larger banks now came to lose deposits to others and to join the list of bank failures. A major reason for this was the sharp decline of money incomes in the cities as the industrial depression deepened, and the highly uneven impacts on the various urban areas. Banks in cities with relatively stable sales to outside areas must have tended to gain deposits from those areas, while banks in cities that lost a large part of their exports and suffered the greatest decreases of money income tended to lose deposits to banks elsewhere. There must have been very large net outflows or deposits from banks in such depressed cities as Detroit, Birmingham, Cleveland, Chicago, Gary, Akron, Indianapolis, and Toledo. It is no coincidence that banking distress in these cities was acute, with many failures and widespread complaints about the unavailability of credit.

All this is not to deprecate the importance of loss of confidence in banks as a. factor in draining off banking reserves and lending power and in precipitating failures. This was widespread, as evidenced by currency withdrawals, shifts of accounts to the government-sponsored postal saving system, and shifts of deposits from one bank to another in hope of increased safety. However, loss of confidence was in most cases, although not all, related to the types of drains already discussed, and to the deterioration of bank assets.

As shown in Table 5–6, bank failures in the three years 1930–1932 were equal to 21.5 percent of all commercial banks in existence at the beginning of 1930, but the failure rate varied greatly from state to state. No bank failed in the smallest state, Rhode Island, and failure rates were less than 3 percent in Maine, New Hampshire, and Vermont. However, failure rates were 51 percent in Nevada, 49 percent in Arkansas, 45 percent in North Carolina, 39 percent in South Dakota, 38 percent in South Carolina, 37 percent in Arizona, 35 percent in Iowa, 34 percent in North Dakota, and 32 percent in Illinois. Consider what such high failure rates must mean to an area in terms of frozen deposits, losses of loan sources, and attempts to collect outstanding loans. In one sense, these percentages tend to overstate the degree of banking distress, because they relate to numbers of banks rather than to volumes of deposits. On the latter base, they would

Table 5–6.   Commercial bank suspensions, by state

GEOGRAPHIC DIVISION AND STATE	NUMBER OF BANKS AT BEGINNING OF 1930	NUMBER OF FAILURES 1930–1932 INCLUSIVE	FAILURE RATE AS PERCENT OF BANKS AT BEGINNING OF 1930			
			1930	1931	1932	TOTAL 1930–1932 INCLUSIVE
United States	23,695	5,096	5.7	9.7	6.1	21.5
New England	696	53	1.6	4.7	1.3	7.6
Connecticut	161	23	4.3	6.2	3.7	14.3
Maine	100	2	—	2.0	—	2.0
Massachusetts	254	24	0.8	7.5	1.2	9.4
New Hampshire	71	2	—	2.8	—	2.8
Rhode Island	25	0	—	—	—	—
Vermont	85	2	2.4	—	—	2.4
Middle Atlantic	2,977	320	1.0	7.7	2.0	10.7
New Jersey	536	49	0.6	7.1	1.5	9.1
New York	933	73	0.9	5.9	1.1	7.8
Pennsylvania	1,508	198	1.3	9.1	2.8	13.1
East North Central	5,263	1,349	5.4	11.6	8.7	25.6
Illinois	1,764	572	7.1	13.5	11.8	32.4
Indiana	859	251	10.1	11.2	7.9	29.2
Michigan	741	221	2.8	15.2	11.7	29.8
Ohio	946	166	2.6	12.2	2.7	17.5
Wisconsin	953	139	2.5	5.0	7.0	14.6
West North Central	6,335	1,577	6.6	11.3	7.0	24.9
Iowa	1,252	442	6.9	16.6	11.7	35.3
Kansas	1,165	150	3.7	3.3	5.9	12.9
Minnesota	1,041	184	2.1	9.7	5.9	17.7
Missouri	1,278	305	8.1	9.5	6.3	23.9
Nebraska	803	206	5.7	13.6	6.4	25.6
North Dakota	410	139	14.4	16.1	3.4	33.9
South Dakota	386	151	14.2	18.9	6.0	39.1
South Atlantic	2,317	595	9.6	11.4	4.7	25.7
Delaware	47	1	—	—	2.1	2.1
District of Columbia	40	4	—	—	10.0	10.0
Florida	233	67	16.7	7.3	4.7	28.8
Georgia	405	91	7.7	8.6	6.2	22.5
Maryland	215	27	1.4	9.3	1.9	12.6
North Carolina	416	187	22.4	15.1	7.5	45.0
South Carolina	205	79	13.2	16.6	8.8	38.5
Virginia	459	66	4.4	8.1	2.0	14.4
West Virginia	297	73	3.4	19.2	2.0	24.6
East South Central	1,606	398	9.5	9.3	6.0	24.8
Alabama	348	88	9.8	10.3	5.2	25.3
Kentucky	568	95	5.3	4.8	6.7	16.7
Mississippi	307	127	19.2	18.2	3.9	41.4
Tennessee	383	88	7.6	8.1	7.3	23.0

Table 5–6 (continued)

GEOGRAPHIC DIVISION AND STATE	NUMBER OF BANKS AT BEGINNING OF 1930	NUMBER OF FAILURES 1930–1932 INCLUSIVE	FAILURE RATE AS PERCENT OF BANKS AT BEGINNING OF 1930			
			1930	1931	1932	TOTAL 1930–1932 INCLUSIVE
West South Central	2,562	468	7.8	6.8	3.7	18.3
Arkansas	413	204	32.4	13.8	3.1	49.4
Louisiana	225	31	4.4	3.1	6.2	13.8
Oklahoma	616	78	3.6	3.9	5.2	12.7
Texas	1,308	155	2.6	6.6	2.7	11.9
Mountain	931	183	2.7	6.7	10.3	19.7
Arizona	46	17	10.9	10.9	15.2	37.0
Colorado	273	50	1.8	7.7	8.8	18.3
Idaho	137	35	0.7	7.3	17.5	25.5
Montana	195	30	5.6	5.6	4.1	15.4
Nevada	35	18	—	5.7	45.7	51.4
New Mexico	56	2	—	1.8	1.8	3.6
Utah	104	26	2.9	8.7	13.5	25.0
Wyoming	85	5	—	3.5	2.4	5.9
Pacific	1,008	153	1.2	5.4	8.6	15.2
California	435	58	1.6	4.1	7.6	13.3
Oregon	234	42	0.9	6.0	11.1	17.9
Washington	339	53	0.9	6.5	8.3	15.6

Sources: *Federal Reserve Bulletin*, November 1937, pp. 1089–1122, and *Banking and Monetary Statistics*, p. 284.

be somewhat lower because failed banks were on the average smaller than those that remained open. However, in at least two other ways they tend to understate the distress accompanying bank failures. For one thing, they fail to divulge that if, for example, more than 40 percent of the banks in a state fail, there are likely to be large areas within the state virtually devoid of banking facilities. Also, actual failures or even threats of failures tend to make other bankers in the area so fearful that they curtail their lending severely, and some virtually close their lending windows.

■ MUTUAL SAVINGS BANKS   The mutual savings banks, of which there were 609 in 1929 with total assets of $9.9 billion, were largely concentrated in New England and the Middle Atlantic states, although a few were scattered among such states as Indiana, Maryland, Minnesota, and Wisconsin. As a group, they suffered less distress in the depression than most other types of financial intermediaries. Only six failed in the three years 1930–1932, and four more the following year. Most of them were also under less pressure to contract credit. Among the reasons for their more favorable experience were the location of most of them in areas where failure rates of all types of financial institutions were relatively low; the highly conservative investment policies of their managements, especially in New England; and their ability to attract funds away from other financial institutions because of their long record of safety.

In the latter part of the 1920s, deposits at mutual savings banks rose at a rate of about $500 million a year, although the increase in 1929 was considerably less. Virtually all of these funds were used to purchase bonds and real estate mortgages. Flows of funds to these institutions actually increased slightly for a year and a half after the stock market crash, with total deposits rising more than $1 billion between the end of 1929 and mid-1931. All of these funds were used to make new mortgage loans and to purchase bonds. After that there was no further rise. New deposits from regular depositors declined, and some depositors withdrew funds, especially from banks located in depressed industrial areas. These withdrawals were approximately offset by new deposits seeking more safety than that offered by other institutions. After mid-1931, the mutual savings banks joined others in the process of contracting credit, reducing their total loans and investments more than $300 million by the end of 1932. There were widespread complaints, especially in New England and the Middle Atlantic states, that this source of mortgage funds had dried up, and that some of these banks, like other lenders, were foreclosing on mortgages.

Thus, even these conservatively managed and relatively stable institutions added to pressures for credit contraction and liquidation during the latter part of the great slide. Few needed help to survive, but few were performing well their normal function of providing new funds. Many were heavily laden with delinquent mortgages and depreciated bonds.

■ **LIFE INSURANCE COMPANIES**   In 1929, there were 438 private life insurance companies with total assets of $17.5 billion. Nearly half of their investments were in mortgages, and most of the rest in long-term bonds. These companies were a major source of funds for both urban and farm mortgages. Most of them were for several reasons less vulnerable than other types of financial intermediaries. First, those that held the bulk of the assets of the industry were large and did business over wide areas. For example, the Metropolitan Life Insurance Company and several other big ones were truly nationwide institutions, selling policies in all areas, drawing income from all areas, and lending in many areas. Thus, their fate did not depend on any one region or sector of the economy. However, some companies were less fortunate because they were small and more concentrated on narrower regions.

Second, these companies normally enjoyed very large cash receipts relative to their fixed commitments to disburse funds. During the 1920s, their total assets had grown at an average rate of about $1.5 billion a year, largely in the form of receipts of income on investments and premiums on life insurance and annuity policies. In addition, they had large cash receipts from maturing bonds and repayments on mortgages. These cash receipts were so large that they normally provided the companies with ample liquidity, and they could decline considerably without forcing the companies to liquidate any assets.

Third, the claims that they issued, mostly life insurance and annuity policies, were in general of longer maturity than those issued by other types of intermediaries and also of such a nature that their holders would not cash them lightly. Partly because no other asset could provide the type of protection afforded by life insurance, most holders of the policies were reluctant to surrender them. Most of those holding annuity policies to finance their years of retirement would cash them only as a last resort. However, withdrawals by policyholders before expiration of their contracts increased sharply as the depression deepened, unemployment rose, and incomes fell. Some surrendered their policies for their cash value. Others borrowed on policies to pay premiums or to get funds for other purposes.

It was for reasons such as these that the life insurance industry suffered less than most other financial intermediaries. Yet the companies did not come through unscathed; they suffered large losses and provided only dwindling amounts of funds to those who had normally looked to them for credit. One reason for this was the deterioration of their assets. We have already noted their experience with farm mortgages. Millions of mortgages on urban homes fell into the same sad condition. The companies also suffered large losses on their bond holdings when the bond market broke after mid-1931. For these reasons alone, the companies would have become increasingly reluctant to make new mortgage loans and to purchase bonds whose risks were rising.

However, they were also inhibited by decreases in the amount of current income available for these purposes. Their total receipts actually remained a bit above their level in 1929 throughout this period, rising about $200 million from 1929 to 1931, and then losing most of the gain in 1932 and 1933. But the flow of receipts available to make net purchases of mortgages and bonds declined, primarily because of surrenders of policies for their cash value and loans to policyholders. In the latter years of the 1920s, the cash values of policies surrendered averaged less than $400 million a year. This rose to $861 million in 1931 and was above $1,300 million in both 1932 and 1933. The companies also lent increasing amounts to their policyholders, many of whom were unemployed or had otherwise lost most of their income.

Thus, because of rising risks and falling amounts of income available for the purpose, the life insurance companies became at best a shrinking source of new money for bonds and mortgages. Their total holdings of bonds rose about $800 million from 1929 to 1932, almost all of this increase occurring by 1931. Total mortgage holdings rose about $350 million in the same period. However, there were net decreases of more than $300 million in 1932 and more than $500 million in 1933.

A committee witness had this to say about the relation of insurance companies to the mortgage market in March 1932:

> I know, as a life insurance counsel, that there is a considerable number of life insurance companies in this country where their policy loans have reached a point where they absorb their premium incomes, and they are out of the market. There is another group as to which this is so nearly true that they have practically withdrawn from the market. There is a third group of companies, and I imagine the Metropolitan Life Insurance Company is one of them, where they have a very large surplus still available for investment, but there are many companies where they recognize that even though they are not in such a position, the demand for premium loans has reached a point where, if it continues, they will be in a position of having to sell their securities in order to realize the money to loan to their policyholders, and under those conditions they realize that if they were mortgage loans they would have to be sacrificed.[10]

As was true of the mutual savings banks, few of the life insurance companies required assistance for survival. But they could again perform their normal investment functions only if the flow of funds to them was increased, the quality of their asset holdings raised, and the creditworthiness of borrowers improved.

■ **FEDERAL AID TO FINANCIAL INSTITUTIONS**   In short, the position of all major types of financial intermediaries had deteriorated seriously by mid-1931, and deterioration accelerated in the following months. However, it was not until October 1931, when the depression had already been under way for two years, that President Hoover first announced his intention of initiating a definite program to aid financial institutions and stabilize the financial situation. Several actions were taken within a year—actions that must have seemed bold indeed to the President and to the many others who shared his views concerning the proper role of government. Without these measures, the banking crash might have come several months earlier, which might or might not have been desirable. But desirable as most of the actions were, the verdict on the program as a whole must be "far too little, much too late." The approach was largely defensive; the spirit seemed to be, "Let's shore up the financial system until recovery comes." The program itself contained virtually no positive, expansionary forces to produce that recovery.

The lateness and inadequacy of the program reflected in part reluctance to expand the scope of the federal government and a belief of the President, and apparently of others in his Administration, that the financial community could save itself through mutual self-help if stimulated by the government to do so. It also reflected an erroneous estimate of the

---

[10] Hearings before a subcommittee of the House Banking and Currency Committee on H. R. 7620, 72nd Congress, 1st Session, March 1932, p. 72.

economic and financial situation. The President probably did believe that "recovery is just around the corner" and would arrive without further assistance from government if the financial system did not collapse. He must also have failed to see how seriously the entire financial system had been damaged by late 1931. For example, most parts of his program were designed to provide loans to private financial institutions—loans that were to be made on a businesslike basis and to be repaid in full no matter what happened to the value of the collateral. This did indeed increase the ability of the institutions to pay their claims and to do so without dumping more of their assets on the depressed markets. But it did nothing directly to restore the net-worth position of the financial intermediaries, which had been so badly damaged. And it did nothing directly to restore the liquidity and solvency of the millions of potential borrowers who had lost their creditworthiness. Thus, the program had little chance of restoring quickly the normal flow of credit so essential to recovery.

The principal actions initiated by President Hoover in this field were to establish a National Credit Corporation, a Reconstruction Finance Corporation, and a Federal Home Loan Bank System, and to liberalize the lending powers of the Federal Reserve Banks.

The National Credit Corporation reflected President Hoover's preference for systems of mutual self-help. In early October 1931, he asked commercial bankers to form a corporation and provide $500 million of their own money to aid distressed banks. The corporation was established in mid-October but was never of much help. For one thing, the funds at its disposal were grossly inadequate for their purposes. Moreover, its banker-managers did not promote its activities aggressively. The Railroad Credit Corporation, established in December 1931, was also largely ineffective. This was a scheme under which proceeds from a special surcharge on railroad freight rates were paid into the corporation to be lent to distressed railroads. Since most railroads were deeply distressed, the amount of money available was too small to be of much help.

The Reconstruction Finance Corporation (RFC) was authorized in January 1932 and opened for business the next month. This corporation was established by the federal government, which provided its capital of $500 million. It was also authorized to borrow up to $1.5 billion by issuing securities fully guaranteed by the federal government; in July this authorization was increased to $3.3 billion. The RFC was originally authorized to lend to banks, insurance companies, savings and loan associations, liquidating agents of closed banks, specified types of agricultural credit institutions, and, with the approval of the Interstate Commerce Commission, to railroads. In July, it was empowered to lend to state and local governments, to finance sales of farm products abroad, and for other specified purposes. All loans were to be on a businesslike basis, to be adequately secured, and to be repaid in full with interest.

At first the usefulness of the RFC was very restricted by the conservatism of its management, but by mid-1932 it was providing funds on a rising scale. As shown in Table 5–7, it had disbursed nearly $1.4 billion to financial institutions by March 3, 1933. Of this, over $1 billion was to

Table 5–7.   Loans disbursed by the Reconstruction Finance Corporation to financial institutions, Feb. 2, 1932–March 3, 1933 (in millions of dollars)

For distribution to depositors in closed banks	$ 79.6
To banks and trust companies	951.4
To Federal Land Banks	18.8
To Mortgage loan companies	90.7
To regional agricultural credit corporations	41.4
To building and loan associations	101.5
To insurance companies	80.5
To joint stock land banks	4.9
To livestock credit corporations	11.9
To agricultural credit corporations	3.6
To credit unions	0.4

Source: The Public Papers and Addresses of Franklin D. Roosevelt, Vol. 2, Random House, New York, 1938, p. 403.

banks and liquidators of banks, and over $100 million to savings and loan associations. The RFC was undoubtedly helpful in 1932 in providing liquidity and in slowing down the rate of liquidation, but in the end it did not prevent a banking collapse. The story might have been different if it had begun operations at least a year earlier.

In July 1932, President Hoover signed a bill establishing a system of twelve regional Federal Home Loan Banks. The purpose of these banks was to lend on home mortgages to private financial institutions with heavy commitments in this field, such as savings and loan associations, insurance companies, and savings banks. The federal government contributed $125 million of capital to the Home Loan Banks, and more was subscribed by the private institutions that joined as members of the Home Loan Bank System, thus becoming eligible to borrow on home mortgages as collateral. The banks opened for business in mid-October, having already received a flood of loan applications. They progressed only slowly at first, largely because of personnel and procedural problems. By the end of 1932, they had disbursed only $838,000; in the next three months, disbursements were about $22 million, still an amount extremely small relative to the magnitude of the home mortgage problem.

The Glass-Steagall Act of February 1932 liberalized the lending power of the Federal Reserve Banks. We noted earlier that the Reserve Banks could lend only to member banks, and then on only two types of assets—U.S. government securities and certain short-term commercial paper qualifying as "eligible paper." Another provision required that the currency issued by the Reserve Banks—Federal Reserve notes—be backed 100 percent by collateral in the form of gold or eligible paper. The Glass-Steagall Act was designed to deal with two problems that came to the fore in 1931. (1) The collateral requirement became an obstacle to large Federal Reserve purchases of government securities as a means of increasing bank reserves. As the Federal Reserve disbursed funds to pay for the securities, some of the recipient banks would reduce their borrowings and thus reduce the Federal Reserve's holdings of eligible paper. It would therefore have to use more of its gold as collateral for Federal Reserve notes, thereby reducing the amount available to meet reserve requirements against its deposit liabilities. The Glass-Steagall Act solved this problem by permitting government securities to serve as collateral. Senator Glass was never happy about this change, but it permitted the Federal Reserve to purchase more than $1 billion of government securities in the next four months, which was one of the most useful actions taken in 1932. (2) Many member banks had insufficient amounts of government securities and eligible paper to serve as collateral for borrowing at the Reserve Banks, although some had other good assets. The new act liberalized Federal Reserve lending power in two ways. One proved to be virtually useless; it permitted member banks to band together to borrow, each guaranteeing the debts of the others. Under the other provision, the Federal Reserve might lend on collateral not technically eligible, if the loan was adequately secured. The reluctance of Senator Glass was evident: such Federal Reserve loans were to be made only at a higher interest rate and only with the consent of at least five members of the Federal Reserve Board. Nevertheless, the new power was somewhat useful, for under it the Federal Reserve had advanced nearly $29 million to member banks by the end of 1932. It would have been more useful if it had existed throughout the period.

■ **CONCLUSIONS**   The principal actions taken by the Administration in 1932 to ameliorate the financial situation were the establishment of the Reconstruction Finance Corporation and the Federal Home Loan Bank System and the broadening of the lending powers of the Federal Reserve. These were useful at the time and even more useful later. Yet in retrospect, it seems unlikely that these institutions, relying so heavily on loans to private financial intermediaries, could have restored the financial system to normal working order even if they had lent more generously. This technique left too many basic problems unsolved. Millions of borrowers would not be able to meet all their debt obligations and reestablish their creditworthiness while their money incomes and asset values remained so low. Great numbers of financial intermediaries were still laden with depreciated securities and in doubtful net-worth positions, many still hoping to reduce rather than increase their risk exposure. And the confidence of savers in financial institutions was fragile. Reassuring statements that "the banking system is fundamentally sound" lacked credibility. In fact, one is left to wonder why the collapse of the banking system did not come many months before March 1933.

6

Collapse of the International Economy

Perhaps the most dramatic symbol of the breakdown of the international trading and financial system was what amounted to an international banking and monetary crisis that swept across most of the western world in the latter part of 1931. Like the banking collapse in the United States in early 1933, this crisis appeared to happen suddenly. However, in both cases, the collapse came only after grinding deflation had weakened the entire system.

It is still difficult to say whether the downturn of economic activity occurred first in the United States or elsewhere, and to fix precisely the dates of the downturns in the various countries. For example, one study concluded that the downturn started in Germany in April 1929, in the United States in June, in Great Britain in July, and in other industrialized Western countries within a few months. Another concluded that the downturn appeared during the first half of 1929 in Poland, Canada, and Argentina; in the third quarter in the United States, Belgium, and Italy; and within the next few months in most other Western countries.[1] However, almost all agree that the United States was among the first to slide into recession and that most other Western nations had joined by early 1930. By the middle of that year, the depression was worldwide in scope. Almost the only economically important nation to escape was the Soviet Union. That nation suffered during the period, but its problems emanated not from inadequacy of effective demand for its output but from droughts and from mistakes in planning and execution.

Elsewhere, the general pattern was similar to that in the United States, although in most countries the depression was less deep and prolonged. Unemployment was widespread; in 1932 the world's total number of unemployed was at least 30 million. Output, and especially industrial output, declined sharply. Price declines for both output and assets were widespread. As in the United States, price decreases were especially large for agricultural and other raw materials. The level of money incomes fell sharply. Here again, two themes must be emphasized: the almost

[1] R. A. Gordon, *Business Fluctuations*, Harper & Row, New York, 1952, pp. 387–388.

worldwide pervasiveness of the depression, and its uneven impacts on the various nations.

Depressive forces spread and reverberated among nations in much the same way that they were communicated from sector to sector and from region to region within a country. An initial decline of aggregate demand lowered output, prices, and income in a country and led to a decrease in demands for the exports of others, thus lowering their incomes. These nations, in turn, decreased their own demands for both domestic and foreign output. Depressive forces were also communicated from country to country through shifts in international capital movements. International lending and investment fell sharply and then came to a virtual standstill. In large part, this reflected decreased desires to borrow and invest, decreased flows of savings in countries that normally lent abroad, and decreased creditworthiness of potential borrowers. These sharp shifts in both international trade and international capital movements upset international balances of payments, made it impossible or too painful for many countries to maintain both freedom of trade and capital movements as well as existing exchange rates on their currencies, and led to trade restrictions and abandonment of gold standards.

■ NATIONAL RESPONSIBILITY FOR THE DEPRESSION

Which nation was responsible for the depression and its severity? This question was widely debated. As might be expected, each nation tended to proclaim its own innocence and to blame others. The whole debate might be dismissed lightly if its effects had been limited to the reputations and futures of incumbent political parties and their leaders. However, it had serious international policy implications, because a nation that believed its problems originated abroad was more likely to go the autarkic route. Many blamed the United States—the world's richest nation, holder of the largest monetary gold stock, greatest source of international lending, and second largest purchaser in export markets. They pointed to the restriction of credit in the United States in late 1928 and 1929 that had sharply reduced American lending, attracted foreign funds, and led to tightened credit conditions in many other countries; to the shock of the stock market crash; to the subsequent decrease of American demands for imports; and to the virtual cessation of American foreign lending after mid-1930.

President Hoover consistently denied guilt for the United States, and especially for his Administration. That he took such positions was perhaps partly accounted for by candidate Roosevelt's sharp charges during the 1932 campaign that Hoover and his party were responsible for the depression and its severity, not only in the United States but also in the rest of the world.

President Hoover did admit that the "financial debauches" that brought on the stock market crash led to a recession in the United States, but he insisted that the recession would have ended within a few months if the American economy had not been buffeted by new disturbances originating in other countries. He also found the basic causes of the depression in the conduct of other countries—in ". . . the greatest war in history, the inheritances from it, the fears and panics and dreadful economic catastrophes which have developed from these causes in foreign countries. . . ."[2] He contended that even the stock market boom and crash were indirectly caused by the war and conditions abroad, because they resulted from the easy-money policy unwisely adopted by the Federal Reserve in 1927 to help solve problems in other countries, especially in Great Britain.

Who was right in this debate? There is blame enough for all to share. The United States, the world's greatest economic power, certainly contributed strongly to the decline abroad. Before 1933, the U.S. took no effective action to stem the decline of economic activity at home or to lessen its impact on other countries. However, other countries were far from blameless. Many of them took no effective steps to curb the fall of aggregate demands at home, and deflationary policies were widespread. Moreover, such countries, like the United States, adopted measures that throttled world trade and capital movements. Among the many methods used were campaigns to persuade their people to buy only domestically produced goods in order to provide jobs for their own unemployed rather than for workers elsewhere. "Buy American," "buy British," "buy only German-made goods" became familiar slogans. Such nationalistic "beggar-my-neighbor" policies to promote domestic employment by limiting imports became widespread. The depression also brought stricter limitations on international migrations of people. Nations with millions of unemployed did not want more to compete for scarce jobs and limited relief funds.

■ **THE INTERNATIONAL MONETARY SYSTEM**   The international monetary system first weakened under the forces of the depression and then virtually collapsed in the latter part of 1931. This was a type of gold-standard system whose restoration as a truly international system had been completed less than six years before its collapse. The old international gold-standard system, of the type that prevailed before 1914, had been swept away by the inflationary fiscal and monetary policies accompanying World War I and its aftermath. Price inflation was endemic in that period; nations suffered price increases ranging from a mere 100 percent to a trillion-fold. Domestic monetary disorders were prevalent, and exchange rates among currencies fluctuated widely and wildly. Amidst these difficulties, governments of virtually all nations looked back to the prewar international gold standard as a haven. The pertinent question

2 William Starr Myers, ed., *The State Papers and Other Public Writings of Herbert Hoover*, Vol. 2, Doubleday, New York, 1934, p. 339.

was not whether to return to gold but how, when, and under what conditions.

The United States returned to the gold standard at the end of the war with the dollar at its prewar value in terms of gold. Germany returned to gold in 1924 and Great Britain in 1925. The British pound sterling was also restored to its prewar value in terms of gold. After the British return, other countries rapidly followed suit. By the end of 1927, the gold standard was again almost worldwide in scope, thereby establishing a network of stable exchange rates.

However, the new gold standard developed in the 1920s was no mere replica of the prewar international gold standard; it differed significantly in both form and functioning. For one thing, the new system inculcated at least two methods of "economizing gold"—of enabling each unit of monetary gold to support a larger amount of money. One method was to terminate the circulation of gold coins, to redeem money only in gold bars, and thus to concentrate more of the available gold in central banks where each unit could serve as reserves behind a multiple amount of notes or deposits. The United States was the only major nation to continue circulation of gold coins in the postwar period.

The other method of economizing gold was the "gold-exchange system" —an arrangement under which some countries held at least a part of their "gold reserves" not in the form of gold itself but in the form of claims against other currencies, which in turn had fixed values in terms of gold. The two principal centers of this system were the United States and Great Britain, and more specifically New York and London. The American dollar and the British pound sterling became the two great "international reserve currencies." The central banks and governments of many other countries came to hold large parts of their international reserves in the form of claims against these currencies. These claims were of several types: deposits at the Federal Reserve Banks or the Bank of England; deposits at New York or London commercial banks; short-term government securities, bills of exchange, or commercial paper denominated in dollars or sterling; and other liquid short-term claims.

It is estimated that by 1929 such claims constituted nearly 20 percent of the international reserves of all central banks and governments. The proportion was considerably higher for countries other than the United States and Great Britain. For example, Table 6–1 indicates that in May 1929, two central banks held more than 80 percent of their total international reserves in the form of foreign exchange. For six more, the figure was above 50 percent, and for three more it was above 30 percent. These data suggest the heavy dependence of the international monetary system on the foreign exchange component of international reserves. The statistics in Table 6–1 relate only to official holdings of short-term international claims. In addition, there were very large private holdings that could be shifted quickly from one international financial center to another.

Table 6–1.   Gold and foreign exchange holdings of selected
central banks, May 1929

	FOREIGN EXCHANGE AS PERCENT OF TOTAL GOLD AND FOREIGN EXCHANGE RESERVES
Central Bank of Chile	87.7
Bank of Greece	84.7
National Bank of Czechoslovakia	59.5
National Bank of Austria	53.6
South African Reserve Bank	49.7
Banca d'Italia	48.9
Sveriges Riksbank	43.9
Bank of Poland	42.2
Bank of France	41.7
National Bank of Copenhagen	35.2
National Bank of Switzerland	34.5
National Bank of Belgium	33.8
Netherlands Bank	26.9
Norges Bank	23.8
National Bank of Rumania	21.4
Reichsbank	14.5
National Bank of Hungary	9.7
Bank of Spain	3.7
Bank of England	0.0
U. S. Federal Reserve Banks	0.0

Source: Computed from data in C. H. Kisch, "Memorandum on Legal Provisions Governing Reserves of Central Banks," in *The International Gold Problem,* Oxford University Press, London, 1931, pp. 138–140.

The gold-exchange system was indeed an effective method of economizing gold so long as the central banks holding foreign exchange continued to consider it at least as "good as gold" and were willing to hold it. It was also dangerous. Attempts by central banks to convert their holdings of foreign exchange into actual gold could harm the center countries, the central banks holding the claims, and the world economy. The United States and Great Britain could be harmed by a drain on their gold reserves. The central banks holding the claims could be harmed if the latter depreciated in terms of gold. And the world economy could be harmed by the deflationary pressures that would be created by the destruction of this important part of the total supply of international reserves. Attempts to convert these claims into gold were by no means unlikely. Anything that damaged confidence in the stability of the dollar or the pound in terms of gold might well lead some central banks to demand gold for their dollar or sterling claims.

Moreover, the stability and growth of the gold-exchange system were imperiled by a feeling in some quarters that "first-class countries hold their international reserves in gold; only lower rank countries hold foreign exchange." Somehow, reliance on a foreign currency as an international reserve suggested dependence on the center country, or even colonial status. Such feelings did not bother small countries, but some larger and more sensitive ones, especially France, felt it strongly. From the time that country first began to accumulate large amounts of dollars and sterling in 1926, the Bank of France was a reluctant holder, clearly hoping to convert them into gold as this became feasible.

The new international gold-standard system also differed from the pre-war system in the extent to which domestic price levels and exchange rates of the various countries were attuned to each other. There is every reason to assume that they were well attuned before 1914. International gold flows and price adjustments in the various countries had brought price levels into line with exchange rates, so that gold had about the same purchasing power in all countries. This was not so true of the new system. Many countries returned to the gold standard at gold values for their currencies that proved to be out of line with their domestic price levels relative to those abroad. For example, both the dollar and the French franc proved to be undervalued; that is, exchange rates on these currencies were so low relative to price levels in the United States and France that these countries were relatively cheap places in which to buy and poor places in which to sell. Thus, they tended to have persistent excesses of exports over imports and to gain gold.

On the other hand, the British pound was almost certainly overvalued; that is, the combination of the exchange rate on the pound and the level of internal prices made Britain a relatively expensive place in which to buy and a good place in which to sell. Britain could therefore avoid unfavorable balances of payments only by following restrictive, or at best not very liberal, monetary policies. In short, mistakes were made in the initial setting of the relative gold values of currencies, and thus their exchange rates.

Moreover, adjustments of internal price levels to exchange rates were inhibited by an increased reluctance of central banks to permit international gold flows to dominate their monetary policies. As compared with the prewar period, there was more deliberate monetary management by central banks with an eye to such objectives as stabilizing prices and promoting employment and business activity. Gold inflows were often offset in order to prevent or limit price increases. Gold outflows were even more frequently offset, at least in part, in order to escape depressing effects on employment, business activity, and prices. Such policies may have promoted domestic economic stability, but they were not conducive to eliminating deficits and surpluses in balances of payments.

For these and other reasons, there developed what was widely criticized as a "maldistribution of gold." Some countries, notably France and the United States, had too much; others, especially Great Britain, had too little. It was unfortunate for the world as a whole that Great Britain, as one of the two principal international monetary centers, should have so little gold relative to its international liabilities and stood in danger of losing it if expansionary policies were followed. France began to gain gold and foreign exchange almost immediately after her *de facto* stabilization in 1926, and the trend continued into the 1930s. France came to be known as the "sinkhole of gold," absorbing large amounts without letting it raise price levels, induce capital exports, or otherwise redistribute the gold to other countries.

The United States was the other large holder of gold. Largely because of big imports of gold in the 1915–1917 period before entering the war and also in the early postwar years, the United States held more than 40 percent of the world's monetary gold in 1924. Moreover, the U.S. tended to have a favorable balance of payments and to attract even more gold in those years in which capital exports were small. Net exports of goods and services averaged about $1 billion a year during the 1920s. Only by large annual foreign lending could a further concentration of gold in the United States be avoided.

Another important source of change in the functioning of the international gold-standard system was the great shift of financial power from London to New York. It is only a slight exaggeration to say that prior to 1914 the international gold standard was managed through London. While the United States was still a net debtor on international account, Great Britain was the world's largest international trader and net creditor, and possessed in London the world's most highly developed and efficient money and capital markets. The situation had changed markedly by the end of World War I. Britain was still a net creditor, but its net position had been decreased greatly by sales of holdings of foreign securities and by borrowings abroad to help finance the war effort. On the other hand, the United States, which had aided the Allies by purchasing American securities from them and by lending to them, emerged as a very large net creditor on international account. Then as American incomes grew in the 1920s, the United States became the world's greatest source of savings and its greatest international lender.

Thus, economic and financial conditions in other countries came to depend heavily on those in the United States. Through demands for their exports, other nations would quickly feel the effect of a decline of incomes and prices in the United States. They were also highly sensitive to financial conditions in the United States. Low interest rates in New York and a high rate of American international lending improved their balances of payments and helped them maintain liberal monetary and credit policies at home. However, high interest rates in New York and a sharp decline of American foreign lending deteriorated their balances of payments and forced many of them into restrictive policies. Let us now examine the behavior of capital movements during this period.

■ **INTERNATIONAL CAPITAL MOVEMENTS**   American capital exports had been very small during the troubled years before 1924. However, during the four years 1924–1927, U. S. net long-term capital exports averaged about $725 million a year. It was largely because of this outflow of dollars that other countries were able to buy about $400 million of American gold and to increase their holdings of short-term claims against dollars despite large American net exports of goods and services. The outflow of long-term capital continued at a high level through the first half of 1928, aided in part by the easy-money policy followed by the Federal Reserve in 1927. Then, primarily to combat the rising use of credit for stock market speculation, the Federal Reserve shifted to a policy of restriction, selling securities in the open market and raising discount rates. The result was a marked rise of the entire interest rate structure, and especially of short-term rates. Rates on call loans to brokers rose most of all.

The impact on international capital movements was almost immediate. As shown in Table 6–2, new issues of foreign securities in the American market declined abruptly in the latter half of 1928, falling more than 50 percent below their level in the first half of the year and 33 percent below their average level in the four years 1924–1927. By the latter half of 1929, these new issues were 66 percent below their 1924–1927 average. To make matters worse, foreign funds began to flow to the United States in larger volume. Some came to buy American stocks; perhaps more came

Table 6–2.   New foreign security issues in the United States, 1924–1932 (in millions of dollars)

PERIOD	FOREIGN ISSUES FOR NEW CAPITAL	FOREIGN ISSUES FOR REFUNDING	TOTAL	TOTAL AT ANNUAL RATE
1924	971	247	1,218	
1925	1,083	233	1,316	
1926	1,125	163	1,288	
1927	1,388	239	1,577	
First half 1928				$2,120
Second half 1928				898
First half 1929				959
Second half 1929				458
First half 1930				1,620
Second half 1930				560
First half 1931				516
Second half 1931				56
First half 1932				4
Second half 1932				68

Source: Board of Governors of the Federal Reserve System, *Banking and Monetary Statistics*, 1943, pp. 487–489.

to take advantage of the high interest rates on brokers loans. One result of these sharp changes in international capital flows was a reversal of gold movements. The United States had actually lost $404 million of gold between November 1924 and July 1928; from the latter date to October 1929, the U. S. gained $268 million. Gold losses by other countries would undoubtedly have been larger if several foreign central banks had not raised their discount rates and restricted credit to discourage the outflow of funds. Between mid-1928 and October 1929, discount rate increases were from 4½ to 6½ percent at the Bank of England, from 6½ to 7½ percent at the German Reichsbank, from 5½ to 7 percent at the National Bank of Italy, from 4½ to 5 percent at the Bank of the Netherlands, and from 3½ to 5½ percent at the Swedish Riksbank.

There can be little doubt that the American stock market boom, Federal Reserve restrictive policies, the sharp decline of American foreign lending, and the induced inflow of foreign funds played major roles in tightening credit conditions abroad in 1929, not only in European financial centers but also in those nations such as Germany and several Latin American countries that had relied heavily on American loans. It is much more difficult to assess the roles played by these developments in bringing about and intensifying the declines in business activity that appeared in so many countries in 1929 or soon thereafter. At least some of the declines might have occurred anyway. All that one can say with confidence is that the restrictive credit policies of the United States increased depressive forces and inhibited foreign central banks from easing credit quickly in order to fight recession. Many people are still convinced that American policies during this period started the depression, not only in the United States but in several other countries as well.

Foreign central bankers must have breathed sighs of relief when the stock market crashed, for it marked the end of high interest rates in New York. The Federal Reserve quickly reversed its policies, purchasing government securities and lowering its discount rates. Interest rates began to fall, and most of them continued downward until early 1931. Large amounts of foreign funds were withdrawn from the American stock market and from brokers' loans, and American capital exports revived briefly. As indicated in Table 6–2, sales of new foreign securities in the American market during the first half of 1930 were at an annual rate above the average for 1924–1927. Nearly $100 million of gold flowed out of the United States in the three months following the crash. This reversal of conditions enabled most foreign central banks to relax their restrictive policies and to move toward credit ease. But for many of them, this comfortable position would not last long.

The revival of foreign security issues in the United States was short-lived. By the second half of 1930, new issues had again fallen sharply, and by early 1931 they had become a mere trickle. (See Table 6–2.) When not only new flotations but also direct investments and repayments are taken into account, the United States became a net importer of long-term capital funds in 1931. Thus, America shifted from being a net exporter of about $725 million per annum of long-term capital funds in the 1924–1927 period to become a net importer of over $200 million in 1931. Beginning in 1930, there were also sharp decreases of new foreign issues in other principal financial centers, such as London, Paris, Amsterdam, and Zurich. This virtual cessation of normal international lending was a serious blow to the balances of payments of other countries.

Let us now examine a related subject—the behavior of international trade in goods and services.

■ AMERICAN IMPORTS AND EXPORTS

As American output, incomes, and prices fell, the nation decreased its demands for imports of almost every kind. It demanded less raw materials to feed its production processes, smaller imports of finished consumer and capital goods, smaller amounts of services for American tourists, smaller amounts of shipping services from foreign countries, and so on. Part A of Table 6–3 shows that the percentage decline of American imports was greater than that of the nation's GNP. The percentage declines from 1929 in the value of imports at current prices, reflecting decreases of both physical quantities and prices, were 24 percent by 1930, 46 percent by 1931, and 63 percent by 1932 and 1933. Decreases in the physical volume of imports were, of course, smaller. From 1929 levels, the decreases were 11 percent to 1930, 20 percent to 1931, and 35 percent to 1932.

Two direct effects of the sharp decrease of American demands for imports should be noted. First, it tended to decrease prices, to reduce output, or to do both in those foreign industries suffering the decrease of American demands. Second, it tended to worsen the balance of payments of the countries suffering losses of demand, which in some cases forced a tightening of monetary and credit conditions there. But this is by no means the end of the story. For one thing, those countries experienced downward multiplier effects domestically as decreased incomes in their export industries led members of those industries to buy less from other domestic industries. They also demanded less from other countries. Thus, the depression spread and deepened through complex interactions and feedback effects among the nations.

It would be quite wrong to imply either that all the depressive forces originated in the United States or that the American economy was not buffeted by decreases in foreign demands for its own exports. Part A of Table 6–3 shows that the value of American exports at current prices, reflecting declines of both physical quantities and prices, had fallen below 1929 levels by 23 percent in 1930, 49 percent in 1931, and 64 percent in 1932. Decreases in the physical volume of American exports were 11 percent by 1930, 24 percent by 1931, and 39 percent by 1932. The decreases in foreign demands for American exports that these figures reflect added to deflationary forces in the U. S., although

Table 6–3. American imports and exports relative to gross
national product, 1929–1933 (in billions of dollars)

	1929	1930	1931	1932	1933
A. Values at current prices					
U. S. gross national product	$104.4	$ 91.1	$ 76.3	$ 58.5	$ 56.0
Imports of goods and services	6.3	4.8	3.4	2.3	2.3
Exports of goods and services	7.0	5.4	3.6	2.5	2.4
Indexes: 1929 = 100					
U. S. Gross National Product	100	87	73	56	54
Imports of goods and services	100	76	54	37	37
Exports of goods and services	100	77	51	36	34
B. Values at constant (1954) prices					
U. S. gross national product	$181.8	$164.5	$153.0	$130.1	$126.6
Imports of goods and services	10.9	9.7	8.7	7.1	7.7
Exports of goods and services	11.1	9.9	8.4	6.8	6.8
Indexes: 1929 = 100					
U. S. Gross National Product	100	90	84	72	70
Imports of goods and services	100	89	80	65	71
Exports of goods and services	100	89	76	61	61

Sources: Various tables in U. S. Department of Commerce, National Income, 1954
edition, and U. S. Income and Output, 1958.

total decreases of domestic demands were far greater. Some of these
decreases of foreign demand were undoubtedly feedback effects from
the decreases of foreign incomes that had originated in decreases of American demands for imports. However, this was not true of all; America
could hardly be held accountable for the entire decrease of incomes
abroad or for all actions taken abroad to throttle international trade. Many
other countries also made mistakes in their monetary, fiscal, and other
policies relating to the depression.

How did output, employment, and prices in the various countries respond
to these decreases of domestic and foreign demands? In general, patterns
of response were similar to those in the United States. Prices of industrial
products did fall, especially as the depression deepened, but decreases
of demand for these things were reflected to a large extent in reductions
of output and employment. For agricultural products and many other
raw materials, the pattern was also similar to that in the United States:
Output was well maintained but their prices fell early and sharply. Even
in the 1920s, many internationally traded raw materials had tended to be
overproduced relative to demands for them, so that their prices had
declined relative to the prices of industrial goods. Now their prices fell
even more rapidly. For example, price declines in the one year from
1929 to 1930 were 40 percent or more for coffee, rubber, wool, and corn;

and between 20 and 30 percent for raw silk, tin, copper, wheat, and sugar. These prices fell even more as the depression progressed.

Think of the effects on countries heavily dependent on such exports—effects on their real incomes, their balances of payments, their ability to import industrial goods, and their ability to service outstanding foreign debts and to remain creditworthy. We shall see later that these developments were closely related to widespread defaults on outstanding foreign loans and to the virtual cessation of new foreign lending. It may well be, as angry American creditors alleged, that some foreign debtors made little effort to pay their debts. However, it is only fair to note that many had fallen into positions comparable to that of the American farmer: Their incomes and net worth positions had deteriorated so much that they could not pay their debts, whose real burdens had been increased by the deflation.

Both the sharp decline of international lending and the decline of international trade in goods and services had profound effects on balances of international payments, affecting individual nations in widely differing ways. In general, industrial nations that had previously been international lenders enjoyed improved balances of international payments until about mid-1931. For example, the United States gained $700 million in gold from the beginning of 1930 to mid-1931, and several other creditor countries achieved even more favorable balances of payments. The worst sufferers during this period were nations that had earlier borrowed abroad and were heavily dependent on exports of raw materials. It is no coincidence that the nations experiencing the most severe deficits in their balances of payments in 1930 included Brazil, Chile, Venezuela, Paraguay, Peru, Australia, and New Zealand. In the meantime, the deepening depression was weakening the positions of the more industrialized countries, ripening them for an almost worldwide banking and monetary panic.

■ **1931: YEAR OF INTERNATIONAL CRISIS**   The international crisis that was to sweep most countries off the gold standard within a few months began in Vienna with the failure of the Credit Anstalt in May 1931. This was the most important bank in Austria, with large loans to depressed Austrian industry and with large deposit liabilities to foreigners. This failure shook confidence in all Austrian banks and in the ability of the Austrian government to maintain the gold value of its currency. Foreign creditors rushed to withdraw their short-term funds, and they were probably joined by some Austrians. In the tradition of international central bank cooperation developed during the 1920s, foreign central banks offered their aid. The Bank for International Settlements three European central banks, and the Federal Reserve provided about $14 million of assistance, of which $1,083,000 was from the Federal Reserve. This was far too small to meet the drain. Austria did not formally abandon the gold standard, but did impose strict controls over all gold and foreign exchange transactions—a device that was to be adopted by many others and that would help choke international trade and capital movements.

The next victim was Austria's neighbor, Hungary. As withdrawals mounted, the Bank for International Settlements, the Federal Reserve, and several European central banks again gave assistance, this time a total of $21 million, of which $2 million came from the Federal Reserve. Again the operation was unsuccessful, and in July, Hungary imposed strict controls over all transactions in gold and foreign exchange. The run then spread to Germany, which was known to have a large short-term debt to foreigners, a deeply depressed economy, and heavy investments in Austria. Withdrawals began in May, acelerated in June, and reached panic proportions in July as one very large bank failed and others fell into difficulties. Total withdrawals between May and late July approached $700 million. This time the Bank for International Settlements, the Federal Reserve, and other central banks provided credits of $100 million, including $25 million from the Federal Reserve. Also, President Hoover on June 20 proposed a one-year moratorium on all intergovernmental debt payments. Nothing could stem the tide. Withdrawals continued until the German government clamped tight controls on all international transactions in late July. These were to be retained and made even more restrictive until after the end of World War II.

Now the crisis spread to one of the two great international monetary and financial centers—London. Monetary and financial conditions there had actually improved during the first half of 1931. London gained about $125 million of gold during this period, losses to France being more than offset by inflows from other countries. Then the tide turned. Exactly why this occurred in July 1931 is not wholly clear, but two developments were relevant. One was publication of the findings of the Macmillan Report, which revealed that London's short-term liabilities to the rest of the world were even larger than had been suspected. Another was the crisis in Austria, Hungary, and Germany, which had damaged confidence in the stability of national currencies and had frozen large amounts of foreign claims.

In any case, withdrawals from London began in early July and then accelerated despite efforts to arrest them. The Bank of England raised its discount rate from 2½ to 3½ percent on July 28, and to 4½ percent on July 30. On August 1, the Federal Reserve and the Bank of France each granted a credit of $125 million to the Bank of England, and on August 29 the British government borrowed $400 million from private sources in New York and Paris. The outflow persisted, and by Friday, September 18, had exceeded $1 billion. At this stage, the British government threw in the sponge in order to avoid further deflationary pressure; it suspended the convertibility of sterling into gold, effective on Monday, September 21, and raised the bank rate to 6 percent to symbolize its intention of avoiding inflationary policies. The sterling exchange rate in terms of dollars began to fall immediately. In June, it had averaged about $4.86; by September 25, it had fallen to $3.83. It then drifted downward, ranging between $3.75 and $3.28 in 1932 and the first three months of 1933. Many foreigners who continued to hold sterling suffered large losses as measured in their own currencies. One of the largest holders, the Bank of France, lost its entire net worth.

Within a few weeks after Britain's departure from gold, large numbers of other economically important countries had abandoned gold payments, or imposed controls on gold and foreign exchange transactions, or both. (See Table 6–4.) These included all members of the British Empire except Canada and the Union of South Africa, the three Scandinavian countries, and many more. Still others followed suit in December 1931 and in 1932. By late 1932, the only major countries that remained on gold and were permitting relatively free international payments were the United States, France, Belgium, Switzerland, and the Netherlands. The international gold standard was gone; a new one, truly international in scope, was not to be reestablished until well after World War II.

The wave of withdrawals that swept Britain off gold on Sept. 21, 1931, shifted quickly to the United States. If sterling had fallen from its high place, what currency could be trusted? Between September 16 and October 28, a period of only six weeks, the United States lost $712 million of gold, mostly to France, Belgium, Switzerland, and the Netherlands. This served, of course, to drain off bank reserves and to force a more rapid contraction of money and credit. Unfortunately, the period also brought a new wave of bank failures, falling confidence in banks, and large currency withdrawals, the latter amounting to $393 million. Thus, in only six weeks, gold outflows and currency withdrawals drained off $1,105 million of member bank reserves, or nearly half of all member bank reserves existing at the beginning of the period. Although the Federal Reserve took some ameliorative action, it allowed credit to contract sharply, in part because it feared that an easier monetary policy would encourage further foreign withdrawals and force the United States off the gold standard. The outcome was the most rapid rate of deflation of money and credit to be experienced during the depression, with the possible exception of that in February 1933.

During the final two months of 1931, gold outflows stopped and the United States actually gained $170 million of gold, mostly from Canada, Latin America, and the Far East. However, the outflow resumed in January, and by mid-June 1932 amounted to another $550 million. Most of this gold went to the central banks of France, Belgium, and the Netherlands, which now wanted to hold gold rather than foreign exchange. The gold-exchange standard was being liquidated. This time the Federal Reserve followed a much more liberal policy. Now that its "free gold" position had been improved by the section of the Glass-Steagall Act permitting government securities to be used as collateral behind Federal

**Table 6–4.   Countries abandoning gold standards or instituting
control of the foreign exchanges in 1931 and 1932**

PERIOD	COUNTRIES ABANDONING GOLD STANDARDS	COUNTRIES INSTITUTING CONTROL OF FOREIGN EXCHANGES
Before September 1931	Australia Brazil Chile New Zealand Paraguay Peru Uruguay Venezuela	Austria Canada Germany Hungary
September–November 1931	Bolivia Canada Colombia Denmark Egypt Finland India Irish Free State Norway Portugal Sweden United Kingdom	Argentina Austria Brazil Bulgaria Czechoslovakia Denmark Estonia Finland Greece Hungary Latvia Persia Turkey Yugoslavia
December 1931–June 1932	Chile Greece Peru Siam	Paraguay Persia Romania
June–December 1932	Union of South Africa	

Sources: Compiled from various sources, including annual *Reports of the Bank for International Settlements* and *World Economic Surveys* by the League of Nations. Some countries abandoned gold, then attempted to return to gold, and then abandoned again.

Reserve notes, it proceeded to purchase more than $1 billion of government securities between February and mid-summer. This policy was in the right direction, but it was inadequate and could not undo the harm done by the sharp contraction of bank reserves and credit that had followed the impact of the international crisis on the United States in September 1931.

The American economy, and many others as well, were also damaged by the exchange control systems and other types of nationalistic protectionism that became so widespread in 1931 and 1932. A typical exchange control system required that all earnings of foreign currencies be surrendered to a designated government agency or a licensed bank and that no one might purchase or pay out foreign currencies without a license. At first these systems had only limited objectives: to prevent flights of capital to other countries and to limit fluctuations of exchange rates on the nation's currency. By granting or refusing to grant permits to buy foreign currencies, exchange control systems could determine which foreign debts would be paid and which would not, total amounts of imports, types of imports, sources of imports, and so on. Thus, exchange control came to be widely used to protect home industries, to limit total imports and thus to reduce international trade, and to discriminate among sources of supply. American exports suffered, not only from the general decrease of international trade but also because the United States was a favorite target for discrimination. Similar results followed as many countries adopted import licensing and other quantitative restrictions on imports. There were also widespread increases of tariffs. However, the United States was hardly in a position to complain about this; America had been a leader in the movement by enacting in mid-1930 the Smoot-Hawley Tariff, which imposed the highest rates in American history and among the highest in the world.

Following the widespread departures from gold in 1931 and 1932, the world tended to be divided into two monetary groups. One, the "gold group," included the countries that continued to maintain approximately constant gold values for their currencies and relatively free international payments. The principal members of this group were the United States, France, Belgium, Switzerland, and the Netherlands. In the "nongold group" were the countries that had allowed their currencies to depreciate significantly in terms of gold and in terms of the currencies that remained approximately constant in terms of gold. Table 6–5 shows the behavior of the dollar exchange rates on the currencies of 22 of these "nongold" countries. The next to last column of that table indicates that by December 1932 the exchange rate on the British pound sterling had fallen to only 68 percent of its level before September 1931; it had depreciated 32 percent in terms of gold, dollars, and other "gold" currencies. Among the currencies that had depreciated by roughly the same percentage were those of all members of the British Empire except Canada and the Union of South Africa (the latter depreciated at the end of 1932), the Scandinavian countries, and several countries in Latin America and elsewhere. Exchange rates among those currencies that depreciated by about the same percentages in terms of the dollar and gold remained approximately unchanged.

This widespread depreciation of exchange rates amounted, in effect, to a sharp rise of exchange rates on the currencies of the gold group. To say that other currencies depreciated in terms of the dollar is to say that the exchange rate on the dollar rose in terms of those currencies. For example,

**Table 6–5.   Indexes of exchange rates on selected foreign
currencies in terms of dollars (average in 1929=100)**

| COUNTRY | INDEX OF EXCHANGE RATE ON FOREIGN CURRENCY | | | | INDEX OF THE EXCHANGE RATE ON THE DOLLAR IN DECEMBER 1932 (1929 AVERAGE=100) |
	1930 AVERAGE	1931 AVERAGE	1932 AVERAGE	DECEMBER 1932 AVERAGE	
Argentina	88	70	61	62	161
Australia	95	73	58	54	185
Brazil	91	60	60	65	154
British India	100	93	73	69	145
Canada	100	97	89	87	115
Chile	100	100	66	50	200
China	71	54	52	47	213
Denmark	100	94	71	64	156
Egypt	100	93	72	68	147
Finland	100	95	62	57	175
Greece	100	100	64	42	238
Japan	107	106	61	45	222
Mexico	98	99	66	66	152
New Zealand	97	86	66	62	161
Norway	100	94	68	63	159
Portugal	100	95	72	68	147
Spain	80	65	55	56	179
Straits Settlements	100	94	72	70	143
Sweden	100	94	69	67	149
United Kingdom	100	93	72	68	147
Uruguay	87	56	48	48	208
Yugoslavia	100	100	93	46	132

Source: Board of Governors of the Federal Reserve System, *Banking and Monetary
Statistics*, pp. 662–682.

if each pound sterling will buy only 68 percent as many dollars as before,
147 percent as many pounds will be required to purchase a given number
of dollars. The exchange rate on the dollar will have risen 47 percent.
The last column of Table 6–5 shows that the exchange rate on the dollar
as seen by these countries had increased by at least 45 percent in almost
all cases, and in some cases by much more.

The large and widespread decreases of exchange rates on other currencies imposed sharp deflationary pressures on the economies of countries
in the gold group. This is not to say that all the depreciations were un-
justified and had no beneficial effects. Some currencies, such as the British
pound, had been overvalued and should probably have been depreciated
earlier. Moreover, several countries took advantage of their new freedom to initiate expansionary policies that would raise their national
incomes and stop price deflation.

On balance, however, the declines of foreign exchange rates—the rise of the exchange rate on the dollar—had a sharply deflationary impact on the American economy. For one thing, it made imports cheaper in terms of dollars. Domestic industries competing with these imports could hold their markets only by lowering prices. It also inhibited exports, especially those competing with goods from countries whose currencies were now cheaper. Where prices of the goods in these foreign currencies had not risen, American exporters could compete only by lowering their prices enough to offset the high cost of dollars in exchange markets. The deflationary impact on prices was especially severe for those agricultural products of which the United States was a large exporter. This point was stressed by those who wanted higher, not lower, prices for American farm products.

■ THE INTERNATIONAL ECONOMY IN 1933   When the new Administration came into power in March 1933, the international economy, as well as the domestic economy, was in shambles. Only a handful of countries still clung to the debris of what had been, a few years earlier, a truly international gold standard. The foreign exchange component of international reserves was almost completely liquidated. No satisfactory substitute for the gold-exchange standard had been developed or even designed. Exchange rates were fluctuating, in some cases erratically, and there were increasing complaints that various countries were depreciating their currencies in "beggar-my-neighbor" attempts to promote domestic recovery at the expense of foreign producers. International trade in goods and services was at a very low level, partly because of the low levels of income in the trading nations but also because of exchange disorders and increasing trade restrictions through exchange controls, quantitative limitations, and rising tariffs. International capital flows had virtually stopped, many international security issues were in default, and most potential borrowers had lost their creditworthiness. The whole problem of war debts and reparations remained unresolved.

To solve these problems and at the same time promote economic recovery at home would have been extremely difficult even if all nations had been in full agreement on objectives and priorities. By 1933, there was no such general agreement among nations, or even within nations. There were even wide differences on such a basic question as this: Is it desirable to reconstruct a world economic system based on relatively free international movements of trade and capital? Many answered with strong affirmatives, insisting not only that such a system was required in the long run to raise world productivity and living standards, but also that it was necessary for recovery from the depression. They stressed the desirability of reviving demands for exports as a key method of promoting employment. There were equally strong dissents from this view. Some agreed that freer trade and capital movements should be restored in the long run, but they insisted that the first job was to promote recovery at home; all else could wait. Others denied the desirability of reconstructing the international system even in the long run, arguing that under such a system each nation is buffeted by destabilizing forces from abroad. This position was bolstered by members of industries benefiting from the rise of protectionism.

A related question was this: Should the world seek to reestablish some sort of international gold standard or some other arrangement that would establish a network of stable exchange rates among national currencies? Many answered "yes." They believed such a system to be essential, both for promoting efficiency in world trade and capital movements and for protection against undesirable fluctuations of exchange rates. However, there were strong dissents in many countries. Some said, "Yes, but not until after we have recovered from the depression." Others said, "Never. The gold standard or any other system of stable exchange rates is inimical to economic stability and recovery. It serves to transmit economic disturbances from country to country and to limit unduly the ability of each country to pursue expansionary policies to promote recovery at home." Many countries that had departed from gold only with great reluctance were now enjoying their greater freedom.

Still another question was this: If nations do agree to stabilize exchange rates, what should be the rates of exchange among the various national currencies? This would have been a stumbling block even if all nations had been fully agreed on the desirability of an early stabilization. Nations whose exchange rates had fallen were reluctant to give up their advantages. And the United States and other members of the gold group would have fought for lower exchange rates on their own currencies.

In view of the widespread disagreements on such strategic questions as these, it is little wonder that the economic policies of the Roosevelt Administration in the international field were so vacillating or that progress in reconstructing the international system proved to be so slow and incomplete.

7

Monetary and Fiscal Policies During the Great Slide

Having described some of the principal happenings in the American economy during the great slide, impacts on the principal groups and economic sectors, and some of the processes involved, we now turn to an examination of monetary and fiscal policies during the period preceding the advent of the Roosevelt Administration in March 1933.

Americans who have reached their maturity only in the period since World War II find it almost incredible that the government and monetary authorities accepted so little responsibility for combating the depression, did so little, and did what they did so ineptly. It is tempting to try to explain these policies in terms of the peculiar attitudes of President Hoover and the Republican Party. Yet it would be difficult to argue persuasively that a majority of American voters wanted markedly different policies in the late 1920s and the first years of the 1930s, or that the Democrats would have followed much different policies if they had been in power. To understand public policies in this earlier period, one must recognize that since that time, and partly because of the tragic experience of the great depression, there have developed almost revolutionary changes in concepts concerning the responsibility of the federal government for promoting economic stability, in our understanding of causes of depressions and of the instruments that can be used to promote recovery, and in our willingness to use the available instruments.

Few Americans would now question the necessity for federal responsibility in this area. Such responsibility was asserted in the Employment Act of 1946:

> It is the continuing policy and responsibility of the Federal government to use all practicable means . . . in a manner calculated to foster and promote free competitive enterprise and the general welfare, conditions under which there will be afforded useful employment opportunities, including self-employment, for those able, willing, and seeking to work, and to promote maximum employment, production, and purchasing power.

More significant than the existence of this piece of legislation is the political fact that leaders in both major political parties now know that a large majority of Americans expect them to assume responsibility and will hold them accountable if they fail to take effective action to halt a decline of employment, output, and prices. Most Americans also believe that the government has in fact the power to prevent a recession from developing into a deep and prolonged depression. Many may not be familiar with the subtleties of income theory developed since the appearance in 1936 of John Maynard Keynes's monumental *General Theory of Employment, Interest and Money*. However, at least one conclusion of that branch of theory is widely known and generally accepted: The appropriate way to combat recession is to reverse the decline of aggregate money demands for output, and that this can be done with expansionary monetary and fiscal policies.

Federal Reserve officials now know that they are expected to respond to a recession with aggressively expansionary monetary policies. Few now believe that a mounting federal budget deficit in the midst of recession, reflecting increased government payments of unemployment benefits and decreased revenues resulting automatically from decreases in national income, should lead to tax increases or expenditure cuts to reduce or eradicate the deficit. In fact, most now believe that such increasing deficits are beneficial as "automatic stabilizers," or "automatic snubbers." Increased unemployment benefits serve to cushion the decline of private incomes and spending power; and the automatic decline of tax collections leaves a larger part of national income in the hands of the public. In fact, most Americans would use fiscal policy more aggressively if depressive forces appeared to be so strong that an expansionary monetary policy alone could not offset them quickly; they would increase government expenditures, or reduce effective tax rates, or both—this despite the fact that such actions would increase the size of the federal deficit.

■ **ATTITUDES IN 1930**   Such ideas, attitudes, and policy prescriptions would have seemed completely alien and unacceptable at the beginning of the depression, not only to the party in power but also to the great majority of Americans. That the federal government should assume heavy responsibility for promoting "maximum employment, production, and purchasing power" would have been unthinkable in a nation adjusted to only a limited role for government, and especially for the federal government. Nor was there agreement that the federal government could do much to promote economic stability even if it tried, nor what the appropriate policy measures would be.

For this situation, the state of economic understanding and thinking at that time must bear heavy responsibility. Professional economists had made great progress in understanding what is now called "microeconomics" —theories of relative prices, allocation of resources, and distribution of income. However, they had as yet no comprehensive, consistent, integrated, and generally accepted "macroeconomics"—a theory of the determination of the level of income and employment and of their fluctuations. Such a theory was developed only after the appearance of Keynes's book in 1936, and it gained general acceptance only later. This is not to say that there were no theories relating to economic downturns and depressions in the earlier period. After all, Keynes and those who followed him did not invent all the concepts and theoretical elements used to build their comprehensive structure. There were many types of theories of downturns and depression: monetary theories, psychological theories, overinvestment theories, underconsumption theories, and so on. All of them were incomplete and many were contradictory. Either absent or not satisfactorily combined were elements that later came to play key roles in a comprehensive theory of income behavior—consumption functions, savings functions, investment demand functions, and income and employment multipliers. In the absence of some comprehensive and generally accepted theory of income behavior, it was almost inevitable that the advice offered by economists would be conflicting, of limited usefulness, and often wrong.

Economists were not even agreed that the appropriate policy in the early stages of depression was to take measures to increase money demands for output. In fact, some economists—and they were not a small minority—contended that such "artificial" monetary and fiscal measures would only intensify and prolong a depression. They believed that depressions are caused by imbalances and maladjustments that develop during the preceding prosperity period. These could be of various kinds: general overexpansion of credit and debt, overexpansion of debt by particular sectors, overproduction of goods of specific types, excessive stocks of capital goods, and so on. It followed, they believed, that the proper cure for a depression was to purge the economy of its maladjustments, letting this occur through a "natural process of liquidation." To interfere with this process "artificially" would only make matters worse. For example, Professor Lionel Robbins—later to become Lord Robbins—wrote as late as 1935:

> In the course of a boom many bad business commitments are undertaken. Debts are incurred which it is impossible to repay. Stocks are produced and accumulated which it is impossible to sell at a profit. Loans are made which it is impossible to recover. Both in the sphere of finance and in the sphere of production, when the boom breaks, these bad commitments are revealed.
>
> Now in order that revival may commence again, it is essential that these positions should be liquidated. . . .
>
> Nobody wishes for bankruptcies. Nobody likes liquidation as such. If bankruptcy and liquidation can be avoided by sound financing, nobody would be against such measures. All that is contended is that when the extent of mal-investment and over-indebtedness has passed a certain limit, measures which postpone liquidation only make matters worse.[1]

Robbins was by no means alone in holding such views; he was joined by many economists, bankers, businessmen, and officials in the government

[1] Robbins, Lionel, *The Great Depression*, Macmillan, London, 1935, pp. 62–75. For statements of similar views, see Alvin H. Hansen, *Economic Stabilization in an Unbalanced World*, Harcourt, Brace & World, New York, 1932, pp. 188–192, 398. After 1937, Hansen became the leading American exponent of Keynesian views.

and the Federal Reserve. What members of this school never explained persuasively was how a general deflation of national money income, employment, and prices would facilitate and expedite correction of maladjustments in specific sectors of the economy.

There were, of course, many dissenters from the analysis and policy prescriptions just described. However, there were wide differences even among those who believed that an early rise of money demands for output would be desirable. Some thought it could be achieved through an expansionary monetary policy; others did not. A few thought that an expansionary fiscal policy, with increases of government expenditures and reductions of taxes, would be both effective and desirable; others insisted that government deficits would delay recovery. However, as the depression wore on and "the natural processes of liquidation" seemed to be killing the patient instead of curing him, orthodoxy weakened and increasing numbers of Americans came to believe that "something should be done," although there was little agreement on what that should be.

Let us examine monetary policies during this period.

■ **MONETARY POLICIES, 1929–1933**   We have already noted a number of factors that contributed to the vulnerability of commercial banks and other financial intermediaries. (1) The absence of any government agency to guarantee bank deposits or claims issued by other intermediaries. In fact, it was widely believed by economists and others that earlier experience with deposit insurance in several states proved its unsoundness; it did not prevent failures and it encouraged lax banking practices. Not even in February 1933, on the eve of the banking crash, would members of the Federal Reserve Board endorse a program of deposit insurance. (2) The absence of any program to insure assets of intermediaries. (3) The widespread prevalence of small unit banks, heavily dependent on local areas. (4) The inadequacy of facilities to provide loans to banks and other intermediaries. We have already noted that at the onset of the depression there were only two sets of such institutions. The Federal Intermediate Credit Banks lent only on the basis of paper resulting from intermediate-term loans to farmers. The Federal Reserve lent only to national banks and to state banks that had elected to become members. Thus, it did not lend to the 15,500 nonmember banks that proved to be so vulnerable, nor to other types of intermediaries. Moreover, it was empowered to lend to member banks on only two types of collateral: securities of the federal government and certain types of short-term loans legally defined as "eligible paper." Together these comprised only a small fraction of total bank assets. This situaion began to be improved only in 1932, when two new federal financial institutions were established—the Reconstruction Finance Corporation and the Federal Home Loan Bank System—and the Federal Reserve was empowered to lend on a wider range of bank assets. By this late date the entire financial system was in distress.

One might have expected that the Federal Reserve, in view of the vulnerability of the financial system, would have flooded the banking system with liquidity—that at an early stage it would have asked Congress to broaden the types of assets that it was empowered to purchase and that by purchasing huge amounts of securities it would have supplied ample funds to meet withdrawals from banks and to enable banks to meet loan demands. The policies actually followed were far less ambitious. The verdict on Federal Reserve policies during this period as a whole must be "much too little and far too late."

To analyze Federal Reserve policies in more detail, it will be useful to divide the period into four parts: (1) October 1929–September 1931. In this period, the Federal Reserve enjoyed maximum freedom to follow expansionary policies if it wished to do so. (2) October 1931–January 1932. Because of large gold withdrawals during the international financial crisis and a surge of currency withdrawals from banks, this was a period of very rapid deflation of money and credit. (3) February 1932–January 1933. Within this period the Federal Reserve bought over $1 billion of government securities to offset gold losses and provide more funds to banks. (4) February–March 1933. This was the period of the banking collapse.

■ **Federal Reserve, October 1929—September 1931**   We have already described the restrictive monetary policy followed by the Federal Reserve from early 1928 until the stock market crash. On the eve of the crash, discount rates were 6 percent at New York and 5 percent at the other Reserve banks, and member banks owed the Federal Reserve about $900 million. The Federal Reserve reversed its policies amost immediately after the crash, purchasing securities and lowering its discount rates. By mid-1930 the System had increased its holdings of government securities by more than $400 million. These purchases, together with gold inflows and net inflows of currency to the banks, enabled member banks to reduce their borrowings at the Federal Reserve by more than $700 million and to add about $50 million to their reserve balance. Discount rates were reduced; the New York rate was decreased in six steps from 6 to 2½ percent, while rates at the other Reserve banks fell to 4 and 3½ percent. In June 1930, it appeared that the Federal Reserve would indeed follow an agressively expansionary policy, first removing pressures for bank contraction and then applying strong pressure for expansion. It was not to turn out that way.

During the period from mid-1930 to September 1931, Reserve Banks made further reductions of their discount rates. The New York rate reached 1½ percent in May 1931, the lowest rate ever posted by a central bank up to that time. Significantly, rate reductions were smaller at the other Reserve banks. One maintained its rate at 3½ percent, five at 3 percent, four at 2½ percent, and one at 2 percent. However, the System made no significant further purchases of securities after mid-1930. It stopped despite the fact that, by today's standards, the reserve position of the banking system was not expansionary. In the autumn of 1931, member banks held only $100 million of reserves in excess of legal requirements, while their borrowings from the Federal Reserve remained above $200 million. Closer scrutiny revealed that most of the excess reserves were concentrated in banks in the larger cities, while many country banks remained heavily in debt to the Federal Reserve.

Why did the Federal Reserve virtually suspend security purchases in mid-1930 and fail to pursue an aggressive expansionary policy? The answer is not to be found in any limitations imposed by legal reserve requirements against Federal Reserve note and deposit liabilities, nor by considerations relating to the nation's balance of payments. Throughout this period, the Federal Reserve's actual gold-reserve ratio was nearly twice its legal minimum, and it held large amounts of free gold; a continuously favorable balance of payments brought new gold inflows almost every month. The System was clearly free to follow much more expansionary policies if it so desired. Its failure to do so reflected deliberate policy decisions by Federal Reserve officials.

The reasons for these decisions are numerous and complex. One factor was clearly the vague diffusion of responsibility and power within the System, which facilitated conflicts between the Federal Reserve Board and officials of the various Reserve banks, and among the Reserve banks. No one inside or outside the System possessed the power to resolve conflicts quickly and to secure prompt action. More fundamental, however, were the wide differences of opinion within the System concerning the responsibilities of the System, the types of policies that would be most appropriate, and the effects and effectiveness of their policy instruments.

Some officials believed that an increase of aggregate money demands for output was desirable, that the Federal Reserve had a responsibility to promote this, and that it could in fact be helpful if it used its instruments aggressively. The outstanding proponents of these views were the officials of the Federal Reserve Bank of New York and Eugene Meyer after he was appointed governor of the Federal Reserve Board in the autumn of 1930. Time after time, they urged larger Federal Reserve purchases of government securities and acceptances.

Such views and policies were quite unacceptable to many Federal Reserve officials, including several members of the Federal Reserve Board and governors of a majority of the Reserve banks. A number of them shared the view that economic maladjustments had developed during the preceding boom and would have to be eradicated through "a natural process of liquidation" before a "sound recovery" could begin. They contended that total bank credit had earlier risen to "excessive levels" and should be reduced, and especially that banks should purge themselves of loans on securities. Many believed that the proper role of the Federal Reserve was to respond to the needs of trade for credit, providing funds when demands increased and withdrawing funds as demands subsided. For this purpose, the Federal Reserve should rely largely on lending to banks. To force funds into the market through purchases of government securities was "artificial" and interfered with the natural process of liquidation. Some also misjudged conditions in financial markets. Looking only at interest rates on the safest short-term securities and at excess reserves in big-city banks, they concluded that credit conditions were already so easy as to be "sloppy."

In the end, such views prevailed and prevented the Federal Reserve from following a really aggressive monetary policy. By September 1931, the money supply had already fallen about 10 percent from its level in mid-1929. The rate of deflation was to be much higher in the next period.

■ **October 1931–January 1932**   After Britain suspended gold payments on Sept. 21, 1931, the international financial crisis swept to the United States, with both foreign central banks and private holders withdrawing funds. Gold losses on September 22 were $116 million, the largest ever suffered by the United States in a single day. By the end of October, $727 million of gold had been lost. A new surge of bank failures and loss of confidence in banks led to net currency withdrawals of $393 million from the banking system during this period. Thus, in only six weeks, gold losses and currency withdrawals drained off $1,120 million of bank reserves.

The Federal Reserve's response conformed to economist Walter Bagehot's classic rule for dealing with crises: Lend freely but at high interest rates. The Federal Reserve did increase its holdings of acceptances, but it bought no government securities and it raised its discount rates. New York increased its discount rate from 1½ to 3½ percent and its minimum rate for buying acceptances from 1 to 3⅛ percent. As a result of these events between mid-September and the end of October, member banks increased their debts to the Federal Reserve by $454 million and suffered a net drain of $189 million from their reserves.

Gold losses stopped at the end of October, and the gold stock actually rose slightly during the remainder of the year. However, the banking system remained under strong pressures to contract credit, and financial markets were demoralized. In the third week of February 1932, member bank debts to the Federal Reserve were $572 million higher and their reserve balances $540 million lower than they had been in mid-September.

Why did Federal Reserve officials allow such strong contractionary pressures to develop? Why didn't they respond by keeping their discount rates low and by purchasing very large amounts of acceptances and government securities? Although the answer is complex, a major reason was their desire to curb outflows of funds and reduce the danger of being forced to suspend gold payments. They knew that several foreign central banks, and especially the Bank of France, had incurred large losses on their holdings of sterling and that they were becoming fearful about the safety of their remaining holdings of dollars. High discount rates and abstention from purchasing securities would reassure foreign creditors that America was determined to defend the gold value of the dollar.

However, there were also other reasons. One was technical—a scarcity, or potential scarcity, of "free gold." The Federal Reserve Act required that Federal Reserve notes be collateraled 100 percent by gold and eligible paper, and that gold used as collateral for notes could not be counted as reserves against Federal Reserve deposit liabilities. Federal Reserve officials who had earlier and for other reasons opposed large purchases of securities now advanced another reason: At least some of the funds provided through security purchases would be used by banks to reduce their borrowings at the Federal Reserve. The latter, with decreased holdings of eligible paper, would have to use more gold as collateral and would be unable to meet reserve requirements against their deposit liabilities.

Still another reason for abstaining from large security purchases was a widespread feeling within the system that conditions had become so unfavorable that monetary actions alone could not improve the situation. Officials pointed to the frozen and shaky position of many banks and other financial institutions, to demoralized bond markets, and to mounting fears that continuing and rising deficits in the federal budget would undermine the government's credit and topple the entire financial structure. They agreed that large purchases should be undertaken only as part of a much broader program, which would include at least these elements: (1) Amendment to the Federal Reserve Act to permit government securities to be used as collateral for Federal Reserve notes, thus solving the "free gold" problem. (2) Establishment of a Reconstruction Finance Corporation to lend to financial institutions. (3) Wage cuts for railroad workers to improve railroad earnings and raise the values of railroad bonds, of which large amounts were outstanding and many heavily depreciated. (4) Elimination of the federal deficit, or at least a sharp reduction, by increasing taxes, reducing expenditures, or both.

By the latter part of February 1932, these measures had either been adopted or were far enough along for the Federal Reserve to begin purchasing securities.

■ **February 1932–January 1933**   On Feb. 24, 1932, the Federal Reserve began what was to be the largest program of open-market purchases in its history up to that time. Between that date and August 10, its holdings of government securities increased $1,110 million, raising total holdings to the unprecedented level of $1,851 million. This was partially offset by gold losses of nearly $350 million, reflecting withdrawals of nearly all of their remaining dollar balances by France, the Netherlands, Switzerland, and Belgium. The gold-exchange system was now almost completely liquidated. However, member banks were able to reduce by $383 million their debt to the Federal Reserve and to add $184 million to their reserve balances.

Federal Reserve purchases were reduced sharply in July and stopped completely in early August. Some Federal Reserve officials wished to go further. However, those who had earlier opposed aggressive expansionary policies now returned to form; they had acquiesced only reluctantly to the last purchases that were made and would go no further. Thus, no further purchases were made until February 1933, when the banking crisis was already developing. However, a resumption of gold inflows in the latter part of 1932 did provide some additional reserve funds.

There can be little doubt that Federal Reserve policies in 1932 relieved some of the contractionary pressures built up by gold outflows and currency withdrawals in the latter part of 1931. For example, from February 24 to the end of 1932, member banks were able to reduce their debt to the Federal Reserve by $568 million and to add $604 million to their reserve balances. A comparison of conditions in December 1932 with those in mid-September 1931, before the international crisis but when banks were already under contractionary pressure, makes the 1932 policy appear less ambitious and adequate. During this period as a whole, total bank reserves increased only $60 million, and bank debts to the Federal Reserve actually rose by $4 million. (See Table 7–1.) Although banks held over

Table 7–1.   Changes in member bank reserves and selected related items (in millions of dollars)

	CHANGE, FEB. 24, 1932– DEC. 28, 1932	CHANGE, SEPT. 16, 1931– DEC. 28, 1932
Total member bank reserves	+$604	+$ 60
Borrowings at the Federal Reserve	− 568	+ 4
Excess reserves	+ 527	+ 347

Source: Board of Governors of the Federal Reserve System, *Banking and Monetary Statistics*, pp. 386–387.

$500 milion of reserves in excess of legal requirements in December 1932, it is almost certain that they felt under no pressure to expand their credit. For one thing, they wanted to hold more excess reserves rather than use them as a basis for lending, in view of the illiquidity of their other assets and their fear of withdrawals. Moreover, large numbers of banks, and especially country banks, had no excess reserves and remained in debt to the Federal Reserve.

In any case, neither Federal Reserve policies, nor the activities of the Reconstruction Finance Corporation, nor both together were able to prevent a collapse of the banking system.

■ **February–March 1933**   The rate of bank failures, which had declined in the preceding months, began to rise again in late December 1932. Failures in that month were 161, followed by 236 in January. Currency withdrawals began in January and accelerated during February. The first statewide bank holiday, aside from one declared in Nevada the preceding

October, came in Louisiana on February 4, when the governor declared a one-day holiday to give one of the largest banks in New Orleans time to arrange for an RFC loan. Not wishing to reveal the real reason for his action, he first thought of declaring a holiday in honor of the great pirate, Jean Lafitte, but finally settled on celebrating the anniversary of America's severance of diplomatic relations with Germany.[2] Acute banking difficulties in Detroit led the governor of Michigan to proclaim, on February 14, an eight-day statewide bank holiday, later extended into March. Troubles now spread like wildfire. Currency hoarding rose, funds were withdrawn from other states to send to Michigan or to meet payments that would otherwise have been met from deposits in Michigan banks, deposits were shifted from weaker to stronger banks, and bankers drew down their interbank deposits. New York City banks alone lost $520 million of interbank deposits during the last two weeks of February, bringing their total losses for the month to $757 million. Maryland declared a statewide holiday on February 25, and at about the same time Arkansas, Indiana, and Ohio authorized restrictions on withdrawals. The end was fast approaching. By March 3, virtually all states had closed their banks or limited withdrawals. When President Roosevelt, in one of his first official actions, declared a nationwide bank holiday, he did little more than prolong the existing situation.

Between mid-January and the crash, currency withdrawals from banks amounted to more than $1,900 million and gold losses to more than $300 million, thus draining off more than $2,200 million of bank reserves. Again the Federal Reserve stood ready to lend freely but at higher discount rates. Its loans to banks increased by $1,165 million, and the New York bank raised its discount rate from 2½ to 3½ percent. Purchases of acceptances and securities were small. However, it is doubtful that even extremely large purchases at this stage could have been helpful. The time for effective action had passed.

Thus, monetary policy had failed to arrest the great contraction of money, credit, and economic activity, not because aggressive expansionary policies were tried and failed, but because they were not tried. The money supply shrank by 25 percent from 1929 to the end of 1932. The rate of decrease of the money supply was highest during the six months following the onset of the international financial crisis in September 1931, but the money supply had been allowed to decline by 10 percent before that crisis reached the United States. An aggressively expansionary monetary policy initiated in the early months of the depression might well have prevented the liquidation and induced recovery. Such a policy would have had less and less chances of success as the depression ground on, decreasing the solvency and liquidity of financial intermediaries, creating more excess capacity in industry, deteriorating the creditworthiness of borrowers, and worsening expectations concerning the profitability of new investment.

[2] *The New York Times*, Feb. 12, 1933, p. 1.

■ **GOVERNMENT TAXES AND EXPENDITURES**   While monetary policy was not aggressively expansionary, neither was fiscal policy. There were no large-scale attempts to raise private disposable incomes and spending power by lowering taxes, or to increase demand for output and raise private incomes through large increases of government expenditures.

Because of the small size of government budgets relative to GNP, it would have been very difficult, politically and administratively, to make fiscal policies highly expansionary even if government officials had been determined to do so. Table 7–2 shows that in 1929, total revenues of all governmental units—federal, state, and local—were only $11.4 billion, or less than 11 percent of GNP, while total expenditures were only $10.4

Table 7–2.   Government receipts and expenditures, on income and product account, 1929–1932 calendar years (in millions of dollars)

	1929	1930	1931	1932	1933
Receipts					
Federal	3,804	3,047	2,047	1,708	2,670
State and local	7,571	7,835	7,743	7,312	7,157
Total	11,375	10,882	9,790	9,020	9,827
Expenditures					
For goods and services					
Federal	1,261	1,372	1,495	1,456	2,000
State and local	7,236	7,823	7,727	6,637	6,047
Total	8,497	9,195	9,222	8,093	8,047
For all other purposes					
Federal	1,368	1,392	2,686	1,729	1,985
State and local	528	609	767	414	1,179
Total	1,896	2,001	3,453	2,143	3,164
Total expenditures					
Federal	2,629	2,764	4,181	3,185	3,985
State and local	7,764	8,432	8,494	7,592	7,266
Total	10,393	11,196	12,675	10,777	11,251
Surplus or deficit on income and product account					
Federal	1,175	283	− 2,134	− 1,477	− 1,315
State and local	− 193	− 597	− 751	− 280	− 69
Total	982	− 314	− 2,885	− 1,757	− 1,384

Source: U. S. Department of Commerce, *The National Income and Product Accounts of the United States, 1929–1965*, pp. 52–54.

billion, or about 10 percent of GNP. Moreover, about two-thirds of these receipts and expenditures were at the state and local government levels.

It would be unrealistic to expect state and local governments to reduce taxes or increase expenditures in order to buoy up economic activity unless all, or virtually all, of the financial costs were borne by the federal government. For one thing, a state or local government would be highly reluctant to increase its own financial burdens in order to increase business activity in general, knowing that a large part of the benefits would accrue to other areas. Moreover, few would have been able to borow enough to finance a large expansionary program.

If an effective expansionary fiscal program were to be undertaken, it would have to be at the federal level. However, the federal budget was very small relative to GNP in 1929. At $3.8 billion, total federal revenues were equal to only about 3.6 percent of GNP. A very large percentage decrease of taxes, or even an elimination of all federal taxes, would have offset only a small part of the decline of private investment spendings. Federal expenditures, at $2.6 billion, were equal to only 2.5 percent of GNP. Extremely large percentage increases of these expenditures would have been required to offset a significant part of the decrease of private investment. Such tax cuts or expenditure increases would have brought large deficits and additions to the national debt, an outcome that few were willing to contemplate.

However, virtually no public officials, and very few others, thought that the government should undertake such programs for the express purpose of buoying demands for output. For this there were many interrelated reasons. It was not the responsibility of the federal government to assure stability in the economy. The government should operate on businesslike principles, undertaking only those projects whose direct benefits were worth their cost. Also, intervention would do more harm than good, partly by interfering with "natural processes of liquidation and adjustment."

■ **Fiscal Theory**   Partially responsible for such widely held beliefs was the state of economic thinking and understanding at the time. In the absence of a comprehensive and generally accepted theory of income determination, there could be no consistent and generally accepted fiscal theory relating the behavior of government taxes and expenditures to the behavior of aggregate demands for output. Crucially absent was the "multiplier" concept. It was not recognized that an initial reduction of taxes or increase of government expenditures could bring a multiple increase of total expenditures for output by inducing increases of private consumption expenditures, and perhaps also of investment expenditures. Thus, it was easy to believe that as more credit and output were taken by the federal government, less would remain for the private sectors.

Especially adverse to the use of tax cuts and expenditure increases for stabilization purposes were the current ideas of economists and others concerning budget deficits and increases of government debt. If economists did not provide a fiscal theory, they did provide general rules for fiscal conduct, and the principal rule was that of an annually balanced budget. Every governmental unit should match its tax revenues and expenditures in every twelve-month period, and if it had outstanding debt it should have a tax surplus to retire a part of the debt each year. There were, of course, permitted exceptions to the general rule. For example, deficits during a major war were conceded to be inevitable although unfortunate, and a government was not to be criticized for a small deficit resulting from an honest miscalculation of revenues and expenditures. It might also borrow to finance self-liquidating public works, such as water-supply systems or toll roads, which would themselves yield enough revenues to service and retire the debt. Moreover, a local government might also borrow to pay for a large nonrecurring item, such as a new school, which would be useful over a long period of time. There were few other exceptions to the rule of an annually balanced budget, and among them were not deficit spending, tax reductions, or expenditure increases to raise the levels of aggregate demand, output, and employment.

It was believed that budget deficits and debt increases that did not conform to these rules harmed the economy and the nation in several ways: (1) A government that is thus enabled to spend without raising taxes is likely to become wasteful and to misallocate resources. (2) Government deficits and borrowing retard business recovery. For one thing, they are likely to retard natural processes of liquidation. Also, new government borrowing tends to raise market rates of interest, and thus to raise the cost and decrease the availability of credit for private use. The Federal Reserve could, of course, avoid this outcome by purchasing government securities or otherwise increasing the total supply of money and credit. However, to finance deficits through new money creation was considered "unsound," "inflationary," and likely to destroy "confidence" in the dollar, the government credit, and financial instruments in general. (3) Continuing deficits and rising debt would destroy the credit of the federal government, with dire consequences for all.

It is difficult to understand why so many believed the credit of the federal government to be so frail. The federal debt at the end of 1929 was equal to only 15 percent of that year's GNP, and it was more than $9 billion below its level at the end of World War I. Yet the fear was real, and the consequences of any impairment of the government's credit was believed to be calamitous. In a radio speech on March 12, 1932, Secretary of the Treasury Ogden L. Mills told the nation:

> Our private credit structure is inextricably bound to the credit of the United States Government. Our currency rests predominantly upon the credit of the United States. Impair that credit and every dollar you handle will be tainted with suspicion. The foundation of our commercial credit system, the Federal Reserve banks, and all other banks which depend upon

them, is tied into and dependent upon the credit of the United States Government. Impair that credit today, and the day after thousands of development projects—they are still going on—will stop; thousands of businessmen dependent upon credit renewals will get refusals from their bankers; thousands of mortgages that would otherwise be renewed or extended will be foreclosed; merchants who would buy on credit will cancel orders; factories that would manufacture on part capacity at least will close down. Impair the credit of the United States Government and all that we have sought to accomplish in the course of the last few months is, to a large extent, nullified. The renewed courage and confidence that have replaced the fear and uncertainty, which prevailed almost universally, will once more grow weak and hesitant.[3]

Although Secretary Mills spoke only of effects of confidence in the United States, he may have shared fears of others that continued deficit spending would impair foreign confidence in the dollar, induce gold exports, and perhaps force the United States off the gold standard.

It should be emphasized that such views were by no means confined to members of the Republican administration; they were widely shared by economists, bankers, businessmen, and others.[4] Even as late as 1932, Democratic leaders in both the Senate and the House helped push through large tax increases, and candidate Roosevelt castigated Hoover repeatedly and mercilessly for his continuing deficits, promising that, if elected, he would restore financial order in the government budget. In the meantime, as the depression deepened, increasing numbers of economists and others began to question the old rules of financial orthodoxy.

Such was the state of attitudes, understanding, and thinking about fiscal policy in the early years of the depression. Let us now look at the policies actually followed.

■ Fiscal Policies, 1929–1933   Although not strongly expansionary during any of these years, federal fiscal policies were more favorable to economic stability during approximately the first two years of the depression than might have been expected in view of the state of thinking of the time. For this, the very comfortable state of the federal budget in 1929 was largely responsible. As in earlier years, budgeted expenditures included over $600 million for debt retirement, but receipts for the fiscal years ending June 30, 1930, and June 30, 1931, were expected to yield a surplus over all expenditures, including those budgeted for debt reduction. There was thus an opportunity to reduce taxes or to increase other government expenditures without interfering with the program of debt reduction. Soon after the stock market crash, President Hoover recommended, and in December Congress enacted, a reduction of one percent in personal income and corporate profits tax rates. It was estimated that this would reduce tax collections by $160 million, the reduction to be about equally divided between 1930 and 1931. However, the reduction was to apply only to incomes in the

[3] *Annual Report of the Secretary of the Treasury,* 1932, pp. 259–260.
[4] For many examples, see Hearings on S. Res. 315 before the Senate Committee on Finance, 72nd Congress, 2nd Session, February 1933.

calendar year 1929, and the Ways and Means Committee specifically declared that its intention was only to pass on to taxpayers the surplus achieved in the fiscal 1929.[5] At about the same time, President Hoover recommended an increase of about $200 million in expenditures for public works. A soldiers' bonus of about $1 billion, enacted despite President Hoover's protests, contributed to private incomes in 1931.

Such actions were acceptable while the federal budget remained in surplus. However, attitudes changed sharply as declines of national income and corporate profits brought marked reductions in federal revenues and as the budget surplus was replaced by a large deficit. The federal deficit exceeded $2 billion in the calendar year 1931. President Hoover and many others now called for both tax increases and expenditure reductions. Changes in federal fiscal policies from 1931 to 1932 were sharply restrictive. Federal expenditures were deduced by about $40 million. Far more restrictive was the Revenue Act of 1932, which provided the largest percentage tax increase ever enacted in American peacetime history. By imposing new taxes, lowering exemptions, and raising rates of existing taxes, it was sufficient to double total federal tax receipts at a full-employment level of GNP. This obviously tended to reduce private incomes after taxes and to shift downward private demands for output.

State and local expenditures actually increased from 1929 to 1930, but by less than $600 million. However, as their revenues began to fall and as some faced debt difficulties, these governmental units began to curtail expenditures, reducing their purchases of goods and services more than they increased their relief payments. Although the decrease of total state and local expenditures from 1930 to 1931 was less than $100 million, that from 1931 to 1932 was $1,090 million. (See Table 7–2, page 121.) Also many of these units introduced new taxes, especially sales taxes, and increased rates of existing taxes.

It is very difficult to assess precisely the effects of overall government fiscal policies on total demands for output and on the course of the depression.[6] Two things can be said with confidence. First, fiscal policies were not strongly expansionary in any of these years. Second, fiscal actions in 1932 were definitely and strongly deflationary. The sharp increase of federal taxes, further increases of state and local taxes, and reductions of expenditures by all levels of government served to depress further the already depressed economy.

■ CONCLUSIONS   The two principal instruments on which the nation now replies to combat recession and restore recovery—monetary

---

[5] James A. Maxwell, *Fiscal Policy*, Holt, Rinehard and Winston, New York, 1955, p. 12.

[6] For an attempt to assess these effects and a description of some of the difficulties involved, see E. Cary Brown, "Fiscal Policy in the 'Thirties: A Reappraisal," *American Economic Review*, December 1956, pp. 857–879.

and fiscal policies—were both employed only weakly and too often wrongly in the period preceding March 1933. Costly as these mistakes were, at least some of them seem almost inevitable when one considers the state of understanding, attitudes, and orthodoxies at the beginning of the depression. Merely to list some of them is to suggest their power to inhibit effective action: lack of any valid and generally accepted theory of income determination, beliefs that "natural processes of liquidation" were required for recovery, the tradition of only a limited role for the federal government, devotion to the objective of maintaining a gold standard at whatever cost, and the principle of annually balanced budgets. An effective recovery program within the confines of these limitations and orthodoxies was impossible. Perhaps a bolder, more imaginative leader than President Hoover could have broken these confines sooner, but it is not clear that such a man was available or could have been elected at the beginning of the 1930s. Even after years of depression had weakened orthodoxies and inhibitions, President Roosevelt was by no means free of such limitations.

8

The Period of Recovery

A checklist of conditions in the various sectors of the economy when Roosevelt assumed the Presidency on March 4, 1933 would have looked something like this:

Sector	Conditions
National output and income	Real output more than 30 percent below 1929 levels and at least 35 percent below full employment levels.
	Prices of output down at least one-quarter on average.
	National money income down about 50 percent.
Labor	More than one-fourth of the labor force totally unemployed and a large fraction of those employed working only part-time.
	Wage cuts widespread during the past two years.
	Many of the unemployed receiving no relief; others receiving only inadequate amounts.
	Relief burdens of many lower governmental units becoming unbearable.
Agriculture	Prices of farm products down sharply, far more than most other prices.
	Farm incomes deeply depressed.
	Widespread delinquencies on farm debts and taxes.
	Farmers rebelling against debts and low prices on farm products.
Urban housing	Tax and mortage delinquencies widespread and foreclosure rates high.
	Prices of houses far below reproduction cost.
	Almost no new mortgage money available.
	New construction at a standstill.

Business firms	Most firms operating far below capacity levels.
	Losses more prevalent than profits.
	Failure rates high, many firms illiquid with serious impairment of net worth.
	Many firms without access to credit.
Banking and finance	All commercial banks closed and other financial intermediaries in bad shape.
	Most banks illiquid and insolvent if assets valued at current market prices.
	Possibility of resumption of runs on banks if reopened without careful preparation.
	Most banks too scared to provide credit.
	Resumption of gold outflow possible, if permitted.
State and local governments	Many in bad financial shape because of tax delinquencies and relief costs.
	Most have cut back sharply on public works and social services
	Some have defaulted on debts; others are meeting debt service only precariously.
	Increasing numbers encountering difficulties in borrowing.
	Financial prospects bleak if must carry mounting relief costs.
Foreign trade and finance	The depression worldwide in scope.
	International trade in goods and services very depressed.
	International lending at a standstill.
	Official restrictions on trade and capital movements widespread and increasing. Most nations off gold standards, with fluctuating exchange rates.
	Lower exchange rates on many foreign currencies exerting downward pressures on prices of American exports and imports.

In short, the economy and the financial system were in shambles. Fortunately, this marked the trough of the depression. However, the process of economic rehabilitation and recovery proved to be difficult, slow, and incomplete before the expanding rearmament program rescued the economy in 1941, more than eight years after Roosevelt assumed office.

■ **THE COURSE OF RECOVERY**   Although real GNP rose and remained above its low level of 1933, it did not again reach its 1929 level until 1937, and then it fell in 1938. (See Table 8–1.) Only in 1939 and later years did it remain above the level achieved in 1929. Real output remained far below its potential levels until 1941, and even in that year it was at least 8 percent below its potential.[1] Unemployment declined from its 1933 high, but the average unemployment rate never fell below 14.3 before 1941, and in that year it was 9.9 percent. This refers only to the totally unemployed; part-time unemployment persisted. Such is a bare outline of the sluggish recovery.

Table 8–1.   Selected indicators of economic activity, 1932–1941

YEAR	INDEX OF GNP AT 1929 PRICES (1929=100)	ACTUAL GNP AS PERCENTAGE OF POTENTIAL GNP AT CONSTANT PRICES	UNEMPLOYMENT AS PERCENTAGE OF LABOR FORCE	AVERAGE PRICE LEVEL OF OUTPUT (1929=100)	INDEX OF GROSS NATIONAL INCOME AT CURRENT PRICES (1929=100)
1929	100		3.2	100	100
1932	72	66	23.6	79	56
1933	70	62	24.9	78	53
1934	76	66	21.7	83	62
1935	84	71	20.1	84	69
1936	95	78	16.9	84	79
1937	101	80	14.3	88	87
1938	96	74	19.0	87	81
1939	104	78	17.2	85	87
1940	113	82	14.6	87	96
1941	137	92	9.9	93	119

Sources: For basic data, see first three tables in Chapter 1, pp. 4, 5, and 7.

Since the preceding indexes are based on annual aggregates or averages, they cannot reflect movements within years. To indicate intrayear movements, we shall use the Federal Reserve index of industrial production, which is available on a monthly basis. (See Figure 3.) It should be noted, however, that this measure of real output is much less comprehensive than GNP and that it tends to move more quickly and widely.

In March 1933, industrial production was only 47 percent of its level during the summer of 1929. It then rose sharply into July, only to suffer a relapse that lasted until January 1934, by which time it had lost nearly half the gains achieved between March and July 1933. A new recovery began in February 1934 and continued into the spring of 1937. At the latter time, industrial production was actually 5 percent above its level in mid-1929. Real GNP for 1937 as a whole was one percent above its 1929 level. However, the economy was still operating far below its potential. Actual

---

[1] It will be remembered that "potential real GNP" is computed by applying a 3 percent annual compound increase to the level achieved in 1929.

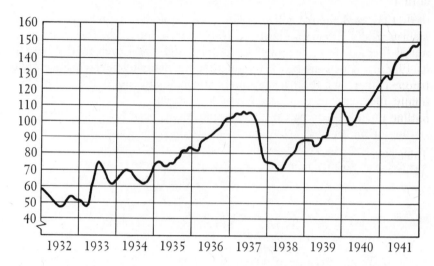

FIG. 3. Federal Reserve Index of Industrial Production, 1932–1941
(average of June–July 1929 = 100)

output was 20 percent below its potential, more than 14 percent of the labor force remained totally unemployed, and part-time unemployment was still common.

Then came what is best described as "a sharp recession within a depression"; this lasted from the spring of 1937 until the spring of 1938. Industrial production fell by one-third during this period, and at its low point was 30 percent below its level in mid-1929. Real GNP in 1938 was 5 percent below that of the preceding year and 26 percent below its potential. The average unemployment rate jumped to 19 percent.

Although the 1937–1938 recession was sharp, painful, and discouraging, it was happily short. In the late spring of 1938 a new recovery began. In 1939, the last full year before the economy came to be influenced significantly by the new war, real GNP was 4 percent above its level in 1929. However, it was still 22 percent below its potential. The number of unemployed averaged 9.5 million, and the unemployment rate was over 17 percent. While the labor force had increased by 6 million between 1929 and 1939, the number employed decreased by 1.8 million.

World War II broke out in September 1939, but its expansionary effects on the American economy did not begin to be significant until 1940. Then they were of two major types: increased demands for American exports, and increased demands for output by the federal government for its expanding national defense program. Belligerent countries that were later to become America's allies took more American exports to help meet their civilian and war needs, and nonbelligerents turned increasingly to American exports as supplies from belligerent countries decreased. U. S. exports had averaged below $4.4 billion in the years immediately preceding 1940; in 1941, they were $1.5 billion higher. (See Table 8-2.)

Table 8–2. U. S. exports and federal purchases of goods and
services, 1936–1941 (in millions of dollars at current prices)

YEAR	U. S. EXPORTS	FEDERAL PURCHASES OF GOODS AND SERVICES		
		TOTAL	NATIONAL DEFENSE	OTHER
1936	$3,539	$ 4,935	—	—
1937	4,553	4,664	—	—
1938	4,336	5,409	—	—
1939	3,432	5,105	$ 1,249	$3,856
1940	5,355	6,015	2,214	3,801
1941	5,925	16,882	13,750	3,132

Source: The National Income and Product Accounts of the United States, 1929–1965,
p. 2.

Far greater was the increase of federal expenditures for output to be used in the expanding national defense program. This expansion began in the spring of 1940 and accelerated thereafter. In the years immediately preceding 1940, total federal expenditures for goods and services for all purposes ranged below $5.4 billion; in 1941, they were $16.9 billion, and expenditures for national defense were nearly $13.8 billion. Thus, the government was spending for national defense alone about two and a half times as much as it had spent for all purposes in the years before 1940. This combination of increased demands for American exports and rising government purchases for defense purposes raised output much closer to full employment levels; they did so by directly increasing both demands for output and private incomes, through multiplier effects on consumption expenditures, and by raising productive activities and prospects for profits enough to revive private investment spending.

Not until the nation had been in the war for well over a year did Americans come to recognize fully how far below its potential the economy had been operating in the prewar period. It is very difficult to compare in a meaningful way wartime and peacetime rates of real output, and there is reason to believe that the estimates for wartime output have an upward bias. However, if one takes the official estimates at face value, real GNP in 1944, the peak year of the war effect, was more than 75 percent above its levels in 1929 and 1939. This also suggests that our estimates of potential real GNP in the latter part of the 1930s may be overly modest, so that we have underestimated the extent of lost output.

Table 8–3 shows the behavior of the two major components of private demands for output–personal consumption and gross private domestic investment. Both are indexes of real output, or output measured at constant prices. In 1933, personal consumption in real terms was only 81 percent of its 1929 level. It then rose, and in the years 1936–1938 it fluctuated around its 1929 level. It would, of course, have been higher if

Table 8–3.   Indexes of GNP and selected components at
constant prices, 1932–1941 (1929=100)

YEAR	TOTAL GNP	PERSONAL CONSUMP- TION	GROSS PRIVATE DOMESTIC INVESTMENT			
			TOTAL	RESIDEN- TIAL CON- STRUCTION	NONRESIDEN- TIAL CON- STRUCTION	PRODUCERS' DURABLE EQUIPMENT
1929	100	100	100	100	100	100
1932	72	82	12	26	31	30
1933	70	81	13	20	29	34
1934	76	85	23	28	35	44
1935	84	90	45	39	43	60
1936	95	99	59	49	60	82
1937	101	103	74	54	71	94
1938	96	100	42	55	52	64
1939	104	106	61	79	58	75
1940	113	112	82	89	71	96
1941	137	119	103	94	84	113

Sources: Computed from data in The National Income and Product Accounts of the United States, 1929–1965, principally p. 4. One component of gross private domestic investment—change in business inventories—is not shown in the table. This item was negative in the years 1932–1934 and in 1938, and positive but small in relation to total private investment in the other years.

the public's real income had been larger. Gross private domestic investment—the amount of output demanded for the purpose of maintaining and increasing the stock of privately owned capital goods—behaved far worse. In 1933, it was only 13 percent of its 1929 level. In no year prior to 1941 did it come close to the 1929 level. Its closest approaches were to 82 percent in 1940 and to 74 percent in 1937. In most of the other years it was at least 40 percent below. Residential construction, which normally accounts for a sizable fraction of total private investment, never recovered fully during this period. During most of the years it was deeply depressed. The same was true of nonresidential construction. Purchases of new producers' durable equipment performed a bit better, but rose above their 1929 level only in 1941.

The failure of the New Deal to bring about an adequate revival of private investment is the key to its failure to achieve a complete and self-sustaining recovery of output and employment. Full-employment levels of real income and output—what we have called potential output—could be reached and maintained only if the amount of real personal and business savings out of that full-employment level of income were fully offset by expenditures for private investment, net foreign investment, and government expenditures in excess of current government income. The sum of these offsets remained far below the large amounts that households and business would have saved out of a full-employment level of income.

It would have been unrealistic, under the circumstances existing in 1933, to expect any large part of the gap to be filled by an increase of net foreign investment, which involves, in effect, lending to foreigners who use the funds to purchase American exports. Too many conditions were adverse to an early recovery of American foreign lending: the deteriorated creditworthiness of foreign borrowers; demoralized markets for securities, and especially for foreign securities; the continued reluctance of lenders to make risky loans; increasing social, political, and military disturbances abroad; and a network of official restrictions on international trade and capital movements.

If the offset gap were to be closed, it would have to be largely through increases in the level of government deficit spending, of private investment, or both. As we shall see, government fiscal policies were far too weak and erratic to close more than a small part of the offset gap. And the combined efforts of fiscal, monetary, and other government policies did not induce an adequate recovery of private investment. These points will later be discussed in more detail.

■ **NEW DEAL RECOVERY POLICIES**   Under the chaotic conditions prevailing when he assumed office, Roosevelt was in a strong political position to change policies and to initiate new ones if he wished to do so. He was fully justified in believing that he and the Democratic party had a mandate from the people "to do something." He had won the Presidency by a landslide, polling 22.8 million votes to Hoover's 15.8 million, and commanding 472 electoral votes to Hoover's 59. Aside from the three traditionally Republican New England states—Maine, New Hampshire, and Vermont—Hoover won only Connecticut, Pennsylvania, and Delaware. The House included 310 Democrats and 117 Republicans, while the Senate comprised 60 Democrats and 35 Republicans. Roosevelt would be in a powerful position if he could command the support of even a majority of his large Democratic majorities in both branches of Congress. He was to find that this was no reluctant, recalcitrant Congress; many of its members wished to move faster and further than he did. His problem was often to prevent Congress from enacting unwanted mandatory measures, which he cleverly avoided in many cases by persuading it to grant him sweeping permissive powers.

Although Roosevelt had ample political power when he assumed office to initiate new economic programs, he had no economic program in any meaningful, operational sense of the term. Neither at the time of his inauguration nor soon thereafter did he have either a well-defined, ordered set of objectives or a set of strategies and tactics for promoting those objectives. Roosevelt was not highly sophisticated in economic matters. He thought much more in terms of goals and objectives than in terms of methods of promoting them. Seeking many objectives, he sometimes failed to evaluate realistically their compatibility or incompatibility and the trade-off values among them. On the methods to be used to promote objectives, he was even less committed and sophisticated. He was far less committed than Hoover to orthodoxies, such as defending the gold standard at any price, striving for an annually balanced budget, and maintaining only a very limited role for the federal government. He was pragmatic, experimental, willing to take chances, and open to advice and compromise. A superb politician, he both yielded to pressures and played off one pressure group against another to further his own ends.

The numerous, diverse, and often-conflicting measures known collectively as the New Deal were not preplanned by Roosevelt as a coherent and consistent program. Instead, most of them were responses to strong pressure groups, each demanding relief of its own plight and redress of its own grievances. Thus, the Roosevelt recovery program came to include not only general measures to increase aggregate demands for output but also a myriad of specific measures to help individual sectors: to provide relief to the unemployed and to provide jobs on federal projects, to raise farm prices and farm incomes, to reduce and rehabilitate farm debts and to do the same for home mortgages, to raise prices and profits for industrial firms, to assist state and local governments, to rehabilitate financial institutions, and so on. Many of the measures adopted were not primarily for the purpose of economic recovery, or necessarily compatible with it. Once the barrier to sweeping government action had been broken, a flood of other measures became politically feasible. Thus, there were also measures to reform financial institutions and financial practices, to facilitate unionization of labor, to conserve natural resources, to institute social security programs, and so on.

Roosevelt's program for economic recovery might have been simpler and probably more effective if from the beginning he had relied primarily on macroeconomic measures that would increase aggregate money demands for output. Through aggressively expansionary monetary policies, tax reductions, and large increases of government expenditures, he might have raised aggregate money demands for output enough to induce full employment, raise incomes in all sectors, and make unnecessary the many measures directed toward relief of conditions in specific sectors. Such a strategy was not adopted and for several reasons could not have been adopted in 1933. Still crucially absent was any comprehensive and generally accepted theory of income determination.

Not before the late 1930s, if at all, were Roosevelt's policies influenced by the new Keynesian type of analysis. The actions taken that were consistent with the Keynesian prescription were taken largely for other reasons and therefore were unlikely to conform in either timing or magnitude to those required to raise aggregate demands for output to full-employment levels. Roosevelt's understanding of monetary policies was defective, and monetary policies in 1933 were inadequately expansionary.

The development of adequately expansionary fiscal policies was hampered not only by the absence of a systematic, valid theory of fiscal policy but also by a continued unwillingness to incur very large deficits in the federal budget.

Roosevelt had formulated no set of monetary policies when he assumed office. These were hammered out amidst conflict and compromise only during the following year or more. Most Americans were highly orthodox in monetary matters at the onset of the depression, and a large number remained so. However, increasing numbers defected as the grinding deflation of prices, incomes, and employment continued. The prestige of the Federal Reserve declined sharply, partly because it had permitted such large reductions of the money supply and bank credit, perhaps more because it failed to prevent the banking panic. Banks and bankers were widely criticized for bank failures, for losses on deposits, and for their niggardly lending. Even the gold standard came under sharp attack as an intolerable limitation on domestic recovery. Many pointed to the deflationary effects of gold outflows in late 1931 and 1932 and again in February 1933. Others stressed the deflationary effects on prices of American imports and exports, and especially of agricultural exports, as the United States maintained the gold value of the dollar while so many other countries depreciated their currencies.

Well before Roosevelt came into office, there were widespread demands for "inflation" of money, and many bills for this purpose were introduced in Congress. These were of various types. Some would direct the Federal Reserve to purchase large amounts of securities or to raise commodity prices to their levels in 1929 or 1926. A few called for large issues of greenbacks or some other type of government fiat money. Several proposed increased monetary roles for silver. These ranged from reestablishment of a full bimetallic standard at the historic mint ratio of 16 to 1, to large purchases of silver until its market price had been doubled, to accepting limited amounts of silver from other countries in payment of war debts. Some such advocates, but by no means all, were more interested in the price of silver than in the general price level. Proposals for modification of the monetary role of gold were also numerous. Some advocated suspension of gold payments, thus freeing the dollar from any tie to gold. Other proposed a sharp devaluation of the dollar in terms of gold, primarily as a means of lowering the exchange rate on the dollar.

It was in the midst of this welter of proposals, pressures, and interests that the new Administration fashioned new monetary arrangements and policies during 1933 and the early months of 1934. The most important of these were policies relative to gold and silver. The Administration first ended the redeemability of the dollar in terms of gold; then depressed the value of the dollar in terms of gold and foreign currencies during the remainder of 1933; and at the end of January 1934, reduced the gold value of the dollar by about 40 percent. This was reflected in a 69 percent increase in the price of gold, from $20.67 to $35 an ounce. Also, beginning in 1934, large amounts of silver were purchased and added to the monetary base. The actions taken in 1933 to reduce the exchange rate on the dollar did tend directly to raise the prices of American exports and imports. However, it was not until 1934 that gold and silver purchases began to add large amounts to the monetary base and thus to bring pressure for an expansion of the supply of money and bank credit. Thus, the adoption of strongly expansionary monetary policies was delayed for nearly a year after Roosevelt assumed office.

■ FISCAL POLICIES   The myth persists that from the beginning Roosevelt followed a set of fiscal policies directed specifically at, and adapted to, the objective of increasing aggregate demands for output to the levels required to restore acceptable levels of real output and employment. This is indeed a myth. Roosevelt had formulated no definite fiscal policy before he became President. As already noted, he excoriated Hoover repeatedly during the 1932 campaign for his budget deficits and the alleged threat to the government's credit, and he promised to put the government's financial house in order. On March 19, a week after becoming President, he again denounced the Hoover deficits and lamented their effects on the economy.

> With the utmost seriousness I point out to the Congress the profound effect of this fact upon our national economy. It has contributed to the recent collapse of our banking structure. It has accentuated the stagnation of the economic life of our people. It has added to the ranks of the unemployed. Our Government's house is not in order and for many reasons no effective action has been taken to restore it to order.
>
> Upon the unimpaired credit of the United States Government rest the safety of deposits, the security of insurance policies, the activity of industrial enterprises, the value of our agricultural products and the availability of employment. The credit of the United States Government definitely affects those fundamental human values. It therefore becomes our first concern to make secure the foundation. National recovery depends upon it.
>
> Too often in recent history liberal governments have been wrecked on the rocks of loose fiscal policy. We must avoid this danger.[2]

During his first weeks in office, Roosevelt actually cut federal expenditures by about $450 million, principally veterans' benefits and salaries of federal employees.

Of course, Roosevelt did not balance the budget; there were federal deficits during every year of his Administration. Yet there is no reason to doubt that in 1932 and later he was sincerely concerned about deficits and that he felt constrained to limit their size. It is significant that tax rates were never decreased under Roosevelt; in fact, there were some tax increases even before the rearmament program began to expand in 1940. Moreover,

[2] *The Public Papers and Addresses of Franklin D. Roosevelt*, Vol. 2, Random House, New York, 1938, p. 49.

the primary justification of expenditure increases seems to have been the direct benefits to recipients, such as the unemployed and farmers. There were, of course, many references to their general contributions to incomes and purchasing power and to indirect benefits to other sectors. However, increased expenditures were not directed primarily to raising aggregate demands for output, and they were far below the levels required to restore full employment.

Table 8–4 provides information about receipts and expenditures of all governmental units in the United States during the years 1933–1941. We shall not deal with the years 1940 and 1941 because tax and expenditure

Table 8–4. Government receipts and expenditures on income and product account, calendar years 1933–1941 (in billions of dollars at current prices)

	1933	1934	1935	1936	1937	1938	1939	1940	1941
Receipts									
Federal	2.7	3.5	3.9	5.0	7.0	6.5	6.7	8.6	15.4
State and local	7.2	8.6	9.1	8.6	9.1	9.3	9.6	10.0	10.4
Total	9.8	12.1	13.1	13.7	16.1	15.8	16.4	18.6	25.8
Expenditures									
For goods and services									
Federal	2.0	3.0	2.9	4.9	4.7	5.4	5.1	6.0	16.9
State and local	6.0	6.8	7.1	7.0	7.2	7.6	8.2	8.0	7.9
Total	8.0	9.8	10.0	11.9	11.9	13.0	13.3	14.0	24.8
All other									
Federal	2.0	3.4	3.6	3.8	2.7	3.2	3.8	4.0	3.6
State and local	1.2	1.2	1.5	1.1	1.2	1.4	1.4	1.3	1.2
Total	3.2	4.6	5.1	5.0	3.9	4.6	5.2	5.3	4.8
Total expenditures									
Federal	4.0	6.4	6.5	8.7	7.4	8.6	8.9	10.0	20.5
State and local	7.2	8.1	8.6	8.1	8.4	9.0	9.6	9.3	9.1
Total	11.2	14.5	15.1	16.8	15.8	17.6	18.5	19.3	29.6
Surplus or deficit (−) on income and product account									
Federal	−1.3	−2.9	−2.6	−3.6	−0.4	−2.1	−2.2	−1.3	−5.0
State and local	−0.1	+0.5	+0.5	+0.5	+0.7	+0.4	+0.1	+0.6	+1.3
Total	−1.4	−2.4	−2.1	−3.1	+0.3	−1.7	−2.1	−0.7	−3.8

Source: The National Income and Product Accounts of the United States, 1929–1965, pp. 52–54. (Items may not add to totals because of rounding.)

increases in those years were primarily for the purpose of financing the expanding rearmament program. The rate of total federal expenditures during the years 1933–1939 was generally higher than the levels in 1929–1932, which were as follows.

CALENDAR YEAR	TOTAL FEDERAL EXPENDITURES (IN BILLIONS)
1929	$2.6
1930	2.8
1931	4.2
1932	3.2

Although the increase from the 1929–1932 levels was large in percentage terms, except in 1933, the absolute increase was far too small to offset the very large deficiency of private investment. We shall find that the expansionary effect of the increase of federal expenditures was at least partially offset by increases of effective federal tax rates, and that the fiscal policies of state and local governments became less expansionary.

E. Carey Brown has attempted to measure the "net contributions" of government fiscal policies, including both government expenditures and tax policies, to aggregate demands for output during this period.[3] He measures "net contribution" as the net shift of aggregate demand by government taxes and expenditures, this being stated for any year as a percentage of that year's full-employment level of GNP. For example, a positive figure of one percent indicates that fiscal policy shifted aggregate demand for output upward by an amount equal to one percent of that year's full-employment level of GNP. He then poses two major questions: (1) How did the net contribution of fiscal policies in the various years 1930–1939 compare with that of 1929? (2) How did these contributions during 1933–1939 compare with those during the years immediately preceding the New Deal? To answer these questions involves difficult technical problems and requires many assumptions, but Brown's methods and conclusions seem generally valid.

The answer for state and local fiscal policies is clear. In 1929, when these governments as a group were running deficits to finance public works programs, their net contribution was 1.8 percent. It remained at or above this level in 1930 and for 1931 as a whole, fell sharply in 1932, and was even lower during the remainder of the period. It was slightly negative in 1934 and 1935, and was zero in 1938. This conclusion may seem strange in view of the rise of state and local expenditures after 1933. (See Table 8–4.) However, in this period, there were also extensive increases of effective tax

[3] E. Carey Brown, "Fiscal Policy in the 'Thirties: A Reappraisal," *American Economic Review*, December 1956, pp. 857–879.

rates, and especially of state and local sales taxes. From a small deficit in 1933, these governmental units shifted to surpluses in all of the following years as their revenues were increased by both the rise of their effective tax rates and the rise of receipts induced by the rise of national income. Thus, the fiscal policies of state and local governments after 1932 were less supportive than they had been in earlier years and made virtually no net contribution to aggregate demand for output.

Net contributions of federal fiscal policies behaved erratically. In 1929, when the federal budget was in surplus by nearly $1.2 billion, the net contribution was negative by about four-tenths of one percent. It became zero in 1930 and was positive in all the following years, although by varying amounts. A considerable part of the 1.7 percent net contribution in 1931 was accounted for by the payment of a soldiers' bonus, which Hoover disliked. Only in 1936 was the net contribution as high as 2.5 percent, and a major part of that reflected the payment of another soldiers' bonus, which Roosevelt disliked. Net contributions in the other years after 1932 ranged below 2 percent, in some years considerably below that level. (See Table 8-5.)

Table 8-5.   E. C. Brown's estimates of net shift of demand as percent of full employment level of GNP in constant dollars

YEAR	ALL GOVERNMENTS	FEDERAL	STATE AND LOCAL
1929	1.4%	− 0.4%	1.8%
1930	1.9	0.0	2.0
1931	3.6	1.7	1.8
1932	1.8	1.0	0.9
1933	0.5	0.5	0.1
1934	1.5	2.0	− 0.4
1935	1.6	1.9	− 0.3
1936	2.6	2.5	0.2
1937	0.2	0.1	0.1
1938	1.2	1.2	0.0
1939	2.0	1.4	0.5

Source: "Fiscal Policy in the 'Thirties: A Reappraisal," *American Economic Review*, December 1956. The data appear as Col. 14 in a table on p. 865.

Again, this conclusion may seem strange in view of the large percentage increase of federal expenditures after 1933. A large part of the explanation less in the fact that effective federal tax rates during this period were considerably higher than those prevailing in the preceding years. We have already mentioned the Revenue Act of 1932, enacted in the middle of that year, which brought the largest percentage increase of federal taxes in American peacetime history and was sufficient to double total federal

revenues at a full employment level of national income. These tax rates
became fully effective in 1933 and were retained throughout the period.
There were also increases of federal taxes within the period. For example,
taxes on corporate income were raised gradually to 19 percent, and new
payroll taxes were imposed to finance the social security program enacted
in 1936.

In general, therefore, federal fiscal policies were at best only weakly
expansionary during the period 1933–1939 as a whole. Moreover, they
fluctuated within the period, and one set of changes helped precipitate the
sharp recession of 1937–1938, which set back recovery about two years.
Between 1935 and 1936, federal fiscal policies became considerably more
expansionary. The principal stimulants were a $2 billion increase in the
rate of federal purchases of goods and services, and a $2.2 billion increase
in other federal expenditures. The latter was largely accounted for by the
$1.7 billion soldiers' bonus declared in 1936. These actions were accom-
panied by an acceleration of the rate of recovery; some increase of prices;
and a high rate of accumulation of business inventories, which made the
economy more vulnerable to recession. Then changes in fiscal policy between 1936 and 1937 became sharply deflationary. (1) Federal purchases
of goods and services declined by $200 million. (2) Other federal ex-
penditures fell by $1.1 billion, largely reflecting the fact that no further
soldiers' bonus was declared. (3) Reflecting largely the enactment of new
social security taxes, the public's contributions for social insurance rose by
nearly $1.3 billion. The federal deficit dropped sharply from $3.6 billion
in 1936 to only $400 million in 1937. And the combined budgets of all
American governmental units—federal, state, and local—shifted from a
deficit of $3.1 billion in 1936 to a surplus of $300 million in 1937. These
were indeed large shifts of fiscal policies in the direction of restriction.

Henry H. Villard has estimated monthly figures for "net income-creating
expenditures"—that is, the excess of income-creating government expenditures over income-reducing government receipts—for all governmental
units combined.[4] He finds that the monthly average rose from $266 million
in 1935 to $338 million in 1936, and then fell to $116 million in the first
half of 1937 and to only $18 million in the latter half of that year. They
were actually negative by $67 million in August and by $46 million in
November. Thus, no matter how one measures it, the net contributions
of fiscal policy to aggregate demands fell sharply from 1936 to 1937.

These were not the only official actions in 1937 that were adverse to
continued recovery. Also highly relevant was the Federal Reserve's increase of member bank reserve requirements in the spring of that year,
which reduced sharply the excess reserves of member banks, halted the
expansion of bank credit and the money supply, and induced a contraction.
However, there can be little doubt that the shift in fiscal policy between
1936 and 1937 played an important role, along with the mistake in mone-

[4] Villard, Henry H., *Deficit Spending and the National Income*, Farrar & Rinehart,
New York, 1941, p. 323.

tary policy, in precipitating and making more severe the recession of 1937–1938. Fortunately, both fiscal and monetary policies became more expansionary in April 1938 when Roosevelt announced a new program of increased federal expenditures and actions were taken to increase sharply the supply of excess reserves to the banking system. However, it was the autumn of 1939 before industrial production again reached the levels achieved in the early months of 1937.

After studying the record of this period, one is forced to agree with E. Carey Brown that, "Fiscal policy, then, seems to have been an unsuccessful recovery device in the 'thirties—not because it did not work, but because it was not tried."[5] Of course, fiscal policies could have been worse, and would have been if Roosevelt had really tried to achieve an annually balanced budget, raising effective tax rates and decreasing federal expenditures to the extent necessary to achieve this goal.

■ **OTHER RECOVERY AND AMELIORATIVE POLICIES**   Thus, Roosevelt's recovery strategy did not rely exclusively, or even primarily, on broad macroeconomic measures that would raise aggregate demands for output enough to induce full employment, raise incomes in all sectors, and render unnecessary numerous measures to alleviate distress in specific sectors. It included a multiplicity of actions directed toward "recovery," or at least toward amelioration of conditions, in various specific areas. Four classes of these measures will be mentioned briefly at this point: (1) relief of the unemployed, (2) farm recovery, (3) industrial recovery, and (4) financial rehibilitation.

The absence of an adequate program for increasing aggregate demand was but one of the reasons for the multiplicity of specific measures. Also relevant were the urgent needs for quick assistance in many areas, and the insistent demands of each group that the government take specific actions to solve its peculiar problems, without waiting for general economic recovery to solve them.

We shall later examine in some detail the various measures taken to relieve the problem of the unemployed by providing relief payments to those who remained unemployed and by providing employment on various types of public works projects. These measures were quite consistent with the objective of raising aggregate demands for output to full-employment levels. Relief payments to the unemployed were a quick and effective method of promoting two things simultaneously: of aiding those who were among the neediest and of raising aggregate private incomes and purchasing power. And public works programs, which required some time for organizing, increased directly both employment and incomes of those employed on the projects and enhanced demands for the products of private industry used in the public works projects. The major shortcoming of these programs was that they were too small to provide either adequate

[5] Brown, *op. cit.*, pp. 863, 866.

relief for the unemployed or adequate increases of aggregate demands.

Farm incomes were indeed deplorably low in early 1933 and urgently needed to be raised. If farmers had been told that no specific action would be taken for this purpose and that general economic recovery should be relied upon to raise demands for and prices of farm products, they would have replied both that they were unwilling to wait and that even full-employment levels of demands would not raise farm incomes to "satisfactory" levels.

At least in principle, it would have been possible to increase farm incomes as a part of a general program of raising government expenditures to increase aggregate demands. For example, farmers could have been encouraged to maintain or even to increase their total output, and their incomes could have been raised to "target" levels by payments from the federal government. Market prices of farm products could have been allowed to adjust to the levels required to equate demand and supply, with any resulting "deficiency" of farm incomes being covered by federal subsidies. Or the federal government could have purchased farm output at prices sufficiently high to yield the "target" levels of farm income, and then resold these products at prices low enough to clear the market.

This strategy was used very little. Instead, the prevailing philosophy was that since the deplorable state of farm incomes resulted from low prices for farm products and these low prices resulted from "overproduction," the appropriate way to raise farm incomes was to limit farm output. Various devices were used for this purpose—production controls, acreage reduction, marketing quotas, withdrawals of land from use, and so on. Such measures could indeed raise the incomes of producers of a farm product if the output of that product was effectively limited and if the price-elasticity of demand for that product was sufficiently low—conditions that were not always met. However, it is doubtful that such measures served to promote general economic recovery. For example, such price increases tended to raise the cost of living and to lower the real purchasing power of urban consumers, and to raise costs of production in industries using agricultural raw materials.

Attempts to raise prices and incomes through restriction of output were by no means limited to the agricultural sector. By the summer of 1933, increasing numbers of businessmen and members of government were demanding that industries be permitted to adopt measures comparable to those in agriculture. By far the most extensive program of this type was under the National Recovery Administration (NRA), which was authorized by the National Industrial Recovery Act of 1933. With the approval of government, and often under strong government pressure, industry after industry adopted "codes of fair competition," which provided for industrial self-government under the general supervision of the federal government. The NRA and the code authorities in the various industries used many methods to raise prices and profits. Prominent among them were the establishment of minimum or "floor" prices, output and marketing quotas, and agreements not to sell below full costs. Such measures did not end when the NRA was declared unconstitutional in 1935; they were continued in such industries as petroleum, gas, and coal.

These programs were by no means universally successful in achieving their immediate objective of raising prices and profits in the industries involved, and to the extent that they achieved this objective they probably hindered instead of promoting general economic recovery. For example, a reduction of output and an increase of prices in one industry raised costs for others and did not assure an increase of employment or of business expenditures for capital formation.

The government took many specific actions to rehabilitate the financial system, which was in shambles in early 1933. These included scaling down private debts; refinancing huge amounts of farm and home mortgages; providing large amounts of government funds through loans and subscriptions to equity claims against financial intermediaries; insuring bank deposits and claims against savings and loan associations; insuring some types of private debts, notably home mortgages; and establishing several new types of financial institutions. These actions had several objectives that were not always mutually compatible: to decrease the burdens on debtors, to improve the liquidity and solvency of financial intermediaries, to help those holding claims against these intermediaries, and to restore the flow of savings and investment.

An alternative strategy would have been to avoid taking such specific actions and to rely upon general monetary and fiscal policies to increase aggregate demands, money incomes, and prices to such levels that debtors could meet their obligations fully and promptly. Such a course was politically unacceptable under the conditions reached in 1933. Moreover, at least some degree of financial rehabilitation was a necessary precondition for full recovery, which depended on a restoration of the savings-investment process. In the absence of specific actions to rehabilitate the financial system, there would have been a "credit deadlock"; financial flows could have been revived only after a considerable degree of economic recovery had been achieved, but the latter could occur only after financial flows had been revived. On the other hand, these specific actions for financial rehabilitation were not adequate substitutes for monetary and fiscal policies to increase aggregate demands.

9

Financial Rehabilitation

With virtually all the nation's banks closed or severely restricted in their operations by state-proclaimed holidays, the entire financial system was paralyzed when Roosevelt assumed office. The banks themselves could not supply currency or loans or clear and collect checks, other financial intermediaries could not operate, the securities markets had to remain closed, and foreign exchange operations were at a standstill. It was clear, therefore, that one of the first of the many tasks facing the new Administration was to reopen the banks, or at least a large majority of them, and to prevent a new round of currency and gold withdrawals.

■ **REOPENING THE BANKS**   On March 6, 1933, Roosevelt invoked the Trading with the Enemy Act and issued an executive order proclaiming a nationwide bank holiday extending through Thursday, March 9. At the same time, he called for a special session of Congress to convene on March 9. In the interim, no bank was to pay out any coin, bullion, or currency or to transact any other business whatsoever without permission of the Secretary of the Treasury. The latter permitted only very limited banking operations during this period.

At its first meeting on March 9, Congress passed the emergency banking bill presented to it by the President that morning, and Roosevelt signed it the same day. This Act confirmed the actions taken under executive order and gave the President full power to control banks for the protection of depositors; to open banks found to be in sound condition; to put on a sound basis banks found to require reorganization; and to control foreign exchange transactions, gold and currency movements, and all banking transactions.

The Act also carried three other important provisions: (1) It provided that the Comptroller of the Currency might be appointed as Conservator of national banks. As Conservator, he could reorganize a national bank without declaring it bankrupt and putting it into receivership. He could do this by providing for readjustments of deposit claims and by arranging for the Reconstruction Finance Corporation to subscribe to new preferred stocks issued by the bank. (2) It authorized the Reserve banks to issue Federal Reserve bank notes, which would be collateraled by government securities and subject to no reserve requirements. Thus, any increase in demands for currency could be met without recourse to clearing-house certificates or other substitutes. And (3) it authorized the Reserve banks to lend on a wider range of assets under unusual conditions.

Armed with this legislation, the President extended the bank holiday indefinitely and announced plans for reopening "sound" banks. An executive order issued on March 10 empowered the Secretary of the Treasury to issue licenses to banks found to be in satisfactory condition, permitting them to conduct their usual banking business, except that they should pay out no gold or gold certificates and supply no currency for hoarding. The term "satisfactory condition" appears to have been interpreted generously. On Saturday, March 11, it was announced that reopening dates would be Monday, March 13, for the Federal Reserve banks and sound commercial banks located in the 12 Federal Reserve cities, March 14 for sound banks in about 250 other cities with recognized clearing houses, and March 15 for sound banks located elsewhere. Other banks would be licensed as they were found to be in satisfactory condition, or were put into such condition. President Roosevelt, in a radio address on Sunday, March 12, assured the nation that the reopened banks would be able to meet every legitimate call and that the government was determined not to have "another epidemic of bank failures."

The reopenings proceeded on schedule. It appears that by the end of the week about 75 percent of all member banks had reopened without restrictions. On April 12, the first date after the banking crash for which comprehensive data are available, unrestricted licenses had been granted to members accounting for 90 percent of the total resources of member banks. State authorities had licensed about 7,400 nonmember banks, or 71 percent of the total number of such banks. However, about $4 billion of deposits were still tied up in some 4,200 member and nonmember banks that had been operating prior to the banking holiday but were not yet licensed or freed from restrictions on their operations.[1] Fortunately, the reopening of banks was not followed by a resumption of currency withdrawals. In fact, net inflows of currency to the banks amounted to $1.25 billion by the end of March and to nearly $2 billion by August.

■ **REHABILITATION OF THE FINANCIAL SYSTEM**   Thus, the reopening of a large majority of the banks accounting for an even larger proportion of total bank assets and deposits had been achieved quickly and with relative ease. A much more difficult problem remained—rehabilitating the banks and other parts of the financial system and restoring them to normal working order.

This broad and complex problem had several parts: (1) The problem

[1] *Annual Report of the Federal Reserve Board*, 1933, pp. 14, 22–24.

of financial intermediaries that were either closed or were operating under restrictions on withdrawals or lending operations. These included not only the banks that had closed since the beginning of 1933 but also banks that had closed earlier and other types of distressed intermediaries, such as building and loan associations and mortgage companies. Large amounts of deposits and other financial claims against these institutions were frozen and unavailable for use; attempts to liquidate their assets were depressing prices of securities, real estate, and other assets; and they could not function as lenders. (2) The problem of liquidity and solvency of the institutions that had been reopened. Although they had been adjudged to be in "satisfactory condition," this was in numerous cases a highly generous rating. In fact, many were laden with illiquid assets and would have been insolvent if their assets had been valued at prevailing market prices. While these conditions continued, there was an ever-present danger that new runs on the intermediaries would develop, or at least that the institutions would be unable to attract new flows of funds. Moreover, they could hardly be expected to assume normal risks in making new loans while they remained so illiquid and at best only slightly solvent. (3) The problems of ultimate debtors, such as business firms, farmers, homeowners, and some state and local governments. Millions of debtors were already delinquent or in default and could not meet their obligations fully and promptly under existing levels of money incomes and asset prices. Others were on the verge of delinquency or default. Still more had suffered such serious deterioration of their creditworthiness that they could not command new funds, or could do so only on very onerous terms.

Some resolution of these problems was required in the interests of debtors, creditors, and restoration of normal flows of credit, which were essential for economic recovery.

Although rehabilitation of the financial system was clearly necessary, its achievement proved to be difficult and time-consuming. Many methods were used. One, which was widely employed, involved readjustment of debt claims by postponing payment dates, reducing interest charges, scaling down the principal values, or combinations of these devices. Thus, deposits and other financial claims against banks and other financial intermediaries were scaled down, put into restricted accounts, or exchanged for equity claims. In similar ways, but on a much wider scale, debts of farmers, homeowners, business firms, and local governments were readjusted. Under the circumstances, creditors were not in a strong position to resist such reductions of their claims, and their bargaining position was further weakened by important changes in the bankruptcy laws and in other laws governing debt contracts, which made it more difficult, and in some cases impossible, for creditors to enforce fulfillment of contracts.

Readjustment of debt claims occurred on a broad scale, but it had serious disadvantages as a rehabilitation device, primarily because an action that benefited debtors was likely to harm creditors and to have undersirable side effects. For example, scaling down deposits and other claims against intermediaries did serve to restore solvency and liquidity of these institutions, but it also reduced the wealth and spending power of depositors and jeopardized the future ability of these institutions to attract funds. Similarly, scaling down debt claims against farmers, homeowners, and business firms helped these debtors but injured their creditors, including financial intermediaries. Thus, financial rehabilitation required the use of other methods as well.

Only limited help in financial rehabilitation could be expected from new private investments in equities or loans to private borrowers. Savings were still at a low level; more importantly, private investors were in no mood to assume large risks. It was almost inevitable, therefore, that the government would play an important role in financial rehabilitation, and that it would use its credit, directly or indirectly, to bolster the financial system. It did this by issuing its own securities, guaranteeing securities issued by its agencies, insuring claims against private financial intermediaries, and assuming some or all of the risk on various classes of private debts. Some of the principal avenues through which the government and its agencies, old and new, supplied assistance were these: (1) By lending to banks and other financial intermediaries; (2) by purchasing stock and other equity claims against these intermediaries; (3) by insuring bank deposits and claims against building and loan associations; and (4) by purchasing claims, or assuming risk on claims, against private borrowers other than financial intermediaries.

To supply these types of assistance, the government employed many agencies, only a few of which will be mentioned here. The Reconstruction Finance Corporation (RFC), which had been established in February 1932, was greatly enlarged in both resources and scope of operations, and it was converted into the government's largest general-purpose financial institution. The Federal Farm Mortgage Corporation (FFMC), together with several other official agencies, supplied huge amounts of agricultural credit. The Home Owners Loan Corporation (HOLC) performed similar functions for home mortgages. The Federal Deposit Insurance Corporation (FDIC) was formed to insure bank deposits, and the Federal Savings and Loan Insurance Corporation (FSLIC) guaranteed claims against building and loan associations.

At this point we shall concentrate primarily on the rehabilitation process, which was largely consummated by mid-1936. Financial reforms will be discussed later. We shall not attempt to cover all aspects of financial rehabilitation; to do so would lead us into an almost endless maze. However, we shall be able to indicate the nature and scope of the process.

■ **Rehabilitation of the Banking System**   Three classes of banks were involved in the rehabilitation process. First were the closed banks, with frozen deposits and unliquidated assets. Second were the banks that remained unlicensed to reopen, or were operating under restrictions. Third were the banks that were licensed and unrestricted, but needed improvement in their liquidity, or solvency, or both.

The RFC played a vital role in helping all three classes. By March 4, 1933, it had already lent nearly $80 million to liquidators of closed banks. (See Table 9–1.) These operations were then speeded up, especially

Table 9–1.   Assistance by the reconstruction finance corporation
to private financial institutions, Feb. 2, 1932, through Oct. 23,
1937 (disbursements, in millions of dollars)

	FEB. 2, 1932, THROUGH MARCH 3, 1933	MARCH 4, 1933, THROUGH OCT. 23, 1937
Loans to		
Banks and trust companies	$951.4	$ 186.3
Building and loan associations	101.5	13.2
Insurance companies	80.5	9.2
Credit unions	0.5	0.2
Mortgage loan companies	90.7	199.4
Liquidators of closed banks	79.6	875.2
Liquidators of building and loan associations	—	2.3
Federal Land Banks	18.8	368.4
Regional agricultural credit corporations	41.4	131.8
Joint stock land banks	4.9	13.1
Livestock credit corporations	11.9	0.7
Agricultural credit corporations	3.6	2.0
Purchases of preferred stock and loans on such stock in		
Banks and trust companies	—	1,084.1
Insurance companies	—	34.3

Source: *The Public Papers and Addresses of Franklin D. Roosevelt*, Vol. 2, Random House, New York, 1938, pp. 403–404.

after the establishment, in October 1933, of a Deposit Liquidation Board, whose purpose was to expedite the process. From that time to the end of 1933, the RFC authorized 776 loans, aggregating more than $300 million, to liquidators of banks. Between March 4, 1933, and late October 1937, total loan disbursements of this type aggregated more than $875 million. These served the multiple purpose of making funds available to depositors more quickly, of enabling liquidators to realize more on bank assets by liquidating them in an orderly manner, and of lessening downward pressures on market prices that would have resulted from more rapid sales of the assets of closed banks.

The RFC also made further loans to the other two classes of banks— both those licensed to operate without restriction and those unlicensed or restricted. However, as indicated in Table 9–1, RFC loans to banks and trust companies were only about one-fifth as large in the period following March 4, 1933, as they had been in the preceding period. A major reason for this was that banks were receiving large inflows of funds from other sources. Among these were inflows of currency from circulation; large gold inflows; flows of funds resulting from loans by the Federal Farm Mortgage Corporation and the Home Owners Loan Corporation; and funds resulting from RFC loans to borrowers other than financial institutions, such as the railroads, holders of farm commodities, and local governmental units.

However, the smaller RFC lending to banks after March 1933 also resulted in part from the fact that the RFC resorted to a new method of helping banks—increasing their solvency by subscribing to preferred stocks or other equity claims against them. By late October 1937, total RFC purchases of such equities had exceeded $1 billion. This was closely related to the creation of a new system for insurance of deposits. At first, the Administration seriously considered establishing at least a temporary deposit insurance program to become effective in March 1933 for banks licensed to reopen. However, it finally decided that such a program might fail if it admitted banks that were not really in sound condition, and that the introduction of such a program should be deferred until necessary preparations had been made.

The Banking Act of 1933, approved on June 16, established the Federal Deposit Insurance Corporation (FDIC) and provided for two insurance plans—a temporary plan to become effective Jan. 1, 1934, and a permanent plan to succeed it. Of the capital stock of the FDIC, $150 million was subscribed by the Treasury, $139 million by the Federal Reserve banks, and $37 million by participating banks. All licensed member banks were required to participate; nonmember banks were permitted to do so if they wished and if they could meet entrance requirements. Most of them elected to join. The plan initially provided for insurance of the first $2,500 of each deposit account; this was soon raised to $5,000.

Both federal and state banking authorities worked feverishly during the latter half of 1933 preparing the way for deposit insurance. One huge task was to examine nearly 9,000 nonmembers that had applied for admission, to evaluate their positions, and to determine what financial assistance they needed to qualify for membership in the FDIC. The RFC supplied most of this assistance; it was in this period that the RFC made most of its purchases of equity claims against banks. In addition to providing safety for small deposits, the FDIC strengthened supervision over state banks that were not members of the Federal Reserve, reduced dangers of runs on banks, and perhaps increased somewhat the willingness of banks to lend.

All of these measures specifically designed to rehabilitate banks, together with the indirect effects of other government programs, did increase the liquidity and solvency of banks. However, they did not restore quickly or completely the willingness of banks to lend and assume normal risks.

Borrowers continued to complain, apparently with good reason, that banks shied away from risks, and especially from longer term loans.

■ **Rehabilitation of Farm Debts and Farm Creditors**   The sad state of farm debts in early 1933 has already been described—widespread delinquencies on taxes as well as debt service, use of force by farmers to prevent foreclosures and sales of farms, and proclamations in at least 22 states providing moratoria on farm debts or otherwise limiting the ability of creditors to enforce their claims. While farmers were demanding that their debt payments be postponed and their debt burdens reduced, their creditors were in a far from enviable position. This was true not only of private lenders, such as commercial banks and insurance companies, but also of farm credit institutions established earlier under auspices of the federal government. For example, all the Joint Stock Land Banks, which had been established under federal charters after 1916 and were privately owned, were highly illiquid, and most of them were insolvent. All were placed in liquidation in 1933. Even the twelve Federal Land Banks, also authorized in 1916, were immobilized. Most of their loans had been made through a large number of national farm-loan associations, or groups of cooperating farmers, who were now unable to meet their debt obligations to their Land Banks.

Two principal methods, other than measures to raise farm incomes, were employed to rehabilitate farm debts. One was to stave off foreclosures, postpone payments, and scale down debts. The other was to provide large amounts of credit. To coordinate such activities, all federal programs in the field of farm credit were concentrated in a new agency—the Farm Credit Administration (FCA)—in March 1933.

The federal bankruptcy laws were amended in March 1933 to provide for "agricultural compositions and extensions." Acting under this authorization, the FCA sponsored formation of "debt adjustment committees" in 2,700 counties in 44 states to encourage debtors and creditors to reach agreements and avoid foreclosures. Not all agreements involved scale-downs, but total scale-downs of farm debts approximated $200 million. Creditors were under heavy pressure to compromise claims in order to qualify for refinancing.[2]

Most of the federal funds for rehabilitation of farm debts were supplied by the 12 Federal Land Banks and the Land Bank Commissioner. The Land Banks received additional capital from the government and loans from the RFC. The Land Bank Commissioner derived most of his funds from a government subscription of $200 million and from issues of fully guaranteed bonds by a newly created institution—the Federal Farm Mortgage Corporation (FFMC). The Land Banks lent up to 50 percent of the value of land and 20 percent of the value of permanent improve-

---

[2] The Frazier-Lemke Act of June 1934, which in effect provided a five-year moratorium on farm foreclosures, was declared unconstitutional in 1935. A second act was found to be constitutional, but only a few cases were handled under these acts.

ments, and the Commissioner supplied additional loans. Both evaluated properties not at their current market prices but at "normal appraised value" or "prudent investment value." Also, both reduced interest rates.

These institutions purchased huge amounts of farm mortgages, advancing about $2.1 billion of mortgage loans between May 1933 and the end of June 1936. Of this amount, $1,460 million was used to refinance mortgages, $60 million to pay taxes, $290 million to pay short-term debts, and nearly $90 million to buy land and to redeem land that had been foreclosed. Holders of farm mortgages were major recipients of these proceeds of these loans, with about $295 million going to life insurance companies, $344 million to commercial banks, and $682 million to others in exchange for refinanced mortgages.[3] By the end of 1936, nearly 40 percent of all farm mortgages were held by agencies under the FCA.

Although this emergency lending by the Federal Land Banks and the Federal Farm Mortgage Corporation did much to alleviate the farm debt situation, farmers were not yet satisfied. They wanted still lower interest rates, and achieved several further reductions in the rates charged by federal agencies. They wanted special federal lending facilities to enable tenants to buy farms. And they got them. They also demanded important permanent additions to farm credit facilities. Even in the 1920s, they had complained that credit for farmers was too scarce, too expensive, and too restricted in maturities. Their increased complaints in 1933 were more effective and resulted in the establishment of many new permanent federal credit agencies. Prior to 1933, there were only two sets of such agencies— the 12 Federal Land Banks and the 12 Federal Intermediate Credit Banks. Several more were added. (1) A Central Bank for Cooperatives and 12 Banks for Cooperatives to provide long-term funds to agricultural cooperatives. (2) Twelve Production Credit Corporations, each with a cluster of Production Credit Associations. The latter, managed by farmers, secured most of their funds from the government and from loans by the Federal Intermediate Credit Banks, and made short-term loans directly to farmers. (3) The Commodity Credit Corporation, which lent and guaranteed private loans on farm commodities. Its major purpose was to provide price supports for selected farm products, but in the process it extended and guaranteed large amounts of credit.

Such extensions of federal activity into the field of agricultural credit might have developed later even if the depression had not occurred. At the very least, however, the depression speeded the process.

■ **Rehabilitation of Home Mortgages and Their Holders**   The state of debts on urban residential structures in early 1933 was quite similar to that of farm debts—widespread delinquencies on taxes as well as debt service, and mounting opposition to mortgage foreclosures and sales of homes.

---

[3] The Twentieth Century Fund, *Debts and Recovery, 1929–1937*, The Twentieth Century Fund, New York, 1938, p. 148.

Owners of many mortgaged homes were in distress; so were investors in these mortgages, especially building and loan associations, mortgage companies, insurance companies, and commercial banks.

Here, too, the government used two principal methods to ameliorate the debt situation: postponement and scaling down of debts, and provision of huge amounts of credit. Some funds had been supplied for this purpose before March 1933. For example, the RFC had already lent over $100 million to building and loan associations, nearly $81 million to insurance companies, and almost $91 million to mortgage loan companies. The 12 Federal Home Loan Banks, which had been authorized in July 1932, were of little help prior to 1933, partly because they were organized so slowly and partly because of defects in the law. However, by the end of 1933, they had lent over $88 million to holders of home mortgages. Between March 1933 and late October 1937, the RFC lent another $199 million to mortgage loan companies and small additional amounts to building and loan associations and insurance companies. (See Table 9-1, page 149.) However, a new institution—the Home Owners Loan Corporation (HOLC), authorized in June 1933—bore most of the burden of refinancing home mortgages.

The HOLC derived its funds from two sources: a $200 million capital subscription by the government, and issues of bonds carrying a full government guarantee. From its beginning in mid-1933 to its termination of lending in June 1936, the HOLC made 1,018,000 loans, aggregating $3,093 million. One out of every five mortgaged dwellings received refinancing aid. The HOLC took over mortgages amounting to $768 million from building and loan associations; $500 million from closed commercial banks; $746 million from other commercial banks; $167 million from savings banks; and $1,007 million from mortgage companies, individual lenders, and others.[4]

Thus, the HOLC purchases supplied funds to all types of holders of home mortgages. Two actions were taken for the specific purpose of helping building and loan associations. One authorized federal charters for them. The HOLC Act of June 1933 provided that federal savings and loan association might be chartered, either *de novo* or by conversion of state-chartered institutions. The HOLC was empowered to buy shares in these institutions in areas where such facilities were inadequate. These federally chartered associations soon became a major part of the savings and loan industry. The other action specifically designed to help this industry and to restore it to working order provided insurance of claims against savings and loan associations. An act of June 27, 1934, established the Federal Savings and Loan Insurance Corporation (FSLIC), which insured the first $5,000 of each account in member institutions. Federal savings and loan associations were required to join, and state-chartered

[4] *Annual Report of the Federal Home Loan Bank Board for the Year Ending June 30, 1937,* p. 29.

associations were permitted to do so if they wished and could qualify. Roosevelt explained the purposes in these terms:

> These institutions are custodians of the funds of small savers, and it is essential that they should be given every reasonable protection. Insurance of this type is necessary in order to arrest any further drain on these institutions and to put them in a position to resume their normal useful functions.[5]

The act of June 27, 1934, also established the Federal Housing Administration to insure long-term amortized mortgages on homes.

Thus, federal activities in the field of home finance were of both an emergency and a longer run nature. The HOLC was for purely emergency purposes and made no new loans after mid-1936, and several of the other actions in this field were directed primarily at current problems. However, the actions taken during this period were to have profound and permanent effects on home financing. Prior to mid-1932, the federal government did not participate at all in housing finance. By the end of 1934, these permanent, federally sponsored institutions were operating: (1) Twelve Federal Home Loan Banks, which serve as lenders to savings and loan associations and other holders of home mortgages. (2) The Federal Savings and Loan Insurance Corporation, which guarantees accounts at member institutions. (3) The Federal Housing Administration, which insures long-term amortized mortgages. (4) Large numbers of federally chartered savings and loan associations.

One effect of these innovations has been to make claims against lenders on mortgages safer and more liquid, and thus to attract more funds. These institutions also took the lead in developing long-term, amortized mortgages equal to a large fraction of the value of a property to replace the old system of short-term, unamortized loans equal to only a smaller fraction of the value of properties.

■ Rehabilitation of Business Debt   Although many business firms were delinquent or in default on their debts and many more had suffered serious deterioration of their creditworthiness, the federal government provided them with no specific program comparable to those for farm and home debts. However, some assistance was tendered. For one thing, an amendment to the bankruptcy act in June 1934 made it possible for corporations to reorganize without going into receivership, by scaling down debts, exchanging debts for equity claims, rearranging maturities, and so on. These provisions were used in a large number of cases. The railroads, which remained in desperate financial condition, received another $211 million in loans from the RFC after March 4, 1933. In March 1934, Roosevelt asked Congress to establish twelve Credit Banks for Industry to provide working capital for small- and medium-size established firms that were unable to secure such longer term funds from other sources. Congress did not comply;

[5] *The Public Papers and Addresses of Franklin D. Roosevelt,* Vol. 3, Random House, New York, 1938, p. 234.

instead, it authorized the Federal Reserve banks and the RFC to participate in such loans with private lenders or to make such loans themselves if the loans were sound and if credit was not obtainable on a reasonable basis from the usual sources. Between mid-1934 and the end of November, 1937, these agencies approved about 4,800 loans aggregating $323 million. However, they rejected more applications than they approved, primarily because the loans were ineligible under the conditions imposed by the Act or could not meet the test of soundness.[6] These loans would undoubtedly have been much larger if the standards of "soundness" applied to them had been as lenient as those applied to mortgages granted by the FFMC and the HOLC.

Some funds for financial rehabilitation were supplied by other government credit agencies that will not be discussed here, but the great bulk of them came from the RFC, the Federal Land Banks and the Federal Farm Mortgage Corporation, and the Home Owners Loan Corporation. It is impossible to estimate accurately how many of the funds issued by these agencies after March 1933 flowed directly or indirectly to commercial banks, but the total was huge. We can identify the following flows to commercial banks, including both closed and operating banks.

FROM THE RFC	(IN MILLIONS)
Loans	$1061.5
Stock subscriptions	1084.1
From refinancing farm debt	344.0
From refinancing home debt	1246.0
Total	$3735.6

Further large amounts initially disbursed to other borrowers must have flowed indirectly to commercial banks.

■ **THE REHABILITATION PROCESS: AN OVERVIEW**   The process of rehabilitating debts and financial institutions, which began almost immediately after Roosevelt assumed office, gathered momentum during the remainder of 1933 and in 1934 and was largely completed by the end of 1935. By the latter date, as shown in Table 9–2, government credit institutions were holding $9.4 billion of loans and preferred stock. Loans of financial institutions and preferred stock in these institutions accounted for nearly $1.7 billion, housing mortgages for $2.9 billion, and farm mortgages and other agricultural loans for $3.6 billion. All other loans amounted to only about $1.2 billion. Many of the loans made to others benefited financial institutions directly or indirectly. These figures do not, however, tell

[6] *Ibid.*, pp. 152–155.

Table 9–2. Holdings of loans and preferred stock by U. S. government corporations and credit agencies, Dec. 31, 1935 (in millions of dollars)

Loans to financial institutions	$ 678
Preferred stock	1,018
Loans to railroads	572
Home and housing mortgage loans	2,903
Farm mortgage loans	2,867
Other agricultural loans	750
Other loans	615
Total	$9,402

Source: Board of Governors of the Federal Reserve System, *Banking and Monetary Statistics*, 1943, p. 517. The government credit institutions included are the Reconstruction Finance Corporation, the Federal Land Banks, the Federal Intermediate Credit Banks, the Federal Farm Mortgage Corporation, the Production Credit Corporations, the Commodity Credit Corporation, the Federal Home Loan Banks, and the Home Owners Loan Corporation. Claims of these agencies against each other are excluded.

the full story. For one thing, they do not reflect loans made earlier and repaid by this date. Also, they do not take into account benefits yielded by government insurance of bank deposits and of accounts at savings and loan associations and by insurance of home mortgages by the Federal Housing Administration.

In retrospect, the rehabilitation program appears to have served a useful purpose, however much one may criticize its details. It helped many indebted farmers and homeowners, it restored confidence in financial intermediaries and improved their liquidity and solvency, and it was a necessary step toward restoring flows of credit. Yet it was not fully successful in achieving the latter purpose. Lenders remained wary of assuming risks on new loans, and especially on longer term loans. The most conspicuous gap in the rehabilitation program was its failure to provide adequate assistance to business firms, and especially to those small- and medium-size firms whose liquidity and solvency had been damaged so badly. A more generous government program providing longer term loans, or insurance of such loans, to firms without adequate alternative sources would probably have helped the recovery process.

■**FINANCIAL REFORMS**   Within a month after assuming office, Roosevelt made it clear that efforts for financial relief were to be accompanied by stern measures for reform of financial practices. On March 29, he wrote to the Congress:

I recommend to the Congress legislation for Federal supervision of traffic in investment securities in interstate commerce.

In spite of many state statutes the public in the past has sustained severe losses through practices neither ethical nor honest on the part of many persons and corporations selling securities.

Of course, the Federal Government cannot and should not take any action which might be construed as approving or guaranteeing that newly issued securities are sound in the sense that their value will be maintained or that the properties which they represent will earn a profit.

There is, however, an obligation upon us to insist that every issue of new securities to be sold in interstate commerce shall be accompanied by full publicity and information, and that no essentially important element attending the issue shall be concealed from the buying public.

This proposal adds to the ancient rule of *caveat emptor*, the further doctrine "let the seller beware." It puts the burden of telling the whole truth on the seller. It should give impetus to honest dealing in securities and thereby bring back public confidence.

The purpose of the legislation I suggest is to protect the public with the least possible interference with honest business.

This is but one step in our broad purpose of protecting investors and depositors. It should be followed by legislation relating to the better supervision of the purchase and sale of all property dealt in on the exchanges, and by legislation to correct unethical and unsafe practices on the part of officers and directors of banks and other corporations.

What we seek is a return to a clearer understanding of the ancient truth that those who manage banks, corporations and other agencies handling or using other people's money are trustees acting for others.[7]

The Securities Act of 1933 was approved May 27. This was followed by the Securities Exchange Act of 1934, approved June 6 of that year, which, among other things, established the Securities and Exchange Commission.

These and other measures for financial reform evoked some of the most emotional and bitter battles of the New Deal period. It appeared that two titans were struggling for supremacy—on the one hand the emerging power of the federal government, and on the other the powerful leaders in industry and finance. The latter protested bitterly that the new measures invaded their privacy, violated their prerogatives, were deliberately directed at casting doubt on the honesty and integrity of business, destroyed confidence, and retarded recovery by making security issues more cumbersome and expensive. The President contended that reforms were necessary, not only to ensure ethical conduct in business and finance but also to restore confidence in business and to avoid collapses in the future.

Many circumstances favored the President. There was a widespread belief that excesses in the stock market and in corporate practices were at least a contributing factor to the depression. Many had lost money on securities and were looking for scapegoats. Moreover, it was clear that at least a minority of financiers and businessmen had been guilty of serious mistakes or worse. Most corporate financial statements provided only inadequate information about their managements and financial condition, and some were misleading. Some officers, directors, and major stockholders used

[7] *Ibid.*, Vol. 2, pp. 93–94.

inside information for their own advantage, despite effects on others. Some borrowed from their own firms or otherwise used the funds of their firms for their own purposes. Manipulations of stock prices by individuals and pools had been widely publicized. Investment advisors sometimes concealed the fact that they had interest in the securities they were advising others to buy or sell. Banks that served as underwriters of issues purchased some of these for their trust accounts. And so on. It was to deal with such practices as these that the government introduced several types of regulation, of which the following were the most important: (1) regulation of new issues, (2) regulation of trading on the securities exchanges and over-the-counter markets, (3) regulation of investment advisors, and (4) separation of commercial and investment banking.

■ **Regulation of New Issues**   The general approach of this regulation is well indicated by the name often given to the legislation on which it is based—"The Truth-in-Securities Act." The Securities Exchange Commission does not certify the quality of any proposed new issue. Rather, it prohibits the public offering of a new security until the issuer has filed with the SEC an acceptable prospectus including full and fair disclosure of all facts that could bear significantly upon the value and prospects of the issue. These include not only information about the management, financial condition, and other aspects of the company but also information about interests of the underwriter and of officers of the company that might be relevant. Heavy civil and criminal penalties are provided for omission of relevant information as well as for misleading statements.

■ **Regulation of Trading in Securities**   This regulation had a threefold purpose. (1) To correct unfair practices in securities markets. The SEC was given jurisdiction over both organized securities exchanges and over-the-counter markets, and various practices were outlawed; these included, among others, wash sales, manipulative operations, and circulation of false rumors. (2) To furnish to the public adequate information about the management and financial conditions of corporations whose securities are traded on the exchanges. Every such corporation is required to file a registration statement disclosing full information, and must keep it up to date by filing adequate annual reports. One important provision requires every officer, director, and principal stockholder to make a monthly report of his purchases, sales, gifts, or other transfers of the equity securities of his company. These reports are published. (3) To regulate the use of credit in financing trading in securities. Two principal actions were taken for this purpose. One prohibited banks from acting as agents for other types of lenders in placing funds with brokers and dealers in securities. The other empowered the Federal Reserve Board to fix minimum margin requirements—or maximum loan values—on security loans, and to vary these for the purpose of preventing abuse or excessive use of credit for purchasing or carrying securities.

■ **Regulation of Investment Advisors**   Essentially, this prohibits anyone from providing financial advice to others without full disclosure of any interests he may have in the securities concerned.

■ **Separation of Commercial and Investment Banking**   The Banking Act of 1933 provided that, with certain exemptions, no commercial bank should serve as underwriter or dealer in securities or remain affiliated with any institution performing these functions. A major purpose was to avoid conflicts of interest and violations of arm's-length dealing that had sometimes appeared earlier when a bank or its affiliate underwrote an issue and the bank purchased some of it for its trust accounts or for its own account. Interests of underwriters were not necessarily consistent with those of beneficiaries of trust accounts, of depositors, or even of the stockholders of a bank. However, the provision was approved for quite other reasons by Senator Carter Glass and his advisor, Professor H. Parker Willis. As doctrinaire adherents to the commercial loan theory of banking, they opposed not only bank underwriting of securities but also acquisition by banks for their own accounts of bonds, mortgages, and loans on security collateral.[8]

The SEC also came to regulate other financial practices, including corporate reorganizations and financial structures of public utility holding companies.

■ **CONCLUSIONS**   The financial reform measures that at the time seemed so radical are now taken for granted and generally viewed as desirable. However, it is difficult to appraise the relationship of these reform measures to the progress of economic recovery in the 1930s. Roosevelt surely exaggerated in claiming that such reforms were necessary to restore confidence and promote recovery. On the other hand, business and financial leaders surely exaggerated in contending that these reforms were the major obstacle to recovery. I believe that on balance these reform measures, and the bitter debates surrounding them, did impede recovery, but were not a major factor. The regulations on new security issues were burdensome, especially in the early stages before lawyers, financiers, and corporate officers became accustomed to them, understood procedures, and worked out routines. Compliance was time-consuming and expensive. Also, businessmen were fearful of the civil and criminal penalties that they might inadvertently incur. Separation of investment from commercial banking at that time may also have impeded new issues by upsetting old established relationships.

As obstacles to recovery, these measures would appear to have been minor as compared with others, such as the widespread prevalence of

[8] Hearings before the Senate Banking and Currency Committee on S. 4115 (the Banking Act of 1932), 72nd Congress, 1st Session, March 23–25 and 28–30, 1932.

excess capacity, the deteriorated financial positions of business firms and financial institutions, and the continued pessimistic state of expectations. However, their importance was probably magnified by the distrust and dislike of Roosevelt by large sectors of the business and financial community.

10

Monetary Policies Under the New Deal

Many of the measures and policies discussed in the preceding chapter should be included under "monetary and credit policy" if that term is construed broadly. Like other measures aimed at influencing monetary and credit conditions, these were designed to affect not only the behavior of bank credit but also the availability and cost of credit from all sources. This chapter will consider monetary policies in a narrower sense of the term. More specifically, it will concentrate largely on the government's policies relative to the monetary roles of gold and silver, and on the policies of the Federal Reserve System.

■ AN OVERVIEW OF THE PERIOD   We shall find that the Federal Reserve played only a diminished role during this period. Earlier, when the government asumed almost no functions in this field, the Federal Reserve had primary, and virtually sole, responsibility. Now the government itself seized the initiative, took vigorous actions, and dominated monetary policy. It did so through its gold and silver policies, primarily the former. As will be described more fully later, the government nationalized all gold in 1933 and proceeded to drive up the dollar price of gold, which amounted to decreasing the gold value of the dollar. Then, at the end of January 1934, it formally decreased the gold value of the dollar more than 40 percent. To state this another way, it raised the official price of gold about 69 percent. The Treasury reaped a profit of $2.8 billion on the upward revaluation of its gold stock. The devaluation of the dollar in terms of gold tended to decrease the exchange rate on the dollar in terms of foreign currencies. In 1934 began what has aptly been called a "golden avalanche" into the monetary system. Some of the gold came from domestic mining and melting of scrap, but most of it was imported. At the end of 1933, the monetary gold stock stood at $4 billion; a year later, including the Treasury's gold profit, it had reached $8.2 billion. Gold imports continued in every year, and by the end of 1941, the nation's monetary gold had reached the colossal figure of $22.7 billion. (See Table 10–1.)

These inflows served, of course, to increase the nation's reserve base of "high-powered money."

Table 10–1.   Monetary gold and silver stocks of the United States
on selected dates, 1932–1941 (in millions of dollars)

END OF MONTH	MONETARY GOLD STOCK	MONETARY SILVER STOCK	TOTAL MONETARY GOLD AND SILVER STOCKS
December 1932	$ 4,218	$ 847	$ 5,065
December 1933	4,036	840	4,876
July 1934	7,911	840	8,751
December 1934	8,228	1,064	9,292
December 1935	10,125	1,452	11,577
December 1936	11,251	1,679	12,930
December 1937	12,760	1,858	14,618
December 1938	14,508	2,061	16,569
December 1939	17,620	2,244	19,864
December 1940	21,995	2,370	24,365
December 1941	22,737	2,520	25,257

Source: Board of Governors of the Federal Reserve System, Banking and Monetary Statistics, 1943, pp. 387–394, 419–420. The monetary silver stock includes silver dollars, silver bullion held against silver certificates, and fractional silver coins.

In the summer of 1934, the Treasury began to add large amounts of silver to its monetary stocks. Its net purchases amounted to $224 million by the end of the year, to $612 million by the end of 1935, and to $1,680 million by the end of 1941. These purchases also served to expand the reserve base of high-powered money.

Thus, the combined net contributions of gold and silver purchases to the reserve base of high-powered money after the end of 1933 were $4,416 million by the end of 1934, $6,801 million by the end of 1935, and $20,381 million by the end of 1941. These far exceeded the amounts needed to meet increased demands for currency in circulation, and most of the excess went into bank reserves. In 1933, total member bank reserves had ranged below $2.7 billion. They reached nearly $4 billion by the end of 1934, nearly $5.6 billion by the end of 1935, and almost $12.5 billion by the end of 1941.

These facts help to explain why the role of the Federal Reserve diminished, especially after the end of 1933. For one thing, the huge purchases of gold and silver by the Treasury made unnecessary further Federal Reserve actions to ease the monetary situation. Moreover, as will be explained more fully at a later point, the government had acquired powerful monetary instruments of its own that it could threaten to use if the Federal Reserve did not conform, or could actually use to offset undesired Federal Reserve actions or to bring about desired conditions.

■ **THE ENVIRONMENT OF MONETARY POLICY**   As noted earlier, many members of Congress were clamoring for monetary expansion by the spring of 1933. Various methods of expansion were proposed—expansion by the Federal Reserve, monetization of silver, issues of greenbacks, alteration of the gold value of the dollar, issues of scrip, and so on. There was a real possibility that the impatient new Congress would enact mandatory legislation directing the President to take specific actions. Roosevelt skillfully avoided this, persuading Congress to grant him broad permissive powers. This was done in Title III of the Farm Relief Act, approved on May 12, 1933. This is popularly referred to as "the Thomas Amendment," after its sponsor, Senator Elmer Thomas of Oklahoma. Under this Act, the President himself, or the Secretary of the Treasury acting under Presidential direction, was empowered to do the following.

(1) Enter into agreements with the Federal Reserve Board and the Federal Reserve banks for the latter to acquire U. S. Treasury obligations or obligations of corporations in which the government was a majority stockholder up to $3 billion in addition to those held on May 12. If the actual reserve ratios of the Reserve banks fell below required levels because of such purchases, no penalties would be imposed and no increases of discount rates would be required.

(2) Issue United States notes (greenbacks) in amounts not to exceed $3 billion. These were to be legal tender for all debts.

(3) Fix the gold value of the dollar by proclamation, with the limitation that it should not be reduced more than 50 percent.

(4) Fix the silver value of the dollar and provide for the unlimited coinage of gold and silver at fixed ratios. The President could reestablish a bimetallic standard in this country alone, or he could enter into agreements with other countries to establish international bimetallism.

(5) Accept silver at a price not to exceed 50 cents an ounce in payment of debts by foreign governments, the total accepted in this way not to exceed $200 million. Any silver acquired in this way was to be coined into silver dollars or held as backing for additional silver certificates.

At least two aspects of this legislation are noteworthy. First, it increased greatly the bargaining power of the government relative to the Federal Reserve. In view of the circumstances and the legislation by Congress, the Federal Reserve was hardly in a position to refuse to buy securities if requested to do so. Moreover, refusal by the Federal Reserve to adopt a policy expansive enough to suit the Administration might lead the latter to take action on its own, which most Federal Reserve officials feared. Second, the monetary powers granted to the President were indeed sweeping and permissive. He was free to choose among the powers and to determine the magnitude and timing of his actions, subject always to the possibility of mandatory action by Congress if his policies were not acceptable to it. Two of these discretionary powers were not used: The President did not invoke the power to issue greenbacks, and he did not force the Federal Reserve to purchase securities, although he did apply moral suasion. However, he took massive actions with respect to gold and silver.

■ **GOLD POLICIES**   It is clear that the President's gold policy, involving an increase in the price of gold or a decrease in the gold value of the dollar, was conceived as a part of his program to raise and then stabilize commodity prices. However, it is still difficult to answer some questions about these policies. Was the President's primary emphasis on commodity prices in general, or on prices of agricultural products? Why did he rely so heavily on gold policy rather than on the other available methods of monetary expansion? Through what channels and processes did he expect an increase in the price of gold to raise prices of other commodities?

At least three reasons for changing the relationship of the dollar to gold were presented to the President. (1) To end a fixed relationship of the dollar to gold, or to reduce the value of the dollar in terms of gold, would reduce the danger of gold hoarding and gold exports, such as had occurred in late 1931, early 1932, and February 1933, and thus increase the nation's freedom to pursue expansionary monetary policies. (2) Professor George F. Warren, one of the President's advisors, asserted that an increase in the price of gold would raise domestic price levels quickly and almost in proportion to the increase in the price of gold. His advice was based on his observation of a long-run correlation between the value of monetary gold stocks and the price level, and he never explained satisfactorily why price levels should be expected to respond quickly or the processes through which this might be achieved. (3) To the extent that a decrease in the gold value of the dollar came to be reflected in a decrease of the exchange rate on the dollar in terms of foreign currencies, this would tend to increase directly the dollar prices of both imports and exports, including the prices of agricultural commodities. (4) Large gold purchases were one method of adding sizable amounts to the monetary base of high-powered money, thus bringing pressure for expansions of the money supply and bank credit. It is important to remember, however, that gold policies did not begin to make additions to the monetary base and bank reserves until after the adoption of the Gold Reserve Act at the end of January 1934.

The relative weights that the President attached to these various arguments are not known. Pragmatist that he was, he probably concluded, "They all sound good to me." However, his public statements in 1933 emphasized the desirability of lowering the exchange rate on the dollar. For example, in his radio address on Oct. 22, 1933, he dwelt on the adverse effects on the United States of the depreciation of foreign currencies prior to 1933:

The effect of this had been to contribute to the serious decrease in our foreign trade, not because our own prices, in terms of dollars, had risen, nor because our products were of inferior quality, nor because we did not have sufficient products to export. But because, in terms of foreign currencies, our products had become so much more expensive, we were not able to obtain our fair share of the world's trade. It was, therefore, necessary to take measures which would result in bringing the dollar back to the position where a fair amount of foreign currency could again buy our product. . . .[1]

Efforts to decrease the exchange rate on the dollar inevitably brought conflicts with other countries. After all, a cheapening of the dollar in terms of other currencies meant an increase of the prices of those currencies in terms of dollars—an unwelcome event for nations wishing to expand their exports and to raise their domestic price levels. Wide divergences of national interests and of national views of monetary policy became evident at the London Economic Conference in June 1933. Virtually all participating nations favored "monetary stabilization." However, their definitions of the term and of acceptable conditions of stabilization differed widely. For example, to France and other members of the gold bloc—Belgium, Switzerland, and the Netherlands—stabilization meant stability of currencies in terms of gold. Every nation should adopt a permanent gold value for its currency and follow whatever policies might be required to defend that value. Such views were completely unacceptable to Britain and most members of the British Empire. If they were to stabilize their currencies in terms of gold at all, they would do so only as a part of a broad international program to raise prices, incomes, and international trade. In the absence of such a program, with adequate safeguards, they would retain freedom of action, and would enter into no more than temporary stabilization agreements subject to change. Roosevelt's views were closer to those of the British. In a wireless to the conference in early July 1933, he sharply refused to commit himself to stabilization of the dollar in gold or foreign currencies, and he expressed his determination to raise and then stabilize domestic prices.

Whether or not countries stabilized their currencies in terms of gold, or stabilized exchange rates by other means, or allowed exchange rates to fluctuate more widely, a highly important and controversial issue remained—that of the levels of exchange rates among national currencies. Under depression conditions, each nation favored a low exchange rate on its own money relative to other currencies. For example, in June 1933, the British were willing to consider a temporary stabilization of the pound-dollar rate at the prevailing level of about £1 = $4. Such a low rate on the pound relative to the dollar was unacceptable to Roosevelt. In November, when the pound had risen to about £1 = $5.14, Roosevelt inquired through Federal Reserve officials whether Britain would agree to stabilize at about that level. Britain declined. Such issues continued into the war period.

[1] *The Public Papers and Addresses of Franklin D. Roosevelt*, Vol. 2, Random House, New York, 1938, p. 428.

■ **Development of the Gold Program**   As noted earlier, the President's proclamation of a banking holiday on March 6 prohibited banks from paying out gold and gold certificates domestically and placed under the control of the Secretary of the Treasury all transactions in gold and foreign exchange. The Secretary never again permitted domestic payments of gold and gold certificates. On March 8, the Federal Reserve Board requested the Reserve banks to prepare lists of persons who had recently withdrawn gold and gold certificates and to give publicity to the request. This unsubtle bit of moral suasion was superseded on April 5 by an executive order requiring the public to surrender all gold certificates and gold except rare coins. Another highly important step was taken on June 5, when Congress abrogated gold clauses in all obligations, past and future. Such clauses, which were widely used in both private and governmental debt contracts, typically provided that the debtor should pay in "gold dollars of the present weight and fineness, or their dollar equivalents." A large increase in the official price of gold would not have been feasible if the gold clauses had been upheld, for debtors would have had to pay larger numbers of dollars to meet their obligations. For example, with a 69 percent increase in the official price of gold, debtors would have had to pay $1,690 to retire a $1,000 debt. The Supreme Court later upheld the validity of the abrogation of gold clauses in a highly controversial set of cases.

Thus, by early June 1933, the domestic role of gold had been much reduced. All gold and gold certificates except those held by the Federal Reserve Banks had been called in, no new gold coins or certificates were to be issued, and it was illegal to state contracts in terms of gold. In the meantime, new policies relative to foreign exchange transactions and the international role of gold were evolving. The Secretary of the Treasury gradually restored freedom of dealings in foreign exchange, but he continued to license and to restrict gold exports. This policy was formalized in an executive order issued on April 20, which prohibited exports of gold except gold previously earmarked for the accounts of foreign governments, foreign central banks, and the Bank for International Settlements. The Secretary of the Treasury was empowered to issue licenses for gold exports "as he deemed necessary to promote the pubilc interest," but only with the approval of the President. It was becoming clear that gold would no longer be sold freely to support the dollar in exchange markets.

Thus, doubts were created about the future gold value of the dollar, some exports of capital funds were induced, and the dollar began to depreciate in terms of other national currencies. For example, the rate on the French franc, which had averaged about 3.92 cents at the beginning of 1933, averaged 5.37 cents in August. And the British pound rose in the same period from about $3.43 to $4.50. The dollar had depreciated about 27 percent in terms of the franc and other gold currencies, and 24 percent in terms of sterling. However, these decreases were still considered too small, and the Secretary of the Treasury began, on September 8, to buy all newly mined domestic gold at a price equal to the best price available in free markets abroad. Purchases at home and abroad became larger after October 25 when the RFC, acting under the President's instructions, began to buy gold at gradually increasing prices. These month-end prices were as follows.

DATE	RFC PURCHASE PRICE PER FINE OUNCE	PERCENTAGE OF OLD MINT PRICE
October 31, 1933	$32.12	155
November 29, 1933	33.93	164
December 30, 1933	34.06	165
January 31, 1934	34.45	167

Source: Secretary of the Treasury, *Annual Report, 1934,* p. 205.

By the end of 1933, the official price of gold had been increased by 65 percent; the gold value of the dollar had been reduced by 39 percent.

Although there were differences of opinion within the Administration as to whether the dollar should again be given a fixed value in terms of gold and what that value should be, Roosevelt decided in January 1934 to stabilize at about the existing level. The result was the Gold Reserve Act of 1934, approved at the end of January. Its principal provisions were these:

(1) The President was authorized to fix the gold value of the dollar at not less than 50 percent nor more than 60 percent of the old level. He set the price of gold at $35 an ounce, expressly reserving the right to alter it as the country's interests might require.[2] The President did not use this discretionary power to make further changes in the price of gold, although at times there were rumors that he might do so. The gold content of the new dollar was 13.71 grains, a reduction of 40.94 percent. The Treasury reaped a handsome profit in raising the price of gold from $20.67 to $35 an ounce. It gained $14.33 on each of its nearly 196 million ounces of holdings, or $2,805 million.

(2) It nationalized all gold, including that held by the Federal Reserve Banks, provided that all profits or losses resulting from changes in the price of gold should accrue to the Treasury, and ended the domestic redeemability of currency in gold or gold certificates.

(3) It ended the coinage of gold for domestic use and provided that all existing gold coins should be formed into bars.

(4) It provided that gold might be held, transported, imported, exported, or otherwise dealt in only in accordance with regulations prescribed by the Secretary of the Treasury with the approval of the President.

[2] The buying price is actually one-fourth of one percent below $35, and the selling price is one-fourth of one percent above it.

In practice, these regulations permitted free import and export of gold but limited domestic holding and dealing to "legitimate" commercial, industrial, artistic, and scientific purposes.

(5) It provided that $2 billion of the gold profits should be used to establish an exchange stabilization fund under the Secretary of the Treasury, which he could use to regulate foreign exchange rates and to influence domestic monetary and credit conditions.

In short, the nation had abolished the gold-coin standard, established a limited gold-bullion standard, decreased the gold value of the dollar by 40.94 percent, and raised the official price of gold 69.33 percent. These actions inevitably had profound effects on exchange rates. The dollar rates on French francs and the currencies of other members of the gold bloc were raised about 69 percent above their levels prior to 1933. This greatly increased deflationary pressures on those countries and finally forced them to devalue in 1936. From the beginning of 1934 to the outbreak of war in September 1939, the dollar price of the British pound ranged between $4.67 and $5.09, usually toward the top of this range. This was far above the $3.28–$3.50 range that had prevailed in the latter part of 1932 and early 1933, and often above the $4.86 level that prevailed before September 1931. Although Americans might claim that such depreciations of the exchange rate on the dollar merely corrected the earlier excessive appreciation, many foreigners retorted that America was trying to solve her domestic recovery problem by exporting deflationary pressures to other countries.

■ SILVER POLICIES   As already noted, the Thomas Amendment in May 1933 gave the President broad discretionary powers to accept silver in payment of war debts, to purchase the metal, to establish bimetallism, and to enter into international silver agreements. He did not establish bimetallism, and only limited amounts of silver were received in payment of war debts.[3] Nevertheless, the Treasury acquired very large amounts of silver under other programs.

These purchases were not necessary to promote the nation's monetary objectives. Unlike the increase in the price of gold, they were not required to lower the exchange rate on the dollar. Also, there were plenty of alternative methods, such as gold purchases and Federal Reserve purchases of acceptances and securities, to provide a reserve base for domestic monetary expansion. These silver policies, adopted only reluctantly by Roosevelt, resulted from a coalition of political forces somewhat similar to those of the late nineteenth century. In part, this was a response to the preceding deflation and to a continuing belief in the South and West that a greater use of silver was an especially effective method of monetary expansion.

[3] For an excellent brief description of American silver policies, see G. Griffith Johnson, The Treasury and Monetary Policy, 1932–1938, Harvard University Press, Cambridge, Mass., 1939, pp. 161–200.

Added to this were the interests and political skills of silver-mining groups and of a handful of senators from the silver states. Especially after the price of silver fell below 25 cents an ounce in 1932, there were loud demands that the government "do something for silver." It did. In fairness, however, it should be remembered that silver was by no means the only commodity that received price support under the New Deal.

Senator Key Pittman, one of the most ardent silverites and an American delegate to the London Economic Conference in mid-1933, persuaded a number of silver-producing and silver-using countries to agree to measures to raise the price of silver. The joker in the agreement soon became obvious. In effect, the United States agreed to purchase annually for monetary purposes an amount of silver equal to its entire domestic production, while the commitments of other countries were small indeed. The President ratified the London Silver Agreement in December 1933, ordering the Treasury to buy the entire domestic output at 64.64 cents an ounce, a price about 50 percent above that previously prevailing. This was increased twice in April 1935, rising to 77 cents an ounce.

The December action was not sufficient to satisfy the proponents of silver, including some who were speculating in silver. Pressure on the President mounted until May, when he agreed to a more ambitious program. This was authorized in the Silver Purchase Act of 1934, approved on June 19. The Act directed the Secretary of the Treasury to purchase silver at home and abroad until the monetary value of the silver stock should be equal to one-third of the value of the monetary gold stock, or until the market price of silver should rise to its monetary value ($1.29 an ounce). It also provided that in order to prevent excessive profits to speculators, no more than 50 cents an ounce should be paid for silver located in the United States on May 1, 1934. The President implemented the latter provision in August by nationalizing such silver at this price. Fortunately, the law did not prescribe the speed of purchases by the Secretary of the Treasury. He therefore brought about as slowly as political conditions permitted. Nevertheless, his purchases were very large. From the beginning of 1934 through 1941, he bought about 2.6 billion ounces at a total cost of more than $1.6 billion. Of this silver, about 78 percent came from abroad, 17 percent from domestic mines, and 5 percent from the nationalization of accumulated silver stocks held within the country.

Proponents of silver brought forth a new rationalization that had not been used before in American political debates on the subject: A rise in the price of silver would help silver-standard countries, such as Mexico, China, and several other countries in the Orient, by raising their purchasing power in world markets. Subsequent events demonstrated the gross error of this argument. In fact, earlier declines in the price of silver had lowered exchange rates on silver standard currencies and helped those countries maintain their exports and lessen domestic deflationary pressures. Now the sharp rise in the price of silver had the reverse effect;

it raised exchange rates on their currencies and reduced their ability to export without drastic reductions of their domestic prices. This deflationary pressure was intensified as some of their silver money was melted and exported. In the end, most silver countries abandoned silver standards and adopted inconvertible standards, or tied their moneys to the dollar or the British pound. Thus, a long-run effect of American silver policy was to reduce still further the monetary use of silver abroad.

■ THE BALANCE OF PAYMENTS   It has already been noted that the United States received gold imports during every year following 1933. Table 10–2 shows the size of these imports annually, together with

Table 10–2.   The balance of international payments of the United States, 1934–1941 (in millions of dollars)

	1934	1935	1936	1937	1938	1939	1940	1941
(1) Sports goods and services (+)	$2975	$3265	$3539	$4553	$4336	$4482	$5355	$6896
(2) Imports of goods and services (−)	2374	3137	3424	4256	3045	3366	3636	4486
(3) Net balance on goods and services account (+)	601	128	115	297	1291	1066	1719	2410
(4) Unilateral transfers (−)	172	182	208	235	182	178	210	1136
(5) Net long term capital flows	+ 195	+ 437	+ 780	+ 523	+ 88	+ 13	+ 73	− 652
(6) Net short-term capital flows	+ 230	+ 1069	+ 428	+ 354	+ 353	+ 485	+ 1530	− 379
(7) Total capital flows	+ 425	+ 1506	+ 1208	+ 877	+ 441	+ 498	+ 1603	− 1031
Errors and omissions	+ 412	+ 364	+ 157	+ 425	+ 249	+ 783	+ 1277	+ 476
Change in the monetary gold stock	− 1266	− 1822	− 1272	− 1364	− 1799	− 3174	− 4243	− 719

Key: (+) = receipts.
(−) = payments. Note: a (−) for the monetary gold stock signifies an increase in that stock.

Source: U. S. Bureau of the Census, Historical Statistics of the United States, Colonial Times to 1957, Washington, 1960, pp. 564–565.

the major items in the balance of payments that made these possible. There were net exports of goods and services in every year; those in 1940 and 1941 were especially large. There were also net capital inflows, both long-term and short-term, in every year prior to 1941. The nation did not again assume the role, developed in the 1920s, of net provider of long-term funds to the rest of the world. Foreign flotations of securities in the American market to raise new funds came to a virtual standstill. In the years 1926–1928, these had averaged about $1.2 billion; in no year after 1931 did they rise above $50 million, and in most years they were considerably below this level. At the same time, there were net inflows of long-term funds to the United States as foreigners made net payments on their outstanding obligations and bought American securities. The virtual absence of American long-term lending undoubtedly retarded world recovery.

In general, the net inflows of short-term funds did not occur because interest rates in New York were high relative to those in other international financial centers. Rather, they reflected expectations and fears relating to changes in exchange rates and to economic and political disturbances. Large inflows occurred soon after the dollar was given a new fixed gold value at the end of January 1934; at least some of these were returns of funds that had been withdrawn by Americans and foreigners in 1933.

A considerable part of the inflows during 1935 and the first eight months of 1936 were related to economic and political disturbances in the gold-bloc countries, for which American monetary policies were partially responsible. As noted earlier, the devaluation of the dollar in terms of gold raised the dollar price of these currencies about 69 percent. These currencies also appreciated in terms of most of the nongold currencies. The appreciation of these gold currencies, and the imposition of exchange restrictions by many countries, affected adversely the balance-of-payments positions of the members of the gold bloc and increased deflationary pressures on their economies. These, together with deliberate official deflationary policies adopted to defend the currencies, created both economic and political disturbances. Belgium threw in the sponge in 1935, devaluing the belga by 28 percent, but the other members of the gold bloc persisted, amidst rising controversy, until September 1936, at which time they suspended their old gold standards and devalued their currencies by about 30 percent.[4]

International flows of short-term funds, including flows to the United States, increased as incidents leading to World War II developed. They were especially large after March 1938 when Germany moved into Austria, at the time of the first Czech crisis in September of that year, in the period following the German absorption of Bohemia and Moravia in the spring of 1939, and preceding the declaration of war in September. Net flows to the United States in 1940 exceeded $1.6 billion.

In short, America's freedom to follow expansionary domestic policies during the period after 1933 was in no way inhibited by its international-reserve and balance-of-payments positions. The U. S. accumulated huge gold reserves and had a favorable balance of payments in every year. In fact, as we shall see later, both government and Federal Reserve officials came to fear that gold inflows and the accompanying increases of bank reserves were creating an excessive inflationary potential.

■ **FEDERAL RESERVE POLICIES IN 1933**   The reserve positions of commercial banks had been severely damaged during the banking

---

[4] For a discussion of these actions and the Tripartite Agreement among France, Britain, and the United States, see *Annual Report of the Board of Governors of the Federal Reserve System*, 1936, pp. 4–8.

crisis. Member banks had lost over $700 million of reserves since the beginning of 1933 and had increased their borrowings from the Federal Reserve to more than $1.4 billion. This situation was only partially relieved by the return flow of currency to the banks, which amounted to about $1,250 million by the end of March and nearly $2 billion by August. The government's gold and silver policies added virtually nothing to bank reserves before the end of 1933. Not until 1934 did the golden avalanche and silver purchases begin to add huge amounts to bank reserves. During 1933, the Federal Reserve still had the time and opportunity to seize the initiative and to take positive and ambitious expansionary actions.

However, the Federal Reserve response was slow, reluctant, and limited. It did reduce discount rates. These were at 3½ percent at all the Reserve banks in March 1933. Five banks kept their rates at this level throughout the year, one reduced to 3 percent, five lowered to 2½ percent, and New York reduced its rate in three steps to 2 percent. The minimum discount rate applicable to purchases of acceptances was reduced in steps from 3½ percent to one-half of one percent, at which level it remained through 1941. Federal reserve purchases of government securities were made only belatedly and reluctantly. None occurred before mid-May. At this time, total bank reserves were still $300 million below their level in late 1932, and member bank borrowings were $330 million while their excess reserves amounted to only $311 million. This inactivity by the Federal Reserve is difficult to understand and impossible to justify. However, most Federal Reserve officials thought that more expansionary action at that time was unnecessary and would be ineffective. They pointed to the existence of excess reserves and low interest rates on safe, short-term assets, and they argued that the failure of banks to expand resulted not from a scarcity of reserves but from their need for financial rehabilitation and from a scarcity of creditworthy borrowers. As in earlier periods, they failed to realize that banks wanted to hold excess reserves far in excess of the available supply.

When the Federal Reserve began to purchase securities after May 17, it did so under strong pressures. Time after time, Treasury officials urged the Federal Reserve to buy securities, partly to help support the recovery effort but more immediately to facilitate Treasury borrowing. Highly visible in the background were the powers conferred on the Treasury by the Thomas Amendment. The Treasury could, in effect, force the Federal Reserve to purchase securities if it did not do so "voluntarily." Moreover, Federal Reserve officials came to hope that purchases by them would stave off recourse by the government to its powers to issue greenbacks, buy silver, or raise the price of gold. In a memorandum of his conversation with Federal Reserve Board Governor Eugene Black on September 16, Governor George L. Harrison, of the New York Federal Reserve Board, described the situation:

> As I see the picture, I said, we now have, largely through market opera-
> tions and a return flow of currency, created approximately $700,000,000 of

excess reserves and a very easy money market position. Certainly from the point of view of the credit and banking situation there would appear to be no need for any further purchases of Government securities. Our operations to date, together with other factors, have resulted in placing the banks of the country as a whole in a position to make a very substantial expansion of bank credit as soon as there is a demand for it by borrowers entitled to have it on the basis of good credit risk. Consequently, further purchases of government securities in the open market must be justified by factors outside the immediate banking and credit picture or, to put it differently, outside those matters specifically and immediately within the jurisdiction of the Federal reserve banks, as central banks.

For some weeks now, under the authority granted by the Open Market Committee with the approval of the Federal Reserve Board in May, the Executive Committee has been making weekly purchases partly because of the need for creating an easy banking position but in latter weeks largely because we have been informed by Governor Black, Secretary Woodin, Mr. Acheson, Mr. Sprague, and others from Washington, that this is an important and advisable way for the Federal reserve banks to cooperate with the Government's program of recovery and an especially weighty factor in minimizing the risk of drastic methods of currency inflation, such as greenbacks. I explained to Governor Black, however, that I had some hesitation in recommending a continuance of open market operations for these reasons alone, unless I was definitely sure that his views as to the needs for these purchases represented the views of the Federal Reserve Board as a whole. In other words, there being no clear cut need from the banking and credit position, I wanted to be sure that the Federal Reserve Board considers that a continuance of open market purchases are advisable or necessary as a contribution to the Governmental program of recovery and also as a substantial means of minimizing the risk of greenbacks.

Governor Black said he understood my position perfectly; that he agreed with it entirely; that I was quite right in assuming that the Federal Reserve Board, as well as he, felt that it was advisable to continue open market purchases at about the present rate.[5]

It was under such conditions that the Federal Reserve added $595 million to its holdings of government securities between May 17 and Nov. 29, 1933. No further purchases were made between the latter date and the end of March 1937. In fact, at no time from the end of November 1933 through 1941 were open-market operations used as an important determinant of the volume of bank reserves. Gold and silver purchases took over the job.

There were at least two reasons for the refusal of Federal Reserve officials to purchase any more securities after November 29. For one thing, they thought that monetary conditions were easy enough. Total bank reserves had risen more than $400 million since mid-May, excess reserves exceeded $700 million, and market rates of interest on safe, short-

[5] Minutes of the Meeting of the Executive Committee of the Federal Open Market Committee, Sept. 21, 1933. The men referred to are George L. Harrison, Governor of the Federal Reserve Bank of New York; Eugene Black, Governor of the Federal Reserve Board; William Woodin, Secretary of the Treasury; Dean Acheson, Undersecretary of the Treasury; and Professor O. M. W. Sprague, Economic Advisor to the Treasury.

term obligations were low. Moreover, it had become evident that further purchases would not head off "inflationary" monetary actions by the government. The RFC was already driving down the gold value of the dollar, and silver purchases were in the offing.

■ **MONETARY POLICIES AFTER 1933**   Although its policies did not become insignificant, the role of the Federal Reserve declined markedly after the end of 1933, and especially after the Gold Reserve Act became effective at the end of January 1934. For one thing, the Federal Reserve was no longer the major determinant of the size of the reserve base of high-powered money or of the volume of member bank reserves. The reserve base of high-powered money averaged $8.8 billion in 1933; it then doubled by 1937 and more than tripled by 1941. (See Table 10–3.) The

Table 10–3.   The reserve base of high-powered money and member bank reserves, 1932–1941 (annual averages of daily figures, in millions of dollars)

YEAR	TOTAL FEDERAL RESERVE CREDIT	MONETARY GOLD STOCK	TREASURY CURRENCY OUT- STANDING	TOTAL RESERVE BASE OF HIGH- POWERED MONEY	MEMBER BANK RESERVES	
					TOTAL	EXCESS
1932	$2,077	$ 3,952	$2,096	$ 8,125	$ 2,114	$ 256
1933	2,429	4,059	2,271	8,759	2,343	528
1934	2,502	7,512	2,381	12,395	3,676	1,564
1935	2,475	9,059	2,478	14,012	5,001	2,467
1936	2,481	10,578	2,503	15,562	5,989	2,512
1937	2,554	12,162	2,567	17,283	6,830	1,220
1938	2,600	13,250	2,711	18,561	7,935	2,522
1939	2,628	16,085	2,879	21,592	10,352	4,392
1940	2,487	19,865	3,018	25,370	13,249	6,326
1941	2,293	22,546	3,156	27,994	13,404	5,324

Source: Board of Governors of the Federal Reserve System, *Banking and Monetary Statistics,* 1943, p. 368.

Federal Reserve supplied only a minute part of the increase; at no time during the period did total Federal Reserve credit rise by more than $100 million above its level at the beginning of 1934. The increase came largely from the huge rise of the monetary gold stock, aided by an increase in outstanding Teasury currency reflecting the cost of silver purchases.

Some of the increase of high-powered money was used to meet increased demands for currency in circulation and for other purposes, but huge amounts flowed into member bank reserves. At the beginning of 1934, total member bank reserves stood at about $2.7 billion; they had risen more than one billion by midyear and then continued to rise, reaching a peak of $14.4 billion in early 1941. Banks used some of these increased reserves as a basis for expanding their credit and their deposit liabilities, and they also accumulated huge amounts of excess reserves. From an average of $866 million in January 1934, excess reserves rose to $1.8 billion by mid-1934 and to about $3 billion in mid-1936. The Federal Reserve then decreased excess reserves through two increases of member bank reserve requirements, one effective in August 1936 and the other in the spring of 1937. Excess reserves again soared after April 1938 as the Federal Reserve lowered reserve requirements, the Treasury desterilized some of its inactive gold, and gold imports continued. By the spring of 1940, they exceeded $6 billion.

The relative power of the Federal Reserve was also diminished by other increased monetary powers of the government. As already noted, the President or the Secretary of the Treasury still had the power to order the Federal Reserve to purchase securities, to issue greenbacks on its own initiative, and to take further actions on gold and silver. Most immediately relevant, however, was the enhanced monetary power of the Treasury resulting from its $2.8 billion profit on the revaluation of gold. This originally had no effect on bank reserves because it was "sterilized" in an inactive gold account at the Treasury, against which no gold certificates were issued. However, the Secretary could at any time use it to increase bank reserves; he could do this by issuing gold certificates to Federal Reserve banks in exchange for deposits there, and then pay out these deposits to meet government expenses or to retire securities held by banks or the public. Thus, he had his own instrument for monetary expansion, of which Federal Reserve officials were fully aware.

Moreover, the Secretary could, if he wished, "sterilize" new acquisitions of monetary gold and prevent it from expanding bank reserves. He could do this by purchasing the gold with new issues of interest-bearing bonds rather than by issuing gold certificates to the Federal Reserve and paying out the resulting deposits. We shall see later that he did this in 1937 and early 1938 with the full cooperation and approval of Federal Reserve officials. However, in the process, he accumulated a further stock of "inactive gold," which he could, and later did, pay out in an expansionary way, whether or not the Federal Reserve approved.

Legislation during the years 1933–1935 granted several new powers to the Federal Reserve. Among the most important of these were power: (1) To alter member bank reserve requirements between their existing levels and double those levels. (2) To make direct loans, or to participate in loans, to nonbank borrowers unable to secure funds on reasonable terms from normal sources. (3) To fix maximum loan values, or minimum margin requirements, on loans for purchasing and carrying securities. (4) To set ceilings on rates paid by banks on time and savings deposits.

The law prohibited interest on demand deposits. Only the first power, that authorizing alteration of member bank reserve requirements, was directly relevant to control of the total supplies of money and credit.

During this period, there were also important changes in the personnel and internal organization of the Federal Reserve. The most important single change of personnel came with the appointment of Marriner S. Eccles as governor of the Federal Reserve Board in November 1934. A wealthy Utah banker and industrialist of unorthodox views, he was the most active and powerful governor of the Board during the period before World War II. Believing that the government should play an active role in promoting recovery, he had shocked the banking fraternity and others in 1932 by advocating the adoption of a large deficit-spending program. He was also an activist in monetary policy, and favored centralization of control within the Federal Reserve System, especially while he was Governor of the Board. Although it did not go as far as Eccles wished, the Banking Act of 1935 both clarified the location of power and responsibility within the system and provided for considerably more centralization.

Three of the most important provisions of the Act were these: First, it abolished the Federal Reserve Board, which had been composed of eight members including the Secretary of the Treasury and the Comptroller of the Currency, and provided for a new central body to be known as the Board of Governors of the Federal Reserve System. The latter was to be composed of seven members appointed by the President for 14-year terms; neither the Secretary of the Treasury nor the Comptroller was to be a member of the new Board. Two reasons were given for eliminating these *ex officio* members. One was that they were too busy to attend meetings regularly. The other was that their membership might bring undue political pressure on the system. Under the circumstances, it is doubtful that elimination of these members reduced the degree of government influence on the Federal Reserve. Only two members of the old Board were carried over to the new one—Eccles as Chairman and M. S. Szymczak; five new members were appointed. As compared with the old Board, the new one was younger, more activist, and more determined to centralize control within the system.

Second, the Banking Act of 1935 reconstituted the open market committee and increased its authority. The old one had been composed of representatives of the twelve Reserve banks; the new Federal Open Market Committee (FOMC) was composed of the seven members of the Board of Governors and representatives of five of the Reserve banks. The Act also strengthened the authority of the new FOMC by providing that a Federal Reserve bank might engage in open-market operations, or decline to participate in such operations, only in accordance with regulations prescribed by the FOMC.

Third, the Act increased the power of the Board over discount rates. The Act continued the power of the Reserve banks to establish discount rates subject to review and determination by the Board, but added the provision that "each bank shall establish such rates every fourteen days, or oftener if deemed necessary by the Board."

The appointment of a new and more active Board, the greater centralization of power over open-market operations and discount rates, and concentration in the Board of the power to fix and alter member bank reserve requirements greatly altered the balance of power within the system and had important policy implications. Those Reserve banks that had obstructed the adoption and execution of strong expansionary policies would now find it much more difficult to do so. However, there was little need for such Federal Reserve policies during this period.

Let us now look at some of the most important monetary policy actions during the period from early 1934 through 1941. As noted earlier, the Federal Reserve minimum discount rate on acceptance purchases had been reduced to one-half of one percent before the end of 1933, and it remained at this level through 1941. Discount rates were reduced further. By September 1937, they were 1 percent at New York and 1½ percent at the other Reserve banks. Then they remained unchanged except that Boston reduced its rate to 1 percent in September 1939. However, the most interesting actions were those related to the recession of 1937–1938.

■ **Monetary Policy and the Recession of 1937–1938**   At least as early as October 1935, by which time excess reserves of member banks had risen above $2.8 billion, Federal Reserve officials began to worry about the inflationary potential of such huge amounts of excess reserves.[6] Two sets of developments in 1936 particularly increased their concern. One was the continued gold inflow, which by late July 1936 had raised member banks excess reserves to $3 billion. The other was the pace of recovery. Although excess capacity and unemployment were still widespread, business activity was rising rapidly, prices were increasing, and the stock market was becoming more active. Federal Reserve officials wished to take no action that would have current restrictive effects. They insisted that expansionary monetary policies should be continued until recovery was much farther along. However, they did want to eliminate in some way a part of the excess reserves that was currently "serving no useful purpose" in order to be in a position to control the situation later when restriction became appropriate.

They considered three possible ways of doing this—sales of government securities from their open-market portfolio, request to the Treasury to sterilize gold, and increase of member bank reserve requirements. In the end they chose the third method, but only after they had made a careful survey of the distribution of excess reserves among the banks and had convinced themselves that no more than a very small number of banks

[6] See *Annual Report of the Board of Governors of the Federal Reserve System,* 1935, pp. 231–233.

would be left without excess reserves. Reserve requirements on all types of deposits at all classes of member banks were raised 50 percent above their old levels, effective Aug. 16, 1936.[7] This still left more than $1.8 billion of excess reserves. The Board explained in a press release:

> The part of the excess reserves thus eliminated is superfluous for all present or prospective needs of commerce, industry and agriculture and can be absorbed without restrictive influence upon member banks, practically all of which now have far more than sufficient reserves to meet the increase. Furthermore, by this action the remaining volume of excess reserves, which will still be larger than at any time in the System's history prior to the recent large inflow of gold, is brought within the scope of control by the Federal Open Market Committee.[8]

This action appears to have had no significant effects on interest rates or the availability of credit. The outcome was not to be so favorable the next time.

As gold inflows continued, excess reserves again rose, reaching more than $2.2 billion in November 1936. Treasury and Federal Reserve officials agreed that something should be done to stop, or to limit strictly, further increases. On December 22, the Treasury announced, in effect, that until further notice it would sterilize all further additions of monetary gold. By August 1937, it had sterilized over $1.3 billion of the metal.[9] However, Federal Reserve officials considered the existing levels of excess reserves to be too high. On Jan. 30, 1937, the Board of Governors announced an increase of member banks' reserve requirements equal to 50 percent of those in effect before August 1936, thus exhausting its legal power to raise these requirements. One-half of this increase was to become effective on March 1 and the other half on May 1.

This action, which the Board insisted would not restrict credit currently and was designed only to bring excess reserves down to manageable levels, was taken only after careful study and consultation with the Treasury. The Board estimated that excess reserves would still exceed $750 million, and that they would be well distributed among all classes of member banks.[10]

[7] Annual Report of the Board of Governors of the Federal Reserve System, 1936, pp. 216–219. The changes were as follows:

	IN EFFECT PRIOR TO AUGUST 16	EFFECTIVE AUGUST 16
Time deposits—all members	3%	4½%
Demand deposits at		
Central reserve city banks	13	19½
Reserve city banks	10	15
Other members	7	10½

[8] Ibid., p. 216.
[9] Board of Governors of the Federal Reserve System, Banking and Monetary Statistics, 1943, p. 515.
[10] For a summary of the results of this survey, see Annual Report of the Board of Governors of the Federal Reserve System, 1937, p. 4.

It expected that virtually all banks would meet the increased requirements by drawing down their excess reserves and correspondent balances, that virtually none would respond by selling securities or restricting loans, and that interest rates would not be affected. In fact, however, interest rates began to rise at about the same time that the first installment of the increase of required reserves became effective on March 1. The increases were relatively small but unmistakable. (See Table 10–4.) Also, bank credit and

Table 10–4. Selected interest rates, 1937 (in percent per annum)

1937	3-MONTH TREASURY BILLS	3–5 YEAR TREASURY NOTES	4–6 MONTH PRIME COMMERCIAL PAPER	90-DAY PRIME BANKERS' ACCEPTANCES	U.S. GOVERNMENT BONDS
January	0.17	1.18	0.75	0.22	2.47
February	0.15	1.22	0.75	0.31	2.46
March	0.38	1.44	0.75	0.38	2.60
April	0.56	1.59	1.00	0.56	2.80
May	0.41	1.48	1.00	0.53	2.76
June	0.36	1.54	1.00	0.47	2.76
July	0.28	1.44	1.00	0.44	2.72
August	0.29	1 45	1.00	0.44	2.72

Source: Board of Governors of the Federal Reserve System, Banking and Monetary Statistics, 1943, pp. 451, 460, 471.

the money supply, which had been increasing since early 1934, ceased to rise and actually declined about 5 percent in the following year. The Federal Reserve had again made the mistake of underestimating the banks' demands for excess reserves for liquidity purposes.

The Secretary of the Treasury, who had not objected to the increase of reserve requirements, was upset by the rise of interest rates, partly because he feared it would impede recovery and partly because the "disorderly market" complicated Treasury financing. The outcome was an agreement to take actions to ease the transition to higher reserve requirements and to prevent disorderly conditions in securities markets. The Treasury purchased some securities, principally bonds, with funds from its investment accounts. The Federal Reserve took two types of actions: It "swapped" some of its short-term securities for long-term bonds in order to support the prices of the latter, and it increased its total portfolio of government securities by $96 million. These actions were apparently effective in arresting the rise of interest rates, and rates began to drift downward after April, although they remained above the low levels prevailing at the beginning of the year. However, these actions did not prevent decreases in the supply of money and bank credit.

The beginning of the recession of 1937–1938 is usually placed in the spring of 1937 because a cyclical peak was reached at that time. The decline during the summer was slow and small, but by September, it was clear that the economy was in recession. Economists still differ in their assessment of the causes of the very sharp but brief recession of 1937–1938, principally on the relative weights that they assign to the various forces.[11] Some stress the shift of fiscal policies, and still others the Federal Reserve increase of reserve requirements in the spring of 1937.

With the benefit of hindsight, it is now clear that the increase of member bank reserve requirements in the spring of 1937 was a mistake. Federal Reserve officials were wrong in their judgment that the very large volume of excess reserves in 1936 and early 1937 was "serving no useful purpose." These were serving the very useful purpose of satisfying the banks' continued high levels of demand for liquidity, and of bringing pressures on banks to expand their loans and investments. The increase of reserve requirements reduced excess reserves from more than $2 billion in early 1937 to only $750 million in August. The remaining supply was probably below the amounts demanded by banks for liquidity purposes, so that banks sold some investments and restricted loans in efforts to increase their liquidity.The Federal Reserve action, and the initial rise of interest rates and fall of bond prices, may also have created fears of further increases in interest rates and further declines of bond prices.

This Federal Reserve action was not the only development in 1937 that was inimical to continued recovery. We have already mentioned the sharp shift of federal fiscal policy toward restriction from 1936 to 1937. The combined pressure of reduced federal expenditures for goods and services, the decrease of federal transfer payments, and the rise of social security taxes might have precipitated a recession even in the absence of the Federal Reserve action.

The nature of the increase of private investment in 1936 and the first few months of 1937 had increased the vulnerability of the economy to recession. As noted earlier, the recovery of private expenditures for fixed investment was disappointingly incomplete; this was especially true of both residential and nonresidential construction. A considerable part of the recovery preceding the recession was based on accumulation of business inventories. These were increased by $376 million in 1935, $2,066 million in 1936, and $1,726 million in 1937. The increases in 1936 and the early part of 1937 were spurred in part by fears of further price increases and work stoppages; that in the last quarter of 1937 resulted, at least in part, from a decline of sales.

It is still not clear why the rate of inventory accumulation first slowed down and then became negative. There are several possibilities: inventory stocks became adequate, or nearly so, relative to the current rate of sales; businessmen revised downward their expectations of future increases of

[11] For an excellent discussion of this episode, as well as bibliographical references, see Kenneth D. Roose, *The Economics of Recession and Revival: An Interpretation of 1937–1938*, Yale University Press, New Haven, Conn., 1954.

sales and of prices, and therefore lowered their desired rate of increase of inventories; tighter money led them to accumulate at a lower rate; and so on. It is probable that several of these influences were operative.[12] The large earlier losses on business inventories undoubtedly contributed to the sharpness of the decline.

At least these conclusions concerning the causes of the 1937–1938 recession and of its severity seem justified. Both the increase of member bank reserve requirements and the sharp shift of federal fiscal actions toward restriction were policy mistakes. Given the vulnerable position of private investment, the two together exerted downward pressures strong enough to precipitate a recession. And both served to increase the severity of the recession. Whatever may have been its causes, the recession proceeded sharply downward until May 1938, by which time industrial production had fallen by one-third.

Not until September 1937, when the rate of decline had begun to increase, did the Federal Reserve realize that a recession was in progress. Then it responded quickly with mildly expansionary actions. On September 12, it requested the Secretary of the Treasury to desterilize $300 million of gold, which he did during the next three weeks. In November, the Federal Reserve purchased $38 million of government securities. No further actions were taken before April 1938.

On April 14, Roosevelt announced a new fiscal and monetary program to stimulate recovery.[13] He requested and received from Congress additional appropriations of $1,550 million, about two-thirds of this for public works. Two expansionary monetary actions were taken. On April 15, the Board of Governors lowered member bank reserve requirements by one-third, thus adding about $750 million to excess reserves. Also, the Treasury began to desterilize its holdings of $1.4 billion of inactive gold. Some of these funds were paid out to meet government expenditures, but more were used to retire outstanding Treasury bills. Treasury bill rates were driven down both by the increase of excess reserves and by the decrease in the supply of bills. The Treasury also discontinued its sterilization of gold inflows, thus allowing further inflows to be added to the reserve base. Excess reserves reached $3 billion by July 1938 and then continued to climb. Not until November 1941 did the Board again raise reserve requirements to the maximum level permitted by law. Even after this action, member bank excess reserves remained above $3 billion.

■ **MONETARY POLICIES AFTER 1938**   The recovery that began in the late spring of 1938 continued into the war period, slowly until 1940 but more rapidly as the rearmament program expanded. Except for the increase of reserve requirements in 1941, neither the Federal Reserve nor the

[12]For a discussion of these issues, see Roose, *op. cit.*, pp. 179–191.
[13] *The Public Papers and Addresses of Franklin D. Roosevelt*, Vol. 7, Random House, New York, 1941, pp. 221–235.

Treasury took further actions to affect the reserve positions of banks. These positions were increased almost steadily by continued gold inflows. However, the Federal Reserve did intervene on several occasions to prevent or ameliorate "disorderly" conditions in the government securities market, and especially in the bond market. It did this in two ways. One was to swap Treasury bills and other short-term obligations for longer term bonds, or vice versa. The other was to make net purchases and sales. The latter were quite small—too small to have significant effects on the reserve position of the banking system.

Federal Reserve officials insisted that they would not "peg" interest rates and security prices at any fixed level; they would only prevent "disorderly" movements. Concern for promoting business recovery appears to have been no more than a minor reason for these actions. More important were the objectives of facilitating Treasury financing and of protecting banks against disorderly fluctuations in the values of their bond portfolios. From this prewar practice of preventing disorderly markets, it was only a short step to a policy of inflexible pegging of government security prices and yields, which followed during World War II and for some years thereafter.

■ **MONETARY AND FINANCIAL DEVELOPMENTS**   Having surveyed monetary policies during the 1933–1941 period, let us now look briefly at some monetary and financial developments. We have already noted that banks accumulated very large excess reserves and fell far short of expanding bank credit and the money supply to the limits legally permitted by their reserve positions. Nevertheless, the money supply expanded sharply and interest rates declined. Table 10–4 (page 179) indicated that virtually all interest rates declined through 1936, rose slightly during 1937, and declined again through the rest of the period. The decline was very large for short-term rates, and especially for the safest and most liquid types of paper. This is normal for periods of low interest rates when rates are expected to rise later. However, it seems almost certain that during this period investors were willing to pay an abnormally high price in terms of foregone earnings in order to purchase more safety and liquidity.

The money supply was increased by rises in all of its direct determinants—by increases of the monetary gold stock, of Treasury currency outstanding, of Federal Reserve holdings of securities, and of commercial bank loans and investments. Column 1 of Table 10–5 indicates the behavior of the money supply narrowly defined to include only currency outside banks plus demand deposits held by the public. Column 2 presents data relating to a broader definition, which also includes time deposits at commercial banks. Both show the same general trends. As already noted, the money supply, narrowly defined, declined 27 percent during the four years preceding June 1933. Then it began an upward trend that was in-

Table 10–5. The money supply and related items, 1929–1941 (in billions of dollars)

YEAR AND MONTH	Col. 1 CURRENCY PLUS DE-MAND DEPOSITS ADJUSTED	Col. 2 COL. 1 PLUS TIME DE-POSITS AT COMMERCIAL BANKS	LOANS AND INVESTMENTS OF ALL COMMERCIAL BANKS				
			Col. 3 TOTAL LOANS AND IN-VESTMENTS	Col. 4 LOANS	Col. 5 TOTAL INVEST-MENTS	Col. 6 U.S. GOVERN-MENT SECU-RITIES	Col. 7 OTHER SECU-RITIES
1929							
June	$26.2	$45.7	$49.4	$35.7	$13.7	$ 4.9	$8.7
1933							
June	19.2	30.1	30.4	16.3	14.0	7.5	6.5
Dec.	19.8	30.8	30.8	16.3	14.5		
1934							
June	21.4	33.3	32.7	15.7	17.0	10.3	6.7
Dec.	23.1	35.3	33.7	15.0	18.7		
1935							
June	25.2	38.0	34.6	14.9	19.7	12.7	7.0
Dec.	27.0	40.2	36.0	15.1	20.9		
1936							
June	29.0	42.7	38.5	15.6	23.0	15.3	7.7
Dec.	31.1	45.0	39.5	16.4	23.1	15.3	7.8
1937							
June	30.7	45.2	39.5	17.4	22.0	14.6	7.5
Dec.	29.6	44.4	38.3	17.1	21.2	14.2	7.1
1938							
June	29.7	44.5	37.1	16.1	21.1	14.0	7.0
Dec.	31.8	46.5	38.7	16.4	22.3	15.1	7.2
1939							
June	33.4	48.5	39.4	16.4	22.9	15.7	7.2
Dec.	36.2	51.5	40.7	17.2	23.4	16.3	7.1
1940							
June	38.7	54.2	41.1	17.4	23.7	16.6	7.2
Dec.	42.3	58.0	43.9	18.8	25.1	17.8	7.4
1941							
June	45.5	61.4	47.6	20.4	27.3	20.1	7.2
Dec.	48.6	64.5	50.7	21.7	29.0	21.8	7.2

Source: Board of Governors of the Federal Reserve System, *Banking and Monetary Statistics*, 1943, pp. 19–20, 34–35.

terrupted only during the year following June 1937. By the end of 1935, it had reached $27 billion, slightly above its level in mid-1929 and 41 percent above its level in mid-1933. At the end of 1940 it was $42.3 billion, or 61 percent above its level in mid-1929 and 121 percent above its level in mid-1933. These were indeed large increases.

Several aspects of the behavior of commercial bank credit are significant. As shown in Table 10–5, total commercial bank loans and investments declined $19 billion, or 38 percent, during the four years preceding June 1933. This occurred despite an increase of $2.6 in bank holdings of U. S. Government securities; loans fell by $19.4 billion and holdings of other securities by $2.2 billion. This suggests a strong shift of bank preferences toward safer and more liquid types of assets. Decreased demands for credit might help explain the decrease of bank loans but not the decrease of bank holdings of other securities.

Such preferences apparently persisted in the following period, at least until defense expenditures began to expand in mid-1940. For example, between June 1933 and June 1940, total bank loans and investments rose by $10.7 billion. Bank holdings of U.S. government securities accounted for $9.1 billion, or 85 percent, of this increase. Bank loans rose only $1.1 billion and bank holdings of other securities only $0.5 billion. It is difficult to believe that the smallness of the increase of loans was due solely to a weakness of demands for bank credit, and this factor could not explain the actual decline of bank holdings of securities other than federal obligations after the end of 1936.

■ THE MONEY SUPPLY AND GNP   Table 10–6 presents data relating to the rate of expenditures for output (GNP at current prices), the money supply, and the income velocity of money. In quantity-theory terms, the 46 percent decline of GNP from 1929 to 1933 reflected decreases of 25 percent in the money supply and 28 percent in the income velocity of money. Although both GNP and the money supply rose after 1933, their increases were not strictly proportional. Column 3 shows that the income velocity of money ranged between 3.04 and 2.55 during the period, with some downward drift toward the end of the period. At no time, however, did the income velocity of money approach the level of 3.92 achieved in 1929. Stated otherwise, the public appeared to demand in 1929 money balances equal to about 25 percent of its rate of expenditures for GNP. In the period 1933–1941, its demands for money balances ranged between 33 and 39 percent of GNP. One reason for this rise was undoubtedly the lower level of interest rates on other assets, and especially on short-term assets of high safety and liquidity. However, both the increase of demands for money balances relative to GNP and the extraordinary low rates on the safest and most liquid types of earning assets are best viewed as a part of the general rise of demands for safety and liquidity. Considering other assets to be less safe and less liquid than they had been regarded in the earlier

Table 10–6.   Gross national product at current prices, the
money supply, and income velocity, 1929–1941

YEAR	Col. 1 GNP AT CURRENT PRICES (IN BILLIONS)	Col. 2 AVERAGE MONEY SUPPLY	Col. 3 INCOME VELOCITY (COL. 1 DIVIDED BY COL. 2)	Col. 4 INDEX OF INCOME VELOCITY (1929= 100)	Col. 5 MONEY SUPPLY AS PERCENT OF GNP
1927	$103.1	$26.4	3.92	100.0	25.5
1930	90.4	25.3	3.57	91.1	28.0
1931	75.8	23.3	3.25	82.9	30.8
1932	58.0	20.8	2.79	71.2	35.8
1933	55.6	19.8	2.81	71.7	35.6
1934	65.1	21.4	3.04	77.6	32.9
1935	72.2	25.1	2.88	73.5	34.7
1936	82.5	29.0	2.84	72.4	35.2
1937	90.4	30.4	2.97	75.8	33.7
1938	84.7	30.4	2.79	71.2	35.8
1939	90.5	33.8	2.68	68.4	37.3
1940	99.7	39.1	2.55	65.1	39.2
1941	125.5	45.4	2.76	70.4	36.2

Sources: GNP data from U. S. Department of Commerce, *The National Income and Product Accounts of the United States, 1929–1965*, p. 2. The money supply figures were calculated from data in Board of Governors of the Federal Reserve System, *Banking and Monetary Statistics, 1943*, pp. 34–35. Money supply is currency plus demand deposits adjusted. The money supply for a year is the average of beginning of year, midyear, and end of year amounts.

period of prosperity, both individuals and institutions shifted their demands toward safer and more liquid assets, including not only money itself but also earning assets of the safest and most liquid types.

■ LESSONS FROM THIS MONETARY EXPERIENCE   This experience with monetary policies from 1933 to 1941 raises at least two questions: What can we learn from this experience concerning the efficacy of monetary policy as an instrument for combating depressions and inducing economic recovery? Why did the monetary policies of 1933–1941 fail to induce a complete and self-sustaining recovery before 1941?

This episode can shed no light on the ability of aggressively expansionary monetary actions undertaken soon after the onset of recession to restore recovery. No such aggressively expansionary actions were taken until after more than four years of grinding deflation had damaged seriously every sector of the economic and financial system and had created conditions highly unfavorable to monetary policy.

It is impossible to isolate the effects of New Deal monetary policies, largely because so many and such diverse actions of other types were taken by the Roosevelt Administrations. However, we can point to some of the reasons why the New Deal monetary policies were not accompanied by a full and self-sustaining recovery. For this purpose, the longer period will be divided into three subperiods: (1) March 4, 1933, to the onset of the recession in the spring of 1937, (2) the 1937–1938 recession, and (3) the years 1939–1941.

Because it set back recovery so seriously, the 1937–1938 recession will be examined first. The recession phase lasted only about a year—from the spring of 1937 to the spring of 1938. However, recovery was slow, and it was not until the autumn of 1939 that industrial production again reached the levels achieved in late 1936 and early 1937. Thus, this "depression within a depression" set back recovery at least two years. If mistakes in monetary and fiscal policies did not precipitate the recession, they certainly contributed to its severity and duration. The sharp decrease of federal expenditures and increase of taxes were strongly deflationary, and the Federal Reserve's increase of reserve requirements was a major factor in raising interest rates and inducing decreases in the supplies of money and bank credit.

These policies were reversed only after a considerable delay. Federal fiscal policies again became more expansionary only after April 1938. Bank reserves were increased about $300 million in September 1937 when the Treasury, at the request of the Federal Reserve, desterilized the amount of gold, but strongly expansionary monetary actions were not taken until April 1938, when the Federal Reserve reduced reserve requirements and the Treasury began to desterilize its holdings of inactive gold and ceased to sterilize further gold imports.

With the benefit of hindsight, it is not difficult to understand why recovery was slow and inadequate during the first four years following March 1933. Almost all economic and financial conditions at the beginning of this period were adverse to a quick recovery and to the ability of monetary policy to induce a quick increase of financial flows and of spendings for output. Widespread excess capacity in housing and in plants and equipment militated against an early recovery of private investment. The financial distress of farmers, homeowners, and business firms reduced both their willingness to spend for investment and their ability to command funds on reasonable terms, if at all. Financial intermediaries, after their losses and traumatic experiences of the preceding three years, were hardly in a position or mood to provide large amounts of new loans. Some degree of financial rehabilitation was a necessary precondition for a full recovery of financial flows.

The process of financial rehabilitation was slow and time-consuming. It began in 1933, accelerated in 1934, and did not approach completion until after the middle of 1935, at the earliest. Even then, it provided only inadequate financial assistance to a very important class of spenders for investment purposes—business firms, and especially small and middle-size firms that had been damaged so seriously.

Such conditions would have been a drag on recovery even if strongly expansionary fiscal and monetary policies had been initiated soon after Roosevelt assumed office. But they were not. We have already seen that federal fiscal policies made large net contributions to aggregate demands only in 1936, and that fiscal policies of state and local governments were less supportive than they had been in earlier years. The adoption of strongly and broadly expansionary monetary policies were delayed until 1934. The gold policies of 1933 did lower the exchange rate on the dollar and served to raise the dollar prices of imports and exports. However, they added nothing to bank reserves, and thus exerted no pressures on the banking system to expand bank credit and the money supply.

The reserve positions of the banks were improved during 1933 by inflows of currency following the reopening of banks and by Federal Reserve purchases of $595 million of government securities. By December, banks had accumulated $766 million of excess reserves and had reduced their borrowings at the Federal Reserve to $117 million. However, in view of the continued illiquidity of many other bank assets, the weak solvency positions of many banks, and their recent traumatic experiences, it seems likely that banks wished to hold at least this amount of excess reserves for liquidity purposes and that most banks felt under no pressure to expand their loans and investments. Not until after January 1934, when the golden avalanche began and the Treasury started to buy silver at an increasing rate, were additions to bank reserves and excess reserves very large. By mid-1934, excess reserves had risen above $1.6 billion. It was probably not until about this time, or not much earlier, that the process of financial rehabilitation had progressed far enough and excess reserves had become large enough to make banks and other financial intermediaries more receptive to expansion of their loans and investments, although many were still unwilling to assume much risk or to make illiquid types of loans.

The economic recovery was still far from complete, but it had made great progress by late 1936. It might well have continued if the mistakes in fiscal and monetary policies had not occurred in early 1937.

Little more need be said about the period 1939–1941. We have already noted that the recession of 1937–1938 reached its nadir in the spring of 1938 but that industrial production again reached its levels of early 1937 only in the autumn of 1939. This recovery was undoubtedly aided by the more expansionary monetary and fiscal policies adopted in April 1938. Recovery continued, although at a slow rate, from the autumn of 1939 until the spring of 1940, when rising exports and the initiation of an expanding rearmament program accelerated it.

Perhaps another lesson can be drawn from this experience: If you are going to use monetary policy as a recovery device, don't wait until years of depression and deflation have nearly wrecked the economy.

11

Relief of the Unemployed

Accumulated needs for relief were huge by March 1933. At least 13 million members of the labor force who were able and willing to work were wholly unemployed, and millions more were only partially employed. Great numbers who had been without work for a long period or had been unemployed several times had exhausted their resources and their borrowing power. Many local governmental units, especially those in areas where unemployment rates were highest, were providing only pitifully small amounts of relief and were in financial difficulty. Aid from state governments was still quite small in relation to needs. And the unemployed were not the only ones in distress. As the large number of unemployed forced authorities to look into the situation, others in distress became visible, including the blind, disabled, and other unemployables; the indigent aged; broken families; dispossessed farm tenants; farmers who had lost their farms; small businessmen who had gone into bankruptcy.

Some sort of greatly expanded program for relief was clearly needed, and needed quickly. One requirement was much more money, and a large part of it would have to come from the federal government, at least in the short run. Another requirement was a large expansion of administrative facilities to handle an expanded relief program, no matter what shape that program might take. The federal government had no such facilities when Roosevelt assumed office. It had no agency whose specific function was to formulate and administer relief programs. Its only activities in this field before March 1933 had been a public works program of modest size, gifts of wheat and cotton by the Federal Farm Board to the Red Cross for drought and general relief, and modest RFC loans to state governments for relief and work relief. These required only a minimum of administrative facilities.

The President could, of course, call upon the regular departments of the executive branch—the departments of War, Navy, Interior, Agriculture, Commerce, and Labor. These were used to some extent. However, the Washington staffs of these departments were at that time very small and did not include the types of trained personnel required for relief programs. Also, they lacked the widespread field organization that would be needed.

189

Administrative capabilities were somewhat better in state and local governments. At the very least, these provided nationwide offices through which
relief could be administered. In both size and quality of personnel, these
state and local relief agencies varied from quite good to very bad. Some
were not free of graft and political corruption. But good or bad, these
agencies already existed and quick action was imperative.

Thus, the desire for quick action was one reason for using state and
local relief agencies even if most of the additional money came from the
federal government. Another reason was the persistent view that relief was
primarily a responsibility of local and state governments, even if they had
to ask the federal government for financial assistance. Roosevelt was willing,
even anxious, to help; but he made it clear from the beginning that the
federal government would not bear the whole burden, that the effort
should be a cooperative one, and that state and local governments should
bear their "fair share." On signing the Federal Emergency Relief Act on
May 12, 1933, he stated:

> I want to make it very clear to citizens in every community that the
> Bill I have just signed, authorizing an appropriation of $500,000,000 of
> Federal funds for unemployment relief, does not absolve States and local
> communities of their responsibility to see that the necessities of life are
> assured their citizens who are in destitute circumstances.
>
> The Bill in effect is a challenge to Governors, legislatures, and local
> officials to stimulate their own efforts to provide for their own citizens
> in need.
>
> For these and other good reasons citizens who are able should voluntarily
> contribute to the pressing needs of welfare services. . . .
>
> The principle which I have on many occasions explained is that the
> first obligation is on the locality; if it is absolutely clear that the locality has
> done its utmost but that more must be done, then the State must do its ut-
> most. Only then can the Federal Government add its contribution to those
> of the locality and the State.[1]

If the relief program was to be a cooperative venture of federal, state,
and local governments, and if the federal government was to reduce its role
as this became feasible and desirable, it was reasonable to rely heavily on
state and local administrative facilities. However, this did not mean that no
expansion of federal supervisory and administrative capacities in this field
was required. For one thing, some parts of the relief program were to be
administered at the federal level. Also, the federal government could
hardly be expected to supply very large amounts of money without any
supervision or control of the nature and adequacy of programs or of the
efficiency and honesty of their administration. These overlapping relationships inevitably led to intergovernmental conflicts and controversies, many
of which involved Harry L. Hopkins, Roosevelt's number-one man in the
relief field.

[1] *The Public Papers and Addresses of Franklin D. Roosevelt*, Vol. 2, Random House,
New York, 1938, pp. 183–184.

Roosevelt was fortunate to have Hopkins in this important post. After graduating from Grinnell College, Hopkins went to New York City, where he became a prominent social worker and headed several important welfare agencies in the 1920s. Governor Roosevelt appointed him as head of the New York Temporary Relief Administration in 1932, and in May 1933 took him to Washington as Administrator of the newly established Federal Emergency Relief Administration (FERA). He also headed other organizations in the field, such as the Civil Works Administration (CWA) and the Works Progress Administration (WPA), and he was the most influential man in the Administration in the broad fields of social welfare and social insurance. He became almost as widely known and as controversial as Roosevelt himself. Hopkins had extraordinary qualifications for such work. He was passionately humanitarian, determined that the needs of the destitute should be met, and met adequately. In pursuing this goal, he was hard-boiled, hard-driving, and even ruthless. He was completely honest and determined that his program should not be blemished by graft and corruption or used for partisan political purposes. Some questioned his administrative ability, but he created a high morale in his organization. He was not fully successful in preventing graft, corruption, and use of funds for political purposes, but he tried.[2]

■ **THE STRATEGY AND TACTICS OF RELIEF**   The distress of the unemployed could be remedied or ameliorated in two major ways: by increasing employment in the government and in private industry, and by providing relief without work to those who remained unemployed. Almost everyone agreed that the best ultimate solution was to provide full employment, with most of the increased jobs in private industry. However, this would take time—how much time was not then appreciated. In the meantime, the government faced difficult and controversial issues in determining the strategy and tactics of its relief program. Decisions were made more difficult by severe budget restraints; neither the federal government nor all governmental units together were willing to provide enough money to do all that needed to be done. All therefore wanted "to get the most for the dollar." However, there were wide disagreements as to how this could be done, partly because of differences in answers to the question, "The most of what?" To cast light on these differences, let us examine briefly three major types of aid—direct relief, public works of types emphasizing the economic value of the project itself, and work relief.

■ **Direct Relief**   Direct relief refers to direct payments of money or goods to the needy without requiring work in return. It had several merits.

---

[2] For an excellent study of Hopkins and of many aspects of the New Deal relief programs, see Searle F. Charles, *Minister of Relief: Harry Hopkins and the Depression*, Syracuse University Press, Syracuse, N.Y., 1963. For Hopkins' own views, see his *Spending to Save*, Norton, New York, 1936.

It was the fastest way of channeling aid to the neediest. It required no planning and start-up time for projects, and it could begin as soon as applicants were screened. It was the cheapest way of relieving the neediest; grants could be tailored to the needs of recipients. It was also a quick method of initiating an increase of aggregate demands for output. In effect, millions of relief recipients could act as spending agents throughout the country, increasing demands for a wide range of goods and services.

However, direct relief also had its severe critics. Some still claimed that it would destroy the will to work and create an army of loafers. For somewhat different reasons, both Roosevelt and Hopkins were adamantly opposed to direct relief except as a temporary expedient. This method of aid failed to promote two of their important objectives: to restore and maintain the self-respect of recipients, and to preserve, utilize, and develop their skills and capabilities. For these purposes, some sort of work should be required, preferably types of work for which the recipients were best qualified by ability, training, and experience.

In actuality, the federal government itself provided only limited amounts of direct relief. (See Table 11–1.) It did make large grants for this purpose to states and local governments during the years 1933–1935, but in 1935 it returned primary responsibility for this type of assistance back to the lower levels of government. The great bulk of federal aid was in the form of expenditures for public works and work relief.

Table 11–1.   Direct relief payments to persons by all U. S. governmental units, 1929–1941 (in millions of dollars)

YEAR	DIRECT RELIEF BY FEDERAL GOVERNMENT	DIRECT RELIEF BY STATE AND LOCAL GOVERNMENTS	TOTAL OF DIRECT RELIEF	TOTAL FEDERAL GRANTS-IN-AID TO STATE AND LOCAL GOVERNMENTS[a]
1929	—	$ 71	$ 71	$ 117
1930	—	105	105	125
1931	—	176	176	313
1932	—	317	317	134
1933	—	558	558	502
1934	—	745	745	1,633
1935	$ 2	954	956	1,706
1936	20	635	655	724
1937	36	787	823	764
1938	23	965	988	778
1939	22	1,024	1,046	988
1940	63	1,013	1,076	857
1941	137	985	1,122	807

[a] These data show total federal grants-in-aid to state and local governments, not just grants-in-aid for relief purposes.

Source: U. S. Department of Commerce, The National Income and Product Accounts of the United States, 1929–1965, pp. 54 and 58.

■ **Public Works Programs and Work Relief**   Another tool for relieving the unemployed and for raising aggregate demands was a public works program in which the emphasis was on the economic value of each project. The chief proponent within the Administration of this type of public works program was Harold L. Ickes, Secretary of the Interior and head of the Public Works Administration (PWA), which was established in the summer of 1933. An honest, sensitive, prickly, and combative man, Ickes was a self-styled "curmudgeon" and widely referred to as "Honest Harold." He believed that in choosing projects, the primary emphasis should be on the economic values of the projects themselves, that each should be constructed at minimum cost, and that waste of money should be avoided even at the cost of delays. He objected to requirements that those employed on public works projects should be taken from the relief rolls or from among the unemployed who were not on relief, and he wanted to hire those who could do the job most cheaply. He also wanted to be free to use relatively large amounts of capital equipment and materials relative to labor where that would reduce the money costs of projects.

This type of public works program certainly had its merits, and it appealed especially to those who wanted "to get the most for the dollar" in terms of the economic values of the specific projects. However, it had serious shortcomings as an instrument for putting dollars into the pockets of the unemployed and for increasing quickly total demands for output. It was by far the most expensive way of providing direct employment, because such a large percentage of government expenditures went for materials and for purchases or rentals of equipment. Ickes properly replied that critics should take into account not only direct employment on the projects but also the income and employment created in industries supplying materials and equipment for the projects.

However, there were at least two shortcomings that Ickes could not argue away and that Hopkins emphasized repeatedly. One was that such projects were slow to get under way and required time to reach their peak of activity. Many of the projects were large-scale, involving such things as highway construction, dams, large public buildings, and harbor improvements. There was no adequate shelf of preplanned projects on which preliminary work had been completed. Thus, time was required to acquire, clear, and prepare sites; to draw plans and let contracts; and to reach the stage of large-scale employment. Ickes might be willing to countenance such delays in raising employment, but Hopkins and many others were not. Moreover, public works projects of this type could not provide appropriate employment for many types of the unemployed. In view of the extremely depressed state of private construction, there was certainly need to provide employment opportunities for those with previous experience in this industry and for others who would normally enter it. But great numbers of the unemployed had no previous experience in these types of work, had little or no desire to enter the field, had experience in other lines, and aspired to work in quite different types of occupations and professions. Among these were teachers, librarians, accountants, lawyers, doctors, nurses, scientists, artists, musicians, actors, writers, and many others.

Roosevelt and Hopkins also wanted projects with high economic value and were strongly opposed to "boondoggles" with little inherent value, but for them the economic value of a project itself was only one of several values to be maximized within a budget constraint. They also valued highly the quickness with which employment could be provided, the fraction of each dollar of expenditures going to the unemployed, and the preservation and development of the abilities and skills of those employed on projects.

Many projects of the types favored by Ickes were adopted. The PWA began in June 1933 and was continued with various amendments to mid-1941. During this period it made grants and loans aggregating about $2.5 billion. In the end, however, Hopkins' views largely prevailed over those of Ickes. For example, the number of workers employed directly on regular government construction projects rose to a peak of 741,000 in mid-1936 and then declined, while the number employed on work projects under Hopkins reached a peak of 4,855,000 in early 1934 and was well above 2,000,000 during most of the following period.

■ OUTLINE OF THE RELIEF AND WORK RELIEF PROGRAMS

Volumes could be written about the numerous and widely differing measures taken to provide for the unemployed and others in distress, the various shifts in policy emphases, the many changes in administrative arrangements, and the successes and failures of the measures. Our purpose here is the much more modest one of providing an outline of the most important aspects of the programs.

Large numbers of families and persons were aided by the public assistance and federal work programs. Since some received aid from more than one program, it is difficult to arrive at totals without duplications. However, estimates of unduplicated totals are given in Table 11–2. In February 1933, about 4,764,000 households with 18,648,000 members were receiving public assistance or work relief, or both. By early 1934, these numbers had increased to more than 7,900,000 and 28,000,000 respectively. At this stage, about 20 percent of the American people were in households receiving some type of aid. This was the peak. By September 1937, the number of households receiving aid had fallen to 4,483,000, and the number of their members to 13,346,000. The recession of 1937–1938 raised these numbers about 60 percent by the end of 1938, after which they again declined. However, in mid-1941, some sort of aid was still being provided to 4,691,-000 households with 12,375,000 members. We do not know how many different households and persons received aid at one time or another during the period.

It should be noted that "the number of cases of assistance" shown in Table 11–2 includes not only general assistance but also cases of special types of assistance, such as old-age assistance, aid to dependent children,

Table 11–2.   Public assistance and federal work programs:
recipients of assistance and persons employed in the continental
United States, selected months, 1933–1941 (in thousands of
households, cases, and recipients)

YEAR AND MONTH	ESTIMATED UNDUPLICATED TOTALS OF			PERSONS EMPLOYED UNDER FEDERAL WORKS PROGRAMS				
	HOUSE-HOLDS	MEMBERS IN THESE HOUSE HOLDS	NUMBER OF CASES OF AS-SISTANCE	TOTAL	CCC	NYA	CWA AND WPA	OTHER FEDERAL AGENCY PROJECTS FI-NANCED FROM EMERGENCY FUNDS
1933								
February	4,764	18,648	5,045	—	—	—	—	—
October	4,234	16,072	4,233	222	222	—	—	—
1934								
January	7,974	28,093	3,801	4,855	297		4,311	247
February	7,975	28,095	3,983	4,396	293		3,854	249
May	5,825	21,255	5,472	757	284		23	450
1935								
July	6,137	21,669	5,855	790	401			389
August	6,128	21,468	5,648	1,105	481		220	404
1936								
June	5,427	18,195	2,863	3,772	336	409	2,286	741
1937								
September	4,483	13,346	3,583	2,159	233	163	1,454	309
1938								
December	6,954	21,286	5,053	4,210	275	612	3,156	167
1939								
June	6,363	18,761	4,606	3,576	266	494	2,570	246
1940								
June	5,371	15,089	4,572	2,636	240	582	1,735	79
1941								
June	4,691	12,375	4,548	2,321	195	741	1,376	9

Key: CCC = Civilian Conservation Corps.
NYA = National Youth Administration.
CWA = Civil Works Administration. (This operated from November 1933 to the spring of 1934.)
WPA = Works Progress Administration. (This operated after the summer of 1935.)

Sources: Social Security Board, *Social Security Bulletin,* February 1941, pp. 68–70, and April 1942, pp. 28–29. For descriptions of the data, see *Social Security Bulletin,* September 1941, pp. 50–52. Persons employed on federal work programs exclude those on regular federal construction programs.

and aid to the blind. Before 1936, the great majority of these cases were receiving "general assistance," mostly unemployment relief. (See Table 11–3.) However, these dropped sharply after 1935, for two principal

Table 11–3.   Numbers of cases of government assistance, selected months, 1933–1941 (in thousands of cases)

| | | | | | SPECIAL TYPES OF ASSISTANCE | | |
YEAR AND MONTH	TOTAL	CASES RE-CEIVING GENERAL ASSIST-ANCE	CASES AIDED UNDER SPECIAL FERA PRO-GRAMS	CASES CERTIFIED BY FARM SECURITY ADMIN-ISTRATION	OLD-AGE ASSIST-ANCE	AID TO DEPEND-ENT CHILDREN	AID TO THE BLIND
1933							
February	5,045	4,512	—	—	116	392	25
October	4,231	3,647	67	—	104	388	25
1934							
January	3,801	3,135	131	—	123	385	27
February	3,983	3,284	169	—	123	381	26
May	5,472	4,636	297	—	128	385	26
1935							
July	5,855	4,663	471	—	302	385	34
August	5,648	4,515	401	—	314	385	33
1936							
June	2,863	1,556	11	62	650	540	44
1937							
September	3,583	1,270	—	67	1,467	727	52
1938							
December	5,053	1,631	—	115	1,776	1,464	67
1939							
June	4,606	1,568	—	69	1,842	1,059	68
1940							
June	4,632	1,354	—	60	1,969	1,177	72
1941							
June	4,548	934	—	40	2,167	1,333	74

Key: CCC = Civilian Conservation Corps.
   NYA = National Youth Administration.
   CWA = Civil Works Administration. (This operated from November 1933 to the spring of 1934.)
   WPA = Works Progress Administration. (This operated after the summer of 1935.)

Sources: Social Security Board, Social Security Bulletin, February 1941, pp. 68–70, and April 1942, pp. 28–29. For descriptions of the data, see Social Security Bulletin, September 1941, pp. 50–52. Persons employed on federal work programs exclude those on regular federal construction programs.

reasons. First, many of those who would otherwise have received general assistance were helped by new federally sponsored types of special assistance, especially by old-age assistance and aid to dependent children. Second, employment in federal work programs became the major method of aiding the unemployed.

Certain other patterns are worth noting. (1) Direct relief payments were made mostly by state and local governments, with only small amounts by the federal government. (See Table 11–1, page 192.) The latter made large grants-in-aid to lower levels of government for this purpose prior to 1936, but it discontinued such grants after 1935, turned the burden of providing direct relief of the unemployed employable back to the states, and concentrated on federal work programs. (2) The relative roles of the federal government and of lower levels of government in providing work relief changed sharply in 1935. (See Table 11–4.) State and local govern-

Table 11–4.   Average number of full-time and part-time
government employees on work relief (thousands of persons)

YEAR	FEDERAL	STATE AND LOCAL	TOTAL
1929	—	—	—
1930	—	20	20
1931	—	299	299
1932	—	592	592
1933	471	1,724	2,195
1934	1,140	1,834	2,974
1935	990	2,097	3,087
1936	3,653	91	3,744
1937	2,707	56	2,763
1938	3,572	19	3,591
1939	3,216	39	3,255
1940	2,792	38	2,830
1941	2,192	17	2,209

Source: U. S. Department of Commerce, *The National Income and Product Accounts of the United States, 1929–1965*, p. 98.

ments provided well over half of the work relief in the earlier period, although much of this was financed by federal grants. However, almost all work relief was provided by the federal government after 1935. (3) Two agencies provided by far the largest amounts of employment on federal work projects—the Civil Works Administration (CWA) and the Works Progress Administration (WPA). (See Table 11–2, page 195.) The CWA was established by executive order in November 1933 for the purpose of providing 4 million jobs during the winter. It was employing 4,311,000 people in January 1934, after which time it began to phase out and then discontinued operations in the spring of 1934. The WPA began operations in August 1935 and continued into the war period. At its peak in November 1934, it employed 3,330,000 persons, and at no time prior to 1941 did it employ less than 1,454,000. Some of the smaller work programs will be discussed later.

Let us now look at the most important of the specific programs.

■ **The Federal Emergency Relief Administration**   The Federal Emergency Relief Act was enacted on May 12, 1933, and Roosevelt established on May 22 the Federal Emergency Relief Administration (FERA) with Hopkins as administrator. The FERA continued into the war period, although with many changes in programs and policies. It was given an initial appropriation of $500 million to be allocated to the states on a grant-in-aid basis. One-half of these funds was to be allocated on a 1 to 3 matching basis; that is, $1 of FERA money was made available for each $3 of public money, from whatever source, spent on direct or work relief. The other half, or $250 million, was to be used by Hopkins at his discretion to make grants to states where the matching requirement would make it impossible to meet relief needs.

This discretionary power was both a help to Hopkins and a source of trouble for him. On the one hand, this power enabled him to withhold funds, or to threaten to do so, if states failed to contribute their share or did not conform to standards set by the FERA. On the other hand, this power and the fact that both the initial appropriation and subsequent additions were far too small to meet all needs meant that Hopkins was put under tremendous pressure to grant more to each state.

Almost inevitably under the circumstances, there were many controversies between the FERA and the states. Some related to the sharing of costs. As already noted, both Roosevelt and Hopkins were determined that the states should increase their contributions as much as possible. However, many states delayed and objected, making all sorts of excuses —lack of constitutional power, necessary delays until the next meeting of the legislature, financial distress, excessive tax burdens, and so on. Hopkins fought back, threatening to withhold funds and actually doing so in some cases, and informing the people in recalcitrant states that the blame for their lack of relief was on their state governments, not the FERA. However, his bargaining power was reduced by the fact that Hopkins knew, and state governments knew that he knew, that to withhold funds meant hardships for the unemployed.

There were also major controversies over the adequacy of relief payments and the fairness of their distributions among the various classes in a community. The average size of relief benefits in many states was far below what Hopkins considered a minimum level of adequacy. (See Table 11–5.) Average benefits also differed greatly from state to state and even among communities within a state. Moreover, a number of states and communities discriminated against some classes of the unemployed, notably nonwhites and foreign-born. Hopkins fought against these shortcomings, but with only limited success.

Table 11–5. Average monthly relief benefits per family

	MAY 1933	MAY 1934	MAY 1935
Average for all states	$15.15	$24.53	$29.33
Some states with lowest benefits			
Mississippi	3.86	11.04	15.23
New Mexico	3.98	19.01	12.32
Oklahoma	4.51	10.05	11.75
Arkansas	4.55	13.29	16.00
Georgia	5.27	14.58	17.16
Florida	5.81	11.71	14.02
Some states with highest benefits			
New York	33.32	45.12	46.91
Massachusetts	31.58	43.61	49.48
Maine	27.12	38.61	34.59
Maryland	27.06	33.70	30.04

Source: Monthly Report of the FERA, February 1936, p. 8. The families used in obtaining these averages include not only those receiving relief throughout the month but also those receiving relief during only part of the period. Thus the averages understate to some extent the average benefits to families wholly dependent on relief.

FERA supervision over the efficiency and honesty of state and local administrators brought further friction. This was especially true in areas where funds were used for partisan political purposes or to support factions within a party.

Most dismaying of all was the slowness of this cooperative program with the states. In October 1933, the number of cases receiving relief was actually somewhat below the level in March. This was partly because employment had risen somewhat, but there were clearly millions of unemployed persons who needed relief of some sort and were not getting it.[3] This was one of the major reasons, but not the only one, for creating the CWA.

■ The Civil Works Administration   The Civil Works Administration (CWA) was established by executive order on November 9, 1933, with Hopkins as its administrator. This was the first of the big federal work projects. Its major purpose was to provide jobs on economically and socially desirable projects during the winter for 4 million of the unemployed and to increase purchasing power. As already indicated, the program reached its peak in January 1934, when it was employing 4,311,000 persons, and then tapered off and was discontinued in the spring. During this period, it spent about $950 million, of which more than 75 percent was in wages.

[3] For amounts of direct relief payments and numbers of families and members of those families receiving assistance, see Tables 11–1 and 11–2 (pages 192 and 195).

The CWA program differed in important ways from the cooperative federal-state relief program then in effect. For one thing, it was a federal program administered by federal officials in Washington and in the numerous state and local offices established to expedite the program. When state and local officials and employees were used, as they often were, they were sworn in as federal employees. However, the CWA cooperated with state and local governments, as well as other federal agencies, in selecting projects. Also, the philosophy of the CWA work program was quite different from that of work relief under the cooperative program of the FERA and lower governmental units. In the latter, the emphasis in work relief was on "relief." Recipients had to apply for relief, submit to a needs test, and establish the amounts of aid needed. Then they were permitted to earn on work relief only the amount required to cover the deficit between their other income and their minimum budget needs. In contrast, the CWA provided jobs without reference to any needs test. It is true that only the unemployed were eligible for CWA jobs. About one-half of those hired were previously on relief, and the others were unemployed persons not on relief. However, those who were hired received "regular" wages and worked "regular" hours without regard to the number of members in their families or the size of their budget deficits.

Wage policies of the CWA and of other federal work projects became highly controversial. Some insisted that wages paid on these projects should be below prevailing levels in the various areas of the country to save money and also to encourage workers to seek employment in private industry. Others replied that such lower wages would yield only inadequate incomes to those employed and would serve to depress wage rates in the private sectors. In general, the policy became that of paying prevailing wage rates in the various areas except where these were below stated minimum levels. The CWA also established maximum hours of work. At the beginning these were 8 hours a day and 30 hours a week for manual labor, and 8 hours a day and 39 hours a week for clerical workers. However, when it became apparent that CWA funds were inadequate, maximum hours were reduced on Jan. 18, 1934, to 24 hours a week in urban areas and 15 hours a week in country areas. Table 11–6 indicates the approximate

Table 11–6. Average weekly earnings of workers on the Civil Works Program

	WEEK ENDING JAN. 11, 1934	WEEK ENDING FEB. 1, 1934
All workers	$15.18	$10.95
Skilled and unskilled labor	14.57	10.23
Drivers of their own teams and trucks	21.39	14.67
Professional, clerical, and administrative	20.11	17.94

Source: Works Progress Administration, *Analysis of Civil Works Program Statistics*, 1939, p. 20.

weekly earnings of various classes of CWA workers before and after the reduction of hours.

Table 11–7 suggests the broad range of projects undertaken by the

Table 11–7.   Percentage distribution of Civil Works Program costs, by type of project

TYPE OF PROJECT	PERCENT
Highways, roads and streets	33.8
Public buildings	14.9
Sanitation and drainage	9.8
Waterworks and other facilities	2.9
Recreational facilities	3.1
Waterways and flood control	4.1
Erosion control and parks	11.3
Airports and airways	1.4
Other construction	4.6
Goods	1.2
Public welfare and health	3.0
Public education, arts and research	5.9
Administration	4.0
Total	100.0

Source: Works Progress Administration, *Analysis of Civil Works Program Statistics,* 1939, p. 27.

CWA. Although Hopkins emphasized the amount of employment and purchasing power created by CWA, he was proud of the social usefulness of the projects themselves. Among those he listed were 250,000 miles of new and improved roads; bridges; repair of 40,000 schools; drainage of hundreds of thousands of acres of malarial lands; destruction of millions of rats and ticks; 150,000 sanitary privies; 200 swimming pools; 3,700 playgrounds; new hospitals; athletic stadiums; airports; and public buildings.[4]

To appreciate the full range of the types of work provided at that time, one must consider not only the work programs of the CWA but also others, most of which were administered by the FERA. For example, the Civil Works Service Program, established in the fall of 1933, provided work for a wide variety of nonmanual labor. Among these were artists, painters, sculptors, etchers, and mural painters; archeologists; historians; and musicians. The Emergency Education Program begun in October 1933 provided jobs for thousands of unemployed teachers, who served in adult education, vocational education and rehabilitation, and nursery schools for underprivileged children. A Women's Work Program, also established in October 1933, provided employment in sewing clothes, making bedding, canning food, nursing, teaching, research, and making statisti-

4 Hopkins, *Spending to Save, op. cit.* pp. 120–125.

cal surveys. Most of these projects were continued after the end of CWA.

When the CWA was discontinued in the spring of 1934, it was succeeded by the Emergency Work Relief Program (EWRP). This was
administered as a division of the FERA and continued until it was superseded by the WPA in late 1935. We shall not deal with it in detail, noting
only that: (1) It provided fewer jobs than the CWA had done. At its
peak in January 1935, it employed 2,444,000 workers. (2) Its policies continued, in general, to conform to Hopkins' views on work programs. And
(3) it continued to provide a wide variety of jobs to white-collar and professional workers, as well as to manual workers.

The FERA also provided relief for other special groups of the destitute.
One group, which we shall discuss more fully in connection with farm
relief, were destitute farmers. These were aided in many ways, including
relief in the form of goods and cash payments, loans for seeds and other
necessary farm supplies, and relocation on better land. Another special
group were the transients, who included not only people roaming about
the country but also others who had been residents in a state for less than
one year. Many states and localities were unwilling to provide relief for
transients. For this reason, and also because many communities were
afraid of them, especially if they were members of minority groups, transients were virtually forced to keep on the move. The FERA supplied special relief, primarily work relief, for transients, and established 250 work
camps for them. More than 300,000 persons were aided under this program.

■ **The Civilian Conservation Corps**   The establishment of the Civilian
Conservation Corps (CCC) by executive order on April 5, 1933, was
largely in response to the sad plight of many young people, which was
described earlier in this book—the heavy impact of unemployment on the
young, their lack of opportunity to develop skills, rising unhappiness and
dissent among them, and the large number of young nomads roaming the
country. The CCC had two major purposes: to conserve the nation's
natural resources, and to conserve and develop young men physically and
psychologically. For this purpose, CCC camps were established throughout
the country, especially in forests and national parks.

Some 1,600 camps had been established by July 1933, and the total rose
to 2,650 in 1935. These camps were supervised by military officers, but
many of the instructors and experts were supplied by the departments of
Interior, Agriculture, and Labor. The number of young men in these
camps reached 222,000 by October 1933 and rose to a peak of more than
480,000 in August 1935. At no time prior to 1941 did the number fall
below 233,000. (See Table 11–2, page 195.)

Members of the CCC did many types of work: building and repairing
roads and paths in forests and national parks, cleaning out dead trees and
underbrush, constructing fire breaks, planting new trees, and so on. The
CCC was often criticized on several bases—because the camps resembled
military camps too much, because their educational programs were inade-

quate, and because some of the men were allegedly subversive. However, this was probably the most widely approved part of the New Deal's program for relief and rehabilitation. Most Americans liked the idea of taking young men out of idleness or worse and restoring their health, strength, and morale through useful work in the great outdoors.

■1935—YEAR OF CHANGE   The year 1935 brought very important changes in the federal government's welfare and social security programs. For one thing, as we shall see later, it was the year in which the government moved toward the establishment of social insurance systems. Also, as we have already noted, it was the year in which Roosevelt became determined to "take the federal government out of the general relief business" and to return to state and local governments the burden of supplying relief to the employable unemployed. The efforts of the federal government thereafter were largely concentrated on providing employment on work projects and on providing assistance to certain special groups, such as the aged, dependent children, and the blind.

The formulation of a new federal work program brought sharp conflicts between Hopkins and Ickes. These reflected in part a power struggle between the two men, but also conflicting views concerning the nature and purposes of new projects. Hopkins won, although only after a considerable time. After the Works Progress Administration (WPA) was established by executive order on May 6, 1935, Hopkins was named as administrator, while retaining his position as head of the FERA. The number employed on WPA projects is shown in Table 11–2 (page 195). Starting at 220,000 in August 1935, the number rose to 3,019,000 in February 1936, declined to 1,454,000 by September 1937, rose again to 3,330,000 by November 1938, and declined thereafter. However, not until 1941 did the number fall below 1,639,000. From its inception through mid-1943, the WPA provided 13,686,000 man-years of employment.[5]

In a "fireside chat" on April 28, 1935, Roosevelt outlined six fundamental principles that would guide the new works program:

(1) The projects should be useful.
(2) Projects shall be of a nature that a considerable proportion of the money spent will go into wages for labor.
(3) Projects will be sought which promise ultimate return to the Federal Treasury of a considerable proportion of the costs.
(4) Funds allotted for each project should be actually and promptly spent and not held over until later years.
(5) In all cases projects must be of a character to give employment to those on relief rolls.
(6) Projects will be allocated to localities or relief areas in relation to the number of workers on relief rolls in those areas.[6]

[5] See WPA, *Final Report on the WPA Program*, 1946, p. 36. This report contains a wealth of information on the activities of the WPA.
[6] *The Public Papers and Addresses of Franklin D. Roosevelt, op. cit.,* Vol. 4. p 13⁵

These principles were quite general, not always mutually compatible, and left room for considerable discretion in the selection of projects. For our purposes, it is enough to say that the criteria actually employed were similar to those of the CWA, and that many of the controversies, including those relating to wage policies and to white-collar projects, were also similar.

About 75 percent of the jobs provided by the WPA were in engineering and construction; the remainder, reflecting the desire to provide employment opportunities for almost every class of the unemployed, were widely distributed. Table 11–8 suggests the wide variety of WPA projects, the

Table 11–8.   Some major types of WPA projects

TYPES OF PROJECTS	COMMENTS
Engineering and construction projects	
Municipal engineering projects	
New streets	67,000 miles
New sidewalks	24,000 miles
Water supply systems	
Sewage disposal systems	
Recreation	8,000 parks
Airports	
New airports	350
Enlarged or improved airports	700
Public buildings	
State, county, and city government buildings	
Hospitals	
Penal institutions	
Military and naval establishments	
Clearance for housing projects	
Highways and roads	
Improvement of rural roads	572,000 miles
Improvement of other secondary roads	
New bridges and viaducts	78,000
Conservation	
Water	
Mine sealing	
Erosion control	
Engineering surveys	
Geodetic	
Boundaries	
Underground structures	
Hydrographic	
Service projects	
Adult education	Literacy and citizenship classes, vocational training, parent and homemaking education, workers' education, correspondence courses

Table 11-8 (continued)

TYPES OF PROJECTS	COMMENTS
Nursery schools	Employed teachers, nurses, nutritionists, clerical workers, cooks, janitors. Provided not only education but also health inspection and medical services, meals, and play.

Library services
    Extension into rural areas
    Cataloging, indexing, books repair
Museum projects
Writers projects
Music projects
	Purposes: to establish high standards of musicianship, develop music appreciation, and rehabilitate and retrain musicians. Employed instrumentalists, vocalists, composers, teachers, tuners, arrangers, and so on.

Art projects	Projects included painting, murals, sculpture, etching, ceramics, and utilitarian art.
Theater projects	Employed not only actors, actresses, and dancers, but also playwrights, scene designers, and theater employees.

Research and records
    Social and economic surveys
    Housing inventories
    National health survey
Welfare projects
    Sewing
    Mattress making
    Braille books
    School lunches
    Gardening and canning	

Note: For further information on WPA service projects, see WPA, *Government Aid During the Depression to Professional, Clerical, Technical and Other Service Workers,* 1936.

many types of employment provided, and some of the tangible results of this work program.

The service projects of the WPA were widely criticized, especially those employing white-collar, artistic, and professional people. There was still a widespread feeling that such people should be able to take care of themselves. Moreover, some saw no lasting economic value in the products of such projects. There can be no doubt, however, that these not only relieved much distress but also served to preserve and develop the capabilities of hundreds of thousands of people.

■ **The National Youth Administration**   The National Youth Administration (NYA) was established by executive order in June 1935 and continued into the war period. Aubrey Williams, Assistant Administrator of the WPA, was appointed as its Executive Director. The NYA consolidated various types of assistance to youth under other programs and expanded the scope of aid. It provided two programs: an "out-of-school work program," and a "student work program." Those in the age group 18–24 were eligible for the out-of-school work program, although in some cases exceptions were made for those ages 16 and 17. Those accepted in this program worked on almost as wide a variety of projects as those under WPA, and received prevailing wage rates. It is estimated that about 1.8 million different youths were employed by the NYA out-of-school work program between the time of its inception and the end of 1941.[7] (See Table 11–9.)

Table 11–9. Persons employed on NYA work programs (in thousands)

OCTOBER OF	TOTAL	OUT-OF-SCHOOL WORK PROGRAM	STUDENT WORK PROGRAM
1935	184		184
1936	507	166	341
1937	367	123	244
1938	542	220	322
1939	600	238	362
1940	584	232	352
1941	561	288	273

Sources: Social Security Board, *Social Security Bulletin*, February 1941, pp. 68–70, and April 1942, pp. 28–29.

Students in the age group 16–24 were eligible for the student work program if they were in high school, college, or graduate work. The NYA granted money to educational institutions, which in turn provided students with enough work to cover their necessary expenses not met from other sources. Some 28,300 secondary schools and 1,700 colleges and universities participated in the program in the academic year 1939–1940. Average monthly earnings of students in the program during that academic year were $4.55 for high school students, $12.75 for college students, and $21.14 for graduate students. Nearly 2 million different students had been aided by the program by the end of 1941. There is no way of knowing how many students would have had to drop out of school in the absence of such assistance, but in view of the financial plight of many of their

[7] For further information, see NYA, *Final Report of the NYA, Fiscal Years 1936–1943*.

parents and the scarcity of private employment opportunities for the young, the number must be large.

■ **SOCIAL SECURITY**   Most of the types of assistance and work programs just discussed were considered temporary, to be discontinued when employment had been restored. However, one measure adopted in 1935 —the Social Security Act signed by Roosevelt on August 14—was meant to be permanent and is a landmark in the history of American social welfare policy. This Act marked the beginning of two of our most important social insurance programs—unemployment insurance and old-age insurance. It also committed the federal government on what has proved to be a permanent basis to cooperation with the states in providing special assistance to the needy aged, dependent children, and the blind.

Under the old-age assistance program, which was quite separate from old-age insurance, the federal government provided grants to the states to help them meet the cost of pensions allowed under state laws to old people in need of relief. Federal grants were to match amounts contributed by the states, with a maximum federal contribution of $15 per month for each individual plus a small amount for administrative costs. The plan for aiding the blind followed the same pattern. Grants for aid to dependent children were on the basis of $1 of federal money for each $2 spent by the states.

Proposals for the establishment of unemployment insurance by the various states were made long before the onset of the depression, and they became more numerous as the depression dragged on. However, all were defeated prior to 1935. There were many reasons for these defeats, but the most widely used argument was that any state that initiated such a program while other states did not would place its business firms at a competitive disadvantage with firms in other states. Unemployment insurance premiums would raise the costs incurred by firms and lead them to go out of business or to move to other states. There was a deadlock; no state would institute a plan until others had already acted.

The 1935 plan broke this deadlock by using the device of tax credits. The Act levied a federal tax on total payrolls of all employers (with some exceptions), initially 1 percent but rising to 3 percent after 1937, and allowed employers a credit of 90 percent against this tax for any contributions made by them to a state unemployment insurance fund that met standards set by the Social Security Board. Under this arrangement, state taxes up to 2.7 percent on payrolls for unemployment insurance made virtually no net additions to costs of employers. Thus, the Act did two things: It brought effective pressure for the establishment of state plans, and it secured substantial uniformity among the various state plans. At first, there were many exclusions from coverage and unemployment benefits were low. However, coverage was extended and benefits increased with the passage of time.

Proposals for state or federal old-age insurance programs also began before the onset of the depression, and they multiplied as the depression ground on and more of the aged became destitute. By the mid-1930s, radical proposals were widespread; the best known of these was the Townsend Plan, which was being supported by Townsend Clubs all over the country.

The old-age insurance plan adopted in 1935 was a federal plan to be administered by a federal trust fund. To finance the plan, equal taxes, based on payrolls, were levied on all employers and employees (with some exceptions). Each of these was to begin at 1 percent and rise gradually to 3 percent. On reaching age 65, those insured under the plan became eligible for old-age benefits. The initial plan was very limited in its coverage and in the amount of benefits provided. Since that time, the trend has been almost continuously toward broader coverage and larger benefits. Moreover, these unemployment and old-age insurance programs served as forerunners for other social insurance programs to come later.

■ CONCLUSIONS   The great depression brought sweeping and long-lasting changes in American social welfare policies. At the onset of the depression, neither the federal government nor state governments assumed any responsibility for relief of the unemployed. Local governments had no specific programs for unemployment relief—only general facilities for relieving those who were destitute for any reason and had exhausted their own resources and could not get sufficient help from their families or private charities. They relied largely on indoor, or institutional, relief. There was no governmental program of old-age insurance.

All this changed during the depression. Local governments changed the pattern of their aid programs and spent unprecedented amounts for relief. States amended their constitutions, enacted new laws, expanded their social welfare staffs, and increased greatly their relief expenditures. The federal government entered the field and spent billions to help millions of Americans. Once the old barriers had been so shattered, it would never again be possible to restore the old patterns of thinking about matters of relief. And the establishment of unemployment insurance and old-age insurance marked the beginning of broader social insurance programs. How much longer these would have been delayed in the absence of the great depression is a matter for conjecture.

12

Farm Relief

The New Deal adopted a wide variety of measures to relieve the economic plight of farmers. Several of these have already been discussed: readjustment and rehabilitation of farm debts and provision of more liberal and cheaper sources of agricultural credit; direct relief and work relief for some of the poorest farmers; reduction of the exchange rate on the dollar as a means of increasing directly the dollar prices of American exports and of import-competing goods, and especially of farm products; and measures to raise prices in general by increasing aggregate demands for output. This chapter will concentrate on New Deal measures directed specifically toward raising the money incomes of farmers by increasing the prices of their products. Many devices were used for this purpose: limitations of acreages or of output, or both; taxes on "surplus production"; marketing agreements to limit amounts offered for sale or to maintain stipulated levels of prices; government purchases of "surplus supplies"; nonrecourse loans to farmers on products at a "fair value"; benefit payments to farmers; and export subsidies.

The New Deal's adoption of such measures was undoubtedly precipitated by the calamitous decline of farm prices and farm incomes in the years following 1929. However, as we have already seen, farmers had complained about the low level of farm prices throughout the 1920s, and had demanded a "fair exchange value" for their products. This was often interpreted as a "parity ratio"—a price for each product sufficient to give a unit of that product as much purchasing power over other things as it enjoyed in the prewar years 1909–1914. Much of this thinking was carried over into the New Deal period. Also, a number of the measures proposed during the 1920s for raising the prices of farm products were to have profound effects on the New Deal's farm program. It will therefore be useful to survey briefly some of these backgrounds.

■ BACKGROUNDS OF THE NEW DEAL PROGRAMS   To understand the problems and complexities of the farm relief program, it is necessary to bear in mind some aspects of the farming industry at that time. First was the wide diversity in the sizes of farms and in the relation-ships of farmers to the lands that they cultivated. In size, farms ranged all the way from hundreds or even thousands of acres down to plots of ten acres or less. Some farmers owned their own land; others were tenants, renting varying amounts of land; still others were sharecroppers. It was typical for not more than 10 to 20 percent of the farmers producing a given type of product to account for more than half of its total output.

This situation had important implications for farm relief programs. For one thing, it meant that under any program that attempted to increase farm incomes by raising the prices of farm products, the major part of the benefits would accrue to the largest farmers. Only minor relief would accrue to sharecroppers, tenants with small farms, or other farmers with small outputs. Also, benefit payments attached to the ownership of land were likely to accrue to landlords. Unless prevented from doing so, land-lords would collect the benefits and might even evict tenants and share-croppers.

Second, most farm products were produced under conditions approxi-mating those of pure competition. For each type of product, there were very large numbers of producers, each accounting for only a minute frac-tion of the total output. The product of one farmer was almost completely substitutable for those of others, and no farmer believed that a change in his own rate of output would have an appreciable effect on market price. Thus, no farmer was likely to reduce his own output voluntarily for the purpose of raising market prices. It was often alleged during the New Deal period that farmers were philosophically opposed to output restric-tion to create "artificial scarcity" and raise prices. Although a few may have felt this way, the more typical reaction of a farmer was something like this: "Sure, it would be profitable if the production of wheat were reduced, and I hope others do it. However, whether I reduce or not will not affect the production policies of others, so I will maintain my output and even increase it if the price goes up. I suspect that others will do the same."

Under such conditions, it was clear that farmers would not indepen-dently reduce output to raise prices, that cooperative efforts to this end would fail without the support of government sanctions, and that effective restriction required compulsion by the government or payment of benefits large enough to make it profitable for farmers to reduce output. Moreover, to secure compliance would be difficult, for individual farmers found it advantageous to violate.

Third, the total output of the most important agricultural commodities exceeded the amounts demanded for domestic use, so that some had to be exported to equate demand and supply. This meant that so long as sellers were free to choose between domestic and foreign markets, the domestic price of a product could not rise above its price abroad, minus transportation and foreign tariff charges. It also meant that tariffs on foreign agricultural products could not be effective. Many farmers were protectionist in the 1920s, seeing in higher import tariffs the solution to their problem. However, an import tariff, no matter how high, could not be effective so long as there was an export surplus of the commodity and sellers were free to choose between domestic and foreign markets. We shall later examine various schemes for establishing a "two-price system," with domestic prices above those abroad.

Let us now examine some of the schemes proposed in the 1920s and early 1930s to raise farm prices, proposals which influenced significantly the New Deal's farm programs.

■ Farmers' Cooperatives   Large numbers of farmers had an almost religious faith in farm cooperatives as a solution to their problems. Their motto was, "Eliminate the middleman," or "Assume the functions of the middleman and perform them in more orderly and economical ways." They believed that purchasing cooperatives could lower prices paid by farmers for supplies by decreasing the monopoly power of other sellers and generally reducing sellers' margins. Also, marketing cooperatives could increase the farmers' net realization by reducing the margins of buyers and processors, doing this by supplying effective competition and by marketing in more orderly ways. The marketing cooperatives that were highly efficient—many were not—did succeed in reducing marketing margins. However, such gains were disappointingly small relative to the farmers' aspirations, and would inevitably remain so while basic market prices remained low. A number of cooperatives, relying solely on persuasion, attempted to induce farmers to restrict output in order to raise prices. A few of these campaigns, such as those in the citrus industry, achieved limited successes. However, most of them failed.

The Agricultural Marketing Act of 1929, which was approved by Hoover in June of that year and which created the Federal Farm Board, was a response to pressures from the cooperative movement. The Federal Farm Board had several major purposes: to promote education in the principles of cooperative marketing; to promote organization of farm cooperatives; to provide data on demands, supplies, and prices in both domestic and foreign markets; and to make loans to marketing cooperatives to enable them to purchase and hold farm products and to market them in an orderly manner. For the last purpose, the Federal Farm Board was given an appropriation of $500 million, which it could use as a revolving fund to make loans to cooperative marketing organizations. Three major commodities were included in the program—cotton, wheat, and wool. Cooperative organizations, using funds from the Federal Farm Board, bought large amounts of these commodities in attempts to support their prices. Also, officials of both the Federal Farm Board and farm cooperatives launched "educational campaigns" to persuade farmers to restrict output, but with virtually no success.

It is doubtful that this program would have been successful even if prosperity had continued. However, the depression, with falling demands for all types of commodities, assured its failure. The marketing cooperatives incurred very large losses on their stocks of cotton, wheat, and wool, and they began to liquidate their holdings in 1931, thereby depressing prices still more. One major lesson emerged from this experience: Without effective restriction of output, efforts to support prices through purchases and withholding from the market would fail or would succeed only at very high cost.

■ Two-Price Systems   A number of proposals that were widely discussed and that gained strong support from farmers and members of Congress in the 1920s and early 1930s sought to solve the problem through a two-price system for selected farm commodities.[1] In essence, the plans were simple: (1) Select for the product a price for domestic use above the world price, and permit to be offered for domestic use only such amounts as would be demanded at the selected price. (2) Dump the surplus on world markets at the price prevailing there. (3) Impose on imports of the product a tariff sufficiently high to prevent imports from lowering the domestic price below the selected level. The weighted average price of the product would thus depend upon the height of the price for domestic use, the fraction of the output that could be sold at that price, the height of the price in foreign markets, and the fraction of output sold in those markets. Thus, with any given price for domestic use, the average price would be lower the lower were world prices and the larger the fraction of output dumped abroad.

This immediately suggests two potential obstacles to the success of such a plan. First, prices abroad might become very low relative to the price selected for domestic uses. This became a reality during the depression. Also, other countries, and especially those whose farmers produced the product, might resent American dumping and retaliate with high tariffs, import quotas, or even import embargoes. This also occurred. Second, a large fraction of total output might have to be sold abroad. This would occur to the extent that the increased price for domestic uses lowered quantities demanded for these uses and to the extent that an increase in average prices received by farmers led them to expand their total output.

However, even if such a plan succeeded in raising the average prices of farm products, serious problems of implementation were involved. (1) How should quantities offered for domestic uses be limited so as to maintain the higher domestic price? The plan would obviously fail if all sellers were free to choose between domestic and foreign markets, with no limitation on sales for domestic use and no special inducements to export. Also, it would be palpably unfair to allow some farmers to take advantage of the higher domestic price and to force others to export. Some method of sharing the gains was needed. This required a pool of money collected

[1] For further information on all the plans discussed in this chapter, see Murray R. Benedict, *Farm Policies of the United States, 1790–1950*, The Twentieth Century Fund, New York, 1953.

from someone to subsidize or reimburse those who sold abroad. (2) How should the money to cover losses on exports be collected and who should pay it?

One set of answers was provided by the McNary-Haugen Plans, named after their Congressional sponsors, Senator Charles McNary of Oregon and Representative Gilbert N. Haugen of Iowa. Five bills to establish such plans were introduced in Congress, one in each of the years 1924–1928, inclusive. Those in 1927 and 1928 were approved by Congress but vetoed by President Coolidge. Although there were differences among the plans, the following outline indicates their general purposes and methods. (1) These plans applied to "basic agricultural commodities," defined to include wheat, cotton, wool, cattle, swine, and rice. (2) For each covered commodity, a "target price" above the world price was to be selected. In some versions, this was the parity price; in others, it was the world price plus an import tariff. All versions of the plan provided an import tariff to protect the domestic price. (3) The government would provide capital for an export corporation, which would purchase the products on a scale sufficient to maintain their domestic prices at the "target levels"; surpluses were to be sold abroad for what they would bring.

In some versions of the plan, losses or subsidies on exports were to be financed by an equalization fee or tax—a device that was to become a key element in the early New Deal farm programs. This tax was to apply to the total output of the basic commodity and was to be paid by the first buyer or processor of the commodity. Since the tax was to apply to the total output and to all first buyers or processors, it would raise all their costs and tend to increase the margin between prices paid by domestic consumers and those received by farmers. Thus, domestic consumers would bear the burden of the tax in the form of higher prices if the prices received by farmers were supported firmly. Farmers certainly believed and hoped that consumers would foot the bill. Such taxes present serious problems of enforcement because first buyers and processors have strong incentives to evade the tax and bootleg the product domestically.

Another proposal for financing losses on exports was "the export-debenture plan," an almost transparent device for financing the subsidy out of the federal budget. These "debentures" were simply certificates issued by the government and acceptable by the Treasury at face value in payment of import duties. These were to be given to exporters of a supported farm product in an amount equal to the difference between the target domestic price and the world price. Thus, the net realization on exports—the sum of the world price plus the value of the debenture—would be equal to the domestic price. The Treasury would foot the bill, not through expenditures of its money but through decreased revenues from import tariffs.

It is important to note that none of the McNary-Haugen Plans provided for limitation of output of those commodities whose prices were to be supported.

■ **The Domestic Allotment Plan**   The basic ideas of the Domestic Allotment Plan were to influence somewhat the Agricultural Adjustment Act of 1933 and to become an essential element in the Soil Conservation and Domestic Allotment Act of 1936. The plan was first proposed in 1927 and was discussed in detail during the following years by John D. Black, the agricultural economist. However, it is commonly associated with M. L. Wilson, of Montana State College, who publicized it widely in 1931 and 1932, became an advisor to Roosevelt in 1932, and later held several important positions in the Department of Agriculture. Like the McNary-Haugen Plans, the Domestic Allotment Plan provided for a two-price system, but its methods were quite different. It proposed that farmers should receive the world price plus an import duty for the part of their crop consumed in the United States, but only the world price for the part of their crop exported. This was to be achieved through a system of "allotments" or "rights" to individual farmers. These "allotments" were simply rights to sell for domestic use, and they were stated in terms of units of the product, such as bushels of wheat or pounds of cotton.

The essential elements of the plan were these: (1) Fix the total or global amounts of rights to be issued for each covered product each year. This would be set at an amount slightly below the quantities expected to be demanded for domestic use at a price equal to the world price plus the import tariff. This was to assure that the domestic price would in fact be maintained at that level. (2) Allot or allocate the total rights to states, districts, and individual farmers. This was to be done on an historical basis, rights being granted in proportion to acreages or amounts of output during some recent period. (3) Require every buyer or processor of the commodity for domestic use to purchase rights from farmers; to buy or process for domestic use without purchasing a corresponding amount of rights was to be illegal. Since the domestic price was to be equal to the world price plus import tariffs, it was expected that competition would force buyers and processors to pay a price for rights approximately equal to the import tariff. Thus, the price paid for rights was comparable to an equalization or processing tax. (4) Any production in excess of a farmer's allotment could be sold only abroad. Again, it is important to note that the plan did not restrict a farmer's total output; the only penalty for producing in excess of his allotment was that the excess had to be sold abroad at whatever prices prevailed there.

Several difficulties encountered by the Domestic Allotment Plan will be discussed later. However, a few problems will be mentioned here. The plan presented serious enforcement problems. Farmers producing in excess of their allotments had strong incentives to collude with buyers and processors who did not want to pay for rights and to bootleg products in the domestic market. To administer the plan required some sort of nationwide administrative network to weigh the conflicting claims of states, districts, and individual farmers and ultimately to make allocations to individual farmers. The allocation of rights on an historical basis created "grandfather rights" and led to many problems: unfair base periods, new entries without base period experience, inefficiences resulting from penalties on shifting from a crop with price supports to those without price supports, and so on. To regulate an industry composed of a few big firms may be difficult; to regulate effectively one with thousands or hundreds of thousands of firms approaches the impossible.

We turn now to some of the major aspects of the New Deal agricultural program.

■ **THE AGRICULTURAL ADJUSTMENT ACT OF 1933**   The Agricultural Adjustment Act of 1933 was signed by Roosevelt on May 12. Although amended several times and supplemented with other laws, it provided the basic legislative framework for the New Deal agricultural relief programs until its production control aspects were ruled unconstitutional by the Supreme Court on Jan. 6, 1936. The Act provided for the establishment of an Agricultural Adjustment Administration (AAA) within the Department of Agriculture. Henry A. Wallace was then Secretary of Agriculture, and the first Administrator of the AAA was George N. Peek, who had earlier been a leading advocate of the McNary-Haugen Plans. However, sharp policy disagreements and conflicts of personalities led to Peek's resignation in December 1933. He was succeeded by Chester C. Davis.

The avowed goal under the act was to give agricultural products the same purchasing power with respect to things purchased by farmers that they commanded in a base period. The base period for all farm commodities except tobacco and potatoes was 1909–1914; for the latter products it was 1919–1929. Prices were not to be raised to this level precipitately, but only "as rapidly as deemed feasible." Several devices were to be used in the program to raise prices; the most important of these were production controls, benefit payments, loans, government purchases, and marketing agreements. Production controls were to apply to farm commodities designated as "basic." Initially, only seven products were defined as "basic," but eight others were added later. (See Table 12–1.)

Roosevelt insisted on two characteristics for his farm program. First, it should be "voluntary." Farmers should not be forced to join by law, by other coercion, or by penalty taxes. Their voluntary cooperation should be sought through persuasion and payment of benefits to those who did cooperate. Some farmers and Congressmen were not devoted to this principle; they were perfectly willing to use prohibitive taxes to force cooperation. For example, the Bankhead Cotton Control Act of April 24, 1934, levied on cotton ginned in excess of a farmer's production quota a tax equal to 5 cents a pound or 50 percent of the current price, whichever was lower. The Kerr-Smith Tobacco Control Act of June 23, 1934, levied a tax on tobacco produced in excess of quotas at a rate equal to one-third of its average selling price.

Table 12–1.   Basic agricultural commodities under the AAA

Initial list:	Wheat	Rice
	Cotton	Tobacco
	Field corn	Milk and milk products
	Hogs	
Added April 7, 1934:	Rye	Grain sorghums
	Flax	Cattle
	Barley	
Added May 9, 1934:	Sugar beets	
	Sugarcane	
Added August 24, 1935	Potatoes	

Roosevelt also insisted on decentralization of administration. Determination of allotments to each county, locality, and individual farmer was to be made in cooperation with local, county, or district production associations and local allotment committees. These associations and committees wielded great powers as they chose among competing claims of farmers, allocated production quotas, and investigated compliance. Some observers became almost lyrical about this exercise in "grass-roots democracy." The verdicts of others were far less favorable. They found that power was in fact largely concentrated in an agricultural hierarchy dominated in many cases by prosperous farmers, the Farm Bureau, and the Extension Service. Less prosperous farmers, and members of minority groups suffered discrimination. And some of the methods used to "persuade" farmers to join "voluntarily" were far from subtle.

Production control plans for the various products differed in detail, but their essential principles were the same: (1) Farmers entered into agreements to adjust their production in accordance with their individual allotments. (2) Those who signed agreements received benefit payments from the government. Thus, they received both the benefit payments and the advantage of any price increase resulting from output restriction. Nonsigners received only the latter. Such a plan was likely to fail if benefit payments were not large enough to compensate a farmer for his loss of freedom to produce more than his allotment. (3) To provide money for payment of benefits, a processing tax was levied on the first processing of the product for domestic use. The tax applied to the product whether it was of domestic origin or imported. The rate of the tax was to be such as to achieve the "fair exchange value" of parity.

The Agricultural Adjustment Act also empowered the Secretary of Agriculture to enter into marketing agreements with farmers and with processors and distributors of farm products. These agreements were exempt from the antitrust laws. Their major professed purpose was to eliminate unfair practices that might tend to prevent achievement of the declared goals. Among their elements were fixing of marketing quotas, prohibition of price-cutting, and fixing and maintenance of prices.

Both farm incomes and farm prices rose markedly from the low levels reached in 1932. (See Table 12–2.) By 1935, net incomes to persons on

Table 12–2.   Farm incomes and farm parity ratios
(income in millions of dollars)

| | | | PRICE INDEXES, 1909–1914=100 | | |
YEAR	REALIZED NET INCOME OF FARM OPERATORS[a]	NET INCOME TO PERSONS ON FARMS FROM FARMING[b]	PRICES RECEIVED BY FARMERS	PRICES PAID BY FARMERS[c]	PARITY RATIO
1929	$6,264	$7,024	148	160	92
1932	1,928	2,510	65	112	58
1933	2,767	3,012	70	109	64
1934	3,871	3,428	90	120	75
1935	4,605	5,858	109	124	88
1936	5,138	4,954	114	124	92
1937	5,232	6,754	122	131	93
1938	4,273	5,101	97	124	78
1939	4,394	5,189	95	123	77
1940	4,289	5,299	100	124	81
1941	6,153	7,455	124	133	93

[a] Includes cash receipts from farm marketings, government payments, value of home consumption, and rental value of farm dwellings less total farm production expenses.

[b] Realized net income of farm operators plus value of inventory change plus wages paid to farm laborers living on farms.

[c] Prices paid, including interest, taxes, and wage rates.

Source: U. S. Department of Commerce, Historical Statistics of the United States, Colonial Times to 1957, 1960, p. 283.

farms from farming had more than doubled, and the parity ratio had risen from 58 to 75. The latter did not at any time during this period reach the target level of 100, although at times it was as high as in 1929. It is impossible to say how much of the improvement of farm incomes and prices resulted from the specific programs to control production and raise farm prices. A considerable part of the improvement resulted from the general rise of national income, which increased demands for farm products. Also, output and prices were strongly influenced by recurrent, widespread, and severe droughts as the wet-cycle of the 1920s gave way to a dry-cycle in the 1930s. In 1931 and 1932, there were small dust storms in western Kansas and eastern Colorado. By the spring of 1934, they were spreading over a vast midwestern and southern area. The worst year was 1936. These droughts and dust storms reduced drastically outputs of some very important agricultural products. For example, wheat output fell so much that the United States actually imported this grain in 1935 and 1936. Outputs of corn and cotton were also hard hit, and beef production suffered from scarcities of good pasturage, hay, and feed grains. Nature did not rely on voluntary agreements to restrict output.

No attempt will be made to cover all the programs under the AAA, but a few comments on the most important of them may be instructive. Two emergency programs in the spring of 1933 created a furore. One was labeled by its critics as "the murder of 6 million little pigs." A quick survey at that time showed that the population of young pigs was abnormally high, indicating very large pork supplies a few months hence. The National Corn-Hog Committee, the Farm Bureau, the Grange, and the Farmers Union joined in recommending that 6 million pigs be killed. This was done. Protestors were but little mollified by the fact that the baby pork was purchased by a newly established Federal Surplus Relief Corporation and distributed to persons on relief. Several further steps were taken to raise the prices of hogs and pork. Large numbers of hogs were purchased and used for fertilizers and for relief programs. Many pregnant sows were bought up and killed, and many farmers agreed to limit the number of brood sows. However, farmers naturally kept those sows with the highest records of fertility, so that the average number of pigs per litter increased markedly.

The other controversial emergency program in May 1933 was that of plowing under cotton. Cotton planting was already completed when the AAA was established. A survey showed that plantings were at the very high level of 40 million acres, which suggested that output would be so high as to add still further to the carryover stock that was already three times normal levels. It was therefore decided to plow under about one-quarter of the plantings, or 10 million acres. Farmers were compensated with payments that averaged $11 per acre retired. Tenants and sharecroppers, as well as owner-farmers, were supposed to be eligible for these payments. However, many landlords demanded the rental payments for themselves and threatened to evict sharecroppers and tenants who protested. Attempts to prevent this were not wholly successful. Difficulties of this sort continued to beset the cotton programs in later years. Many other actions were taken to support the price of cotton. As we have seen, a production control program that was originally voluntary became coercive in the spring of 1934 when a tax was imposed on amounts ginned in excess of quotas. Cash rentals were paid on land taken out of cotton production. Benefit payments were made on cotton produced within quotas. The Commodity Credit Corporation (CCC), established in October 1933, made nonrecourse loans to farmers with cotton as collateral. The RFC lent to China and the Soviet Union to finance cotton purchases from the United States.

Several measures were adopted to support wheat prices. A plow-up program was considered in 1933 but rejected because of the drought. An International Wheat Agreement, signed in August 1933 and pledging the most important exporting nations to restrict acreage, was of little help because it broke down within a year. Millions of farmers signed agreements to reduce their acreages below their 1930–1932 levels, receiving in return benefit payments on production within their quotas. However, large numbers did not sign, or dropped out after signing, or simply violated their agreements.

Measures to support corn prices included acreage reduction, benefit payments on output within quotas, and nonrecourse loans by the CCC. The support programs for milk and dairy products relied largely on marketing agreements, many of which attempted to fix and maintain prices, and on large government purchases of surpluses.

These examples indicate the general purposes and methods used under the AAA and some of the problems encountered.[2]

By 1935, many people, both within and outside the government, were coming to believe that the AAA methods and policies should be modified, and perhaps changed markedly. Acreage reduction was breaking down in some product areas, such as wheat. Increases in productivity were in some cases offsetting the effects of acreage reduction. Too little was being done in the field of soil conservation. Little was being accomplished in restoring agricultural exports. The processing tax was under fire in the courts. And some felt that in any case, benefit payments should be met out of the federal budget rather than from taxes that were likely to be borne by domestic consumers of the various products.

Such considerations might have led to changes in the AAA methods and policies even if the government had remained free to continue the AAA without substantial change. However, this freedom was removed on Jan. 6, 1936, when the Supreme Court, in the Hoosac Mills Case (United States v. Butler, 297, U. S. Reports 1), declared the processing tax unconstitutional. The Court ruled that the processing tax, in this case the processing tax on cotton, was unconstitutional because its proceeds were dedicated to a function, control of farm production, that was beyond the constitutional power of the federal government. Farm production was in intrastate, not interstate, commerce. However, the Court's decision left intact the federal government's power in the fields of marketing agreements and purchases for surplus removal. This led to the second stage of the New Deal agricultural program, expressed in the Soil Conservation and Domestic Allotment Act, approved Feb. 29, 1936.

■ **Soil Conservation and Domestic Allotment Act**   The Soil Conservation and Domestic Allotment Act reflected the convergence of two lines of development and two purposes. One line was from the domestic allotment plans through the acreage and output restrictions of the AAA, and its major purpose was to raise farm prices and incomes. The other line

2 For further information on these programs, see Edwin G. Nourse, Joseph S. Davis, and John D. Black, *Three Years of the Agricultural Adjustment Administration*, The Brookings Institution, Washington, D.C., 1937.

originated in the broad movement for conservation of natural resources, and its major purpose was to conserve the soil. Interest in soil conservation was greatly increased by the dust storms, but many had earlier pointed to widespread abuses of the soil. These included bringing into cultivation lands, such as those in western Kansas and eastern Colorado, which without their natural cover would inevitably be subject to serious wind erosion during dry cycles; removal of trees and natural cover from hillsides, which not only subjected them to wind and water erosion but also reduced their ability to retain water and thus increased the danger of floods in lower areas; up-hill and down-hill, rather than contour, plowing, which both increased water erosion and decreased water retention; repeated plantings of soil-depleting crops on the same land, which both exhausted its fertility and increased erosion; failure to rotate crops or to plant soil-conserving crops; and inadequate use of fertilizer.

Although the new program clearly had the double objective of conserving soil and of raising prices of farm products, there remained the problem of determining the relative importance of each. Some believed the prime purpose was long-run soil conservation, with crop restriction as an indirect side effect. Others reversed the priorities. The outcomes were compromises between these views, with the nature of the compromises varying from case to case. For the conservation purposes of the Act, crops were classified into three categories. (1) Soil-conserving, which included grasses, legumes, and green manure crops. (2) Soil-depleting, which were the intensively cultivated row crops, and included all the "basic crops" designated as such in 1933 by the AAA. (3) Neutral, which were crops not falling in either of the first two categories.

Annual benefit payments, averaging about $11 an acre, were paid to farmers who reduced acreages planted in soil-depleting crops and left the land idle or planted soil-conserving crops. Farmers were also eligible for benefits, which in many cases were sufficient to cover the entire cost of the projects, for instituting certain soil-conserving practices. Among these were applications of fertilizers; planting forest trees; construction of mechanical erosion controls, such as obstacles in gullies created by erosion; terracing of land to obstruct drainage of water and promote water retention; and contour plowing.

There can be no doubt that this program and those that followed made valuable contributions to soil conservation. The programs themselves, the widespread publicity accompanying them, and the demonstration effects by the most cooperative farmers made farmers in general much more aware of the dangers of soil depletion, and the various benefit payments gave them an incentive to improve their practices. However, the farm-by-farm approach made it virtually impossible to get the maximum benefits in terms of conservation for each dollar spent. Some of the land that remained in use for soil-depleting crops needed conservation more than some of that which was removed from such uses.

To support farm incomes and the prices of farm products, the new program did not rely exclusively on the soil-conservation measures just described; it continued a number of measures instituted earlier. For many crops, it continued to allot quotas and to pay benefits on production within quotas. The CCC made nonrecourse loans on a wide variety of farm products, so that producers could default on loans without loss if the market price turned out to be less than the amounts of the loans. Also, the Federal Surplus Relief Corporation (FSRC) purchased large amounts of many farm products. Stocks accumulated by the CCC and FSRC were distributed for relief purposes, sold for export, or held. Since the processing tax could no longer be used to finance such costs, funds had to be secured from other sources. These came mostly from general appropriations, use of relief appropriations by the FSRC, and earmarking of a fraction of the revenues from import tariffs.

■ The Agricultural Adjustment Act of Feb. 16, 1938   A major innovation in the Agricultural Adjustment Act of Feb. 16, 1938, was the concept of an "ever-normal granary." This had long been a favorite idea of Secretary Wallace. He was distressed by the extremely wide variations in the carryover stock of farm products—from virtually nothing in some years to huge excesses in others. Major reasons for such wide fluctuations were, of course, the alternation of good and bad crop years and variations in domestic demand. However, inflexible price supports, providing almost unchangeable prices despite changes in output and stocks, were also partially responsible. For example, an excessively high price for one farm product relative to others could lead to excessive output relative to domestic demands and to the accumulation of huge stocks. A price could prove to be excessive because it was initially set too high, because technological advances lowered its cost of production relative to costs of other farm products, or because demand for it declined. Wallace's central idea was that steps should be taken to regulate output of the various products in such a way as to maintain "normal carryovers" from year to year—an "ever-normal granary."

The 1938 Act did not abandon measures to support farm prices and incomes. It continued the soil conservation program, production allotments, benefits payments on production within quotas, CCC nonrecourse loans, and federal purchases of surpluses. However, it provided that these measures were to be used more flexibly to adjust supplies to demands and to maintain an ever-normal granary. For example, if carryover stocks of a commodity became excessive, this would be a signal to reduce the net realization of farmers producing it.

To take into consideration the effects of prices not only on the size of farm incomes but also on quantities demanded and on amounts supplied was an important change. It was a step toward allowing flexible prices to equate demand and supply. However, it was only a short step; direct production controls were to be retained. How much price flexibility would have developed and how effective it would have been in equating demands and supplies if the depression had continued and the war had not intervened is impossible to say. Farmers would certainly have opposed large price reductions for the purpose of reducing supplies. Actually, the experiment was cut short by the war, which brought increases of both exports and domestic demands.

■ **Other Elements in the Farm Program**   A few other measures to relieve farmers and farm workers will be mentioned briefly. As already noted, some farm workers, farmers who had lost their farms, and tenants and share-croppers who had been dispossessed received direct relief or work relief. Some went to migrant worker camps. Several thousand families were moved from submarginal land to better land and were given financial assistance in moving, acquiring land, and purchasing necessary supplies. Some tenants received loans to purchase farms. Such measures were helpful in many individual cases, but they hardly dented the huge problem of poverty among sharecroppers and small farmers.

■ **CONCLUSIONS**   How American farm policies would have developed in the absence of the great depression is impossible to say. The federal government might have come to play a more active role in influencing farm prices, and perhaps farm output, even if general prosperity had continued. After all, the McNary-Haugen Plans of 1927 and 1928 failed to be adopted only because they were vetoed by Coolidge, and Hoover approved the establishment of the Federal Farm Board in 1929 while he still expected the New Era to continue. A new President might have been more responsive to the demands of the farm bloc. However, it is difficult to believe that the federal government would have become so deeply involved in farming in the absence of the great depression, which not only created distress for farmers and multiplied their demands for help but also broke down political obstacles to federal action.

In any case, the great depression was the occasion, if not the cause, of revolutionary changes in the relationships of the federal government to agriculture. For the first time, the federal government assumed responsibility for influencing, if not controlling, farm incomes and the prices of farm products. In the process, it came to influence not only prices and the rates of output of farm products, but also the relative supplies of the various types of products, uses of land, and even the production patterns of individual farmers. Once the federal government had admitted such responsibilities and had taken so many actions, a return to its laissez-faire policies of the 1920s proved impossible. Various farm support and soil conservation programs bearing at least a family resemblance to those of the 1930s were still in evidence 40 years after the end of the great depression, despite the intervening period of almost continuous general prosperity and a technological revolution in agriculture.

13

Industrial Recovery Programs

The programs adopted by the New Deal in attempts to provide farm relief and to promote agricultural recovery had their counterparts, in purpose if not in methods, in almost all branches of industry. The most sweeping and spectacular of these were under the National Recovery Administration (NRA).

The National Industrial Recovery Act (NIRA), signed by Roosevelt on June 16, 1933, was composed of two major parts, which were viewed as complementary. One part authorized the Public Works Administration, (PWA), of which Secretary Ickes became Administrator. Its purpose was both to provide employment directly and to raise total purchasing power. The other part authorized the creation of NRA, of which Gen. Hugh S. Johnson became the first Administrator. Roosevelt described the general objectives of the NRA in his request that

> . . . the Congress provide for the machinery necessary for a great cooperative movement throughout all industry in order to obtain wide reemployment, to shorten the working week, to pay a decent wage for the shorter week, and to prevent unfair competition and disastrous overproduction.
>
> Employers cannot do this singly or even in organized groups, because such action increases costs and thus permits cut-throat underselling by selfish competitors unwilling to join in such a public-spirited endeavor.
>
> One of the great restrictions upon such cooperative efforts up to this time has been our antitrust laws. They were purposely designed as the means to cure the great evils of monopolistic price fixing. They should certainly be retained as a permanent assurance that the old evils of unfair competition shall never return. But the public interest will be served if, with the authority and under the guidance of Government, private industries are permitted to make agreements and codes insuring fair competition. However, it is necessary, if we thus limit the operation of antitrust laws to their original purpose, to provide a rigorous licensing power in order to meet rare cases of noncooperation and abuse. Such a safeguard is indispensable.[1]

As it turned out, the two programs authorized by the NIRA did not

[1] *The Public Papers and Addresses of Franklin D. Roosevelt*, Random House, New York, 1938, Vol. 2, p. 202. This recommendation was made to Congress on May 17, 1933.

proceed at anything like the same pace. As we have already seen, the PWA developed only slowly under the cautious Ickes. However, by late July the energetic, ebullient, swashbuckling General Johnson had launched a nationwide campaign with an almost wartime fervor. Not only firms in manufacturing and mining but also those in wholesaling, retailing, service establishments, and almost all other lines were urged to join the NRA. Millions did. The Blue Eagle, insignia of NRA, became a symbol of patriotism. Establishments that met the requirements of NRA and displayed the Blue Eagle gained public approval; those that did not were considered slackers, unfair competitors, or worse. Some observers quipped that things might have turned out better if roles had been reversed, with Ickes as head of NRA and Johnson in charge of PWA.

The NRA was a vast experiment in "industrial self-government under general supervision by government." Each industry was not only permitted but also strongly urged to set up a "code authority" and to formulate a "code of fair competition." The latter typically included two types of provisions: (1) "Fair" conditions with respect to output, prices, and various trade practices, and (2) fair practices with respect to wages, hours of work, conditions of work, and collective bargaining. These codes of fair competition could become effective only after approval by the NRA. However, once approved by the NRA, a code achieved the force of law and became binding on all members of the industry to which it applied, whether or not they had signed an NRA agreement. Code authorities typically tried to achieve "voluntary" compliance, but they could resort to the courts if necessary. Joseph Schumpeter commented about the NRA, "Stripped of phraseological mimicry and apart from provisions about labor, [it] was legal recognition and official encouragement, amounting to compulsion, of a modified form of the German cartel which, quite independently of this legislation, tended to grow out of the activities of trade associations."[2] Some critics described it in sharper language; they found the NRA to be an American version of the corporate state, fascist in form and perhaps in spirit, an experiment in syndicalism.

■ **BACKGROUNDS OF THE NRA**   The NRA does indeed appear to be a bizarre phenomenon when viewed against the background of the professed philosophies of the government and of business leaders. As expressed in the Sherman and Clayton acts, the general policy of the government was to prevent and combat monopoly and restraint of competition and to rely largely on free competition to organize and control the economy. Now the government, including many liberal Democrats who had traditionally been "trustbusters," not only permitted but also urged members of industries to enter into agreements that would inevitably restrain competition in some degree. Businessmen, mostly staunch Republi-

---

[2] Joseph A. Schumpeter, *Business Cycles*, Vol. II, McGraw-Hill, New York, 1939, p. 922.

cans or conservative Democrats, had traditionally extolled the virtues of free enterprise, insisted upon freedom to compete and to run their own affairs, and resisted control by government. Now they cooperated with the government, and in a large majority of cases took the initiative in establishing codes of fair competition and code authorities. These would inevitably limit their individual freedoms to determine their policies and would subject them to an unknown degree of control by government. However, despite these traditions and professed philosophies, other forces were strong enough to make possible the NRA and to gain widespread support for it for a short period.

A major force, of course, was the depression itself and the conditions it generated—unemployment, wage-cutting and inadequate labor incomes, widespread excess capacity, price-cutting and selling below cost, business losses instead of profits, and bankruptcies. These results of "untrammeled competition" undermined faith in the competitive system as a device for organizing and controlling the economy. Many clergymen, intellectuals, and others came to believe that the competitive system had failed, and they demanded its modification or abandonment. Great numbers of businessmen liked the results no better and wanted quick relief.

Although the NRA could not have been adopted in the absence of the great depression, it was not wholly without precedents. Ideas and practices that originated well before the onset of the depression contributed to both the adoption of the NRA and its methods. Among these were the movement for scientific management and planning; certain government policies; the trade association movement; and movements to improve the conditions of labor.

Owing to the work of Frederick Taylor and others, the movement for scientific management and planning had gained great prestige in the 1920s. Since the use of scientific methods and rational planning in individual firms had contributed so much to productivity, why should it not be applied on a much broader scale—on an industry-wide, or even an economy-wide, basis? Surely it would be superior to "unplanned" or "chaotic" competition. Such ideas gained wide acceptance among intellectuals and even among businessmen, although the advocates of planning were generally unclear and often in conflict concerning objectives and methods.

The general government policy of preventing monopoly and of relying on competition to regulate the economy did not enjoy universal support in either principle or practice. Many continued to believe that it would be better to allow business to achieve some degree of monopoly power and to subject it to government supervision and regulation. For example, the Interstate Commerce Commission regulated the railroads and allowed them to enter into rate agreements subject to its approval. A major purpose of the Federal Trade Commission was to prevent "unfair" competition, and the practices that it outlawed were in many cases "unfair" to competitors rather than to consumers. The War Industries Board exercised widespread controls over industry during World War I. It is probably no coincidence that many of the men associated with the NRA and with NRA-type proposals had played roles in the War Industries Board. Among these were General Johnson and Bernard Baruch.

Crucial to the adoption of the NRA and to its methods was the trade association movement of the 1920s. Strongly approved by Herbert Hoover as Secretary of Commerce, trade associations were established in virtually every major industry and in many minor ones. These played major roles in the NRA, usually drawing up the codes of fair competition and controlling the code authorities. Although the activities of the various trade associations in the 1920s varied widely, the following were the most common. (1) Standardization of products by physical characteristics, size, and so on. It was this activity that Secretary Hoover approved most highly because it allegedly increased efficiency in production and inventory management. (2) Standardization of cost accounting and financial reporting. Trade association officials urged their members to use uniform methods for computing costs, telling them what items to include in costs and how to figure each element of cost. Members were often urged to use "standard costs" rather than their own cost experience. This was frequently accompanied by campaigns to persuade members not to sell at prices below "full cost." (3) Open filing of prices. Every member of the industry was required to file his effective price list with the trade association, which would make it fully available to all members. No member was to change his prices without prior notice to the trade association. (4) Proscription of "unfair trade practices." The list of such practices varied from association to association, but it often included misrepresentation of products, secret rebating or price-cutting, selling below cost, and so on.

Many—probably most—of the trade associations restrained competition, unfair and otherwise. Some were accused of violating the antitrust laws, and most of them felt unduly restrained by these laws and sought their modification and liberalization. One outcome was the creation, in 1926, of Trade Practice Conferences under the auspices of the Federal Trade Commission. Under this arrangement, industries were permitted to write their own rules subject to approval by the Federal Trade Commission. However, this liberalization was considered by most associations to be quite inadequate; they wanted much broader scope for self-regulation.

Although it does not pretend to provide a precise statistical summary of the attitudes of businessmen toward trade associations and the proper scope of their activities, the following information is suggestive. Members of the Chamber of Commerce of the United States voted as follows in late 1931 on ten propositions put to them by the Chamber's Special Committee on Continuity of Business and Employment.

> I. The antitrust laws should be modified so as to make clear that the laws permit agreements increasing the possibilities of keeping production related to consumption.   *2,495 yes, 315 no*

II. Modification of the antitrust laws should include provision for government supervision in order that agreements which are not in the public interest in stabilization of business operation and employment may be nullified.   *2,132 yes, 648 no*

III. Businesses desiring to combine should have opportunity to ascertain from a suitable government authority whether or not the proposed combination will be in violation of the antitrust laws.   *2,479 yes, 304 no*

IV. The principles of a national economic council should be placed in effect.   *2,246 yes, 497 no*

V. For each field of business, a representative trade association should perform the functions of an economic council.   *2,457 yes, 281 no*

VI. Aided by increased opportunity for stability of operations, each employer should so plan operations as to assure the greatest possible number of employees there will be work for the greatest possible number of weeks in the year.   *2,647 yes, 128 no*

VII. Aided by increased opportunity for stabilization, employers individually and collectively should provide adequate reserves for unemployment and other benefits for their employees.   *2,146 yes, 511 no*

VIII. Through trade associations, employers should make such reserves and benefits uniform throughout each field of business, in all states.   *2,026 yes, 613 no*

IX. Unemployment which now exists and may presently occur should be dealt with upon an individual basis, locally, through organization to that end.   *2,143 yes, 116 no*

X. Needed relief should be provided through private contributions supplemented by state and local governments, and without any federal appropriations for such purposes.   *2,534 yes, 197 no*[3]

Several businessmen prosposed specific plans consistent with the preceding views. The most widely discussed of these was the "Swope Plan," named for its author, Gerard Swope, President of the General Electric Company.[4]

Thus, one major source of the ideas and pressures that led to the adoption of NRA was the trade association movement, with its emphasis on broader leeway for industrial self-government, including power to "keep production related to consumption." Another major source of the NRA was the labor movement, with its demands for improving the position of labor and labor unions. Among such demands were protection of the rights of labor to organize; abolition or effective regulation of child labor; protection of women workers; and improvement of hours of work, wage rates and working conditions.

Labor unions were in the doldrums during the 1920s and early 1930s.

---

[3] Chamber of Commerce of the United States of America, *Referendum Number Fifty-eight, Continuity of Business and Employment*, Jan. 18, 1932.

[4] See J. George Frederick, ed., *The Swope Plan*, The Business Bourse, New York, 1931.

Total union membership fell from more than 5 million in 1920 to 3.4 million in 1929 and less than 3 million in 1933. Most of these members were in the building trades, mining, and a few skilled crafts. Few unskilled workers belonged to unions.

Union officials protested bitterly, but for the most part ineffectively, against "unfair" methods used by employers to prevent workers from forming and joining unions of their own choosing. One device labor detested was the "yellow-dog contract," under which an employee was required to sign a contract stating that during his period of employment he would not join a labor union. Another detested device was the "company union," formed and usually dominated by the employer himself. An employer would recognize the company union and use it to prevent the formation of an "outside" union. Court injunctions were widely used to prevent violations of yellow-dog contracts, to protect company unions against rivals, to curb strikes, and otherwise to limit the activities of labor.

Strong pressures from labor finally led to the passage of the Norris-La Guardia Anti-Injunction Act of 1932. This Act made yellow-dog contracts unenforceable in the courts, limited the power of courts to issue injunctions against labor, and asserted the right of labor to organize. It served as a background and provided some of the language for what became Section 7a of the NIRA. This stated: "Employees shall have the right to organize and to bargain collectively through representatives of their own choosing, and shall be free from interference, restraint, or coercion of employers— in the designation of such representatives." Virtually every code of fair competition included such a provision, but compliance was not thereby assured.

Attempts to secure federal regulation of child labor had a long history. One federal act was ruled unconstitutional in 1918 on the ground that this labor was in intrastate, not interstate, commerce. A later attempt to abolish child labor by taxing its products in interstate commerce was invalidated in 1922 on the basis that the federal taxing power could not be used to control intrastate commerce. Agitation against the use of child labor continued, but no further federal action was achieved prior to the NRA. However, most of the codes of fair competition either declared the use of child labor to be an unfair practice or introduced safeguards for children. Many codes also sought to improve working conditions for women.

Even before the depression, but increasingly so as the depression deepened, there were demands for the establishment of minimum wages, a shorter workweek, and "decent" incomes for workers. Hoover contributed to the movement through his appeals to employers to maintain wage rates as a means of maintaining purchasing power, and through his sponsorship of a nationwide share-the-work campaign. By the spring of 1933, there were widespread movements to shorten the workweek and to raise money wages for the dual purpose of providing "decent" incomes for workers and of increasing total purchasing power. For example, the Black-Connery bill, introduced in April 1933, proposed that the maximum should be a 5-day, 30-hour week. Most of the codes of fair competition prescribed minimum wages and maximum hours of work.

Thus, at least two sets of interests were to be represented in and served by the NRA codes: those of employers and those of workers. Under the circumstances, it was inevitable that both would exert strong pressures for price increases. Labor would insist upon higher average wages per hour through increasing minimum wage rates, raising other wage rates, reducing hours of work without lowering weekly wages, or some combinations of these. And employers would strive not only to raise prices at least enough to offset increases in labor costs, but also to correct "unreasonably low prices" by outlawing sales below cost, loss leaders, and so on. The interests of consumers were clearly jeopardized, but consumers had no effective organization to protect them and only weak support in the government. An attempt was made to maintain a balance by appointing three advisory boards to the administrator of the NRA—an Industrial Advisory Board, composed of leading industrialists; a Labor Advisory Board, composed of union leaders and others prominent in the labor movement; and a Consumers Advisory Board. It was prophetic that the Consumers Advisory Board was the last to be established and that its members lacked a power base to support their efforts. It should have been evident from the beginning that in each industry there would be sharp conflicts of interest among employers, workers, and consumers of the products. However, many were surprised by the bitter controversies that developed within industries as firms disagreed on price policies, output quotas, and various trade practices.

■ THE WORKING OF THE NRA   Codes of fair competition were of two general types: industry codes, or basic and supplementary codes applying to individual industries; and the "blanket code," or the President's Reemployment Agreements with individual employers.[5]

Almost immediately after Roosevelt's approval of the NIRA on June 16, 1933, General Johnson began a nationwide, whirlwind campaign to induce industries to submit codes of fair competition. The first national industry code, the Cotton Textile Code, was approved on July 9. By July 27, some 209 national industry codes had been submitted. Since this progress was considered too slow, and also because the NRA was becoming bogged down with industry codes, Roosevelt launched on July 27 a nationwide campaign to induce individual firms to sign a "blanket code," or reemployment agreements, with him. Within a few weeks, more than 2.3 million employers with some 16.3 million employees signed such agree-

[5] For further information on the working of the NRA, codes of fair competition, and code authorities, see the following sources: Leverett S. Lyon, Paul T. Homan, Lewis L. Lorwin, George Terborgh, Charles L. Dearing, and Leon C. Marshall, *The National Recovery Administration: An Analysis and Appraisal*, The Brookings Institution, Washington, D.C., 1935. Also, Charles F. Roos, *NRA Economic Planning*, Principia Press, Bloomington, Ind., 1937.

ments, which entitled them to display the Blue Eagle. From the time of its inception until it was ruled unconstitutional in May 1935, the NRA approved 557 basic and 189 supplementary industry codes. It was estimated that 95 percent of all industrial employees were covered by these codes.

In essence, the blanket code employers were asked to sign and to abide by until the end of 1933 or until they had submitted an industry code, whichever came earlier, required employers to meet the following conditions:[6]

I. Not to employ any person under 16 years of age, except that those between 14 and 16 might be employed outside manufacturing and mechanical industries for not more than 3 hours a day if such employment occurred between 7 A.M. and 7 P.M. and did not interfere with hours of day school.

II. To meet the following conditions with respect to maximum hours and minimum wages.
　　1. Accounting, clerical, banking, office, service, and inside sales employees
　　　　a) maximum hours: 40 hours a week
　　　　b) minimum wages: $12 to $15 a week, depending on size of city
　　2. Factory and mechanical workers and artisans
　　　　a) maximum hours: 8 hours a day and 35 hours a week, but with a right to work 40 hours a week for any 6 weeks prior to the end of 1933
　　　　b) minimum wages: 40 cent an hour or the rates in effect on July 25, 1929, whichever was lower, but in no case less than 30 cents an hour

III. Not to reduce any wage rates already above the minima described above, and to increase others so as to maintain equitable relationships.

IV. Not to use any subterfuge to frustrate the spirit and intent of the agreement, which was to remove obstructions to commerce and to shorten hours and to raise wages for the shorter week to a living basis.

V. Not to raise prices above the level prevailing on July 1 by more than necessary to cover increases in costs since that date.

VI. To support and patronize establishments which had also signed the agreement and were listed as members of NRA.

VII. To cooperate to the fullest extent in having a code of fair competition submitted by his industry at the earliest possible date.

VIII. To agree to adjust purchase prices upward on outstanding fixed-price purchase contracts by amounts sufficient to cover the supplier's increased costs resulting from complying with the blanket code or an industry code.

　　[6] These are summaries and omit some qualifications. For the full text of the agreement, see *The Public Papers and Addresses of Franklin D. Roosevelt, op. cit.*, pp. 308–311.

It will be noted that the primary emphasis of the blanket code was on shortening the workweek, supporting wage rates, and minimizing price increases. Most of the industry codes placed far more emphasis on increasing prices.

To understand the working of the NRA, especially during its earlier phase, and the distribution of power over the making and administration of industry codes, it is necessary to bear in mind the central role of the industries and of their trade associations. As Roosevelt later described it:

> From the very outset until the end, codes were developed, as a matter of Administration policy, from proposals initiated from within the industries themselves. All but a few of them were sponsored and originally proposed by at least one trade association. With the passage of NIRA, which extended to industry the opportunity to organize for self-government, many trade associations which had been inactive for years came to life again, and many industries which did not have trade associations hastened to organize them. The proposed codes were of course reviewed in the public interest by NRA, but the principle was always followed that the final form of the code should be as far as possible a result of the meeting of minds of those in the industry, arrived at in a spirit of cooperation.
>
> The principle was also established at the outset that each code, after final approval, would be administered by the industry itself, with as little Government interference and control as possible—the concept of industrial self-government. This principle was, however, greatly modified as the result of experience with the compliance efforts made by code authorities.[7]

Also, the code authority was typically dominated by a trade association or by the same members of the industry that dominated the trade association. This usually meant control by the largest and most powerful members of the industry. Only 37 codes provided for labor representation and only 3 for direct consumer representatives. Many later provided for government representatives, but these were without vote.

The ability of industry to initiate code proposals and to dominate code authorities gave it a great power advantage, and it was only to be expected that this power would be used primarily to improve profits, rather than to benefit labor and protect consumers. This power could, of course, be reduced by strict surveillance, establishment of standards, and modifications of proposed codes by General Johnson and the Labor and Consumers Advisory boards. However, such surveillance was lax, especially so during the earlier phases of the NRA. Johnson's reviews of codes were very tolerant, partly because he was so firmly committed to the idea of self-government by industry and partly because he wanted codes to become effective in a hurry. His passion for haste helps to explain many of the snarls and woes that developed in the NRA. The Labor Advisory Board was interested primarily in the labor provisions of codes, not in industry trade practices or consumer protection. And the Consumer Advisory Board lacked power. Later attempts to accord greater protection to labor and consumers, although only partially effective, brought increasing complaints from in-

[7] *Ibid.*, p. 276.

dustry. After all, trade associations and their members had not sought greater scope for industrial self-regulation for the purposes of encouraging unionization of labor, increases of wage rates, and lower prices for consumers.

Let us now look briefly at some of the issues and problems of the NRA.

■ **Labor Provisions of the Codes**   As already noted, virtually all codes either outlawed child labor or regulated its use and provided special protection for women workers. These appear to have led to little controversy, although compliance was far from perfect. All other provisions with respect to wages and hours—minimum wage rates, other wages, and length of the workweek—led to sharp conflict, not ony between employers and employees but also among the employers in an industry. As might be expected, employees demanded higher basic wage rates, the maintenance of at least the traditional wage differentials, and at least the maintenance of weekly earnings despite reduction of the length of the workweek. Large numbers of strikes developed as employers resisted. Employers often conflicted sharply with each other concerning the wage rate to be prescribed in the codes. In many industries, wage rates for each type of labor had been nonuniform, varying by size of employer, geographic location, and so on. Now some of the employers with the highest levels of wages sought to force others up to the same level, hoping thereby to raise the costs of their competitors and to weaken their competitive positions. Those with the advantage of lower wage rates naturally fought back. This was only one of the ways in which members of an industry jockeyed for favorable positions.

The bitterest controversies developed over the rights of labor to organize. Employers signing a code of fair competition did not thereby renounce their opposition to "outside" unions nor the use of company unions to exclude rival organizations. On the other hand, labor leaders and many others interpreted Section 7a of the NIRA and similar provisions in the codes to mean that employees had the right to organize and bargain collectively through "outside" unions of their own choosing without "interference, or coercion of employers." They were shocked and angered when the NRA ruled that an employer could meet the requirements of Section 7a by "bargaining collectively" with a company union. Great numbers of employers revived company unions or established new ones. Trade associations and employers' counselors not only prepared model plans for their clients but also maintained experts to assist companies in getting them started and keeping them active. By the spring of 1934, one-fourth of all industrial workers were employed in plants maintaining company unions. About two-thirds of these were established during the NRA period, usually after a strike or after an outside union had made headway in a plant.

Official attitudes toward company unions became less favorable after jurisdiction over labor disputes was transferred from the employer-minded

NRA to a newly established, independent National Labor Relations Board (NLRB). However, the right of labor to organize and to bargain collectively through unions of its own choosing was still a bitterly fought issue when the NRA was invalidated in May 1935. In fact, the bitterest contests lay ahead. In accepting Section 7a as a price for the right of industrial self-regulation, employers had unleashed forces that they could not stop. Union membership, which averaged only 3.1 million in 1932, rose to 3.9 million in 1935 and to 8 million in 1938.[8]

■ **Trade Practices Under the Codes**   Many of the codes did prohibit trade practices that were "unfair" in the Federal Trade Commission sense of the term. (See Part I of Table 13–1.) However, most of these practices had already been outlawed by the Federal Trade Commission or the Trade Practice Conferences. The prime purpose of the trade practice provisions of the codes was to raise prices, and many methods were used to this end. A few of the most common of these are listed in Part II of Table 13–1. Comments on some of them may be helpful.

It should be noted that to fix a minimum price was in effect to fix the actual price, if the minimum could be enforced, for in most cases the minimum price was established at a level above that at which individual buyers would be willing to sell if free to do so. Uniform methods of cost finding were usually coupled with prohibitions against selling below cost. In some cases, code authorities proclaimed standard costs of production of a product, usually without much research, and required members to use those rather than their own cost experience. Open price systems required each seller to file his price list and required notification before prices were changed. Some code authorities were empowered to reject filings of "unfair" prices. Specified discount and credit terms were used primarily to prevent price-cutting through larger discounts or longer or otherwise more favorable credit terms. Standardized specifications of products tended to lessen product differentiation and to facilitate the enforcement of uniform prices. Specified transportation terms were most widely used to assure that all sellers would quote identical delivered prices. Specifications concerning the making of bids and quotations also facilitated identical bidding.

Several codes also attempted to control output and production capacity. These provisions were of four general types.[9] (1) Limitations on the number of hours within a given period during which machines or plants might be operated. These were most common in codes applying to various branches of the textile industry, but they also appeared in codes for such industries as glass containers, canning and packing machinery, and cast iron soil pipe. (2) Establishment of maximum production quotas for individual members of an industry. This was used in some form for At-

[8] Florence Peterson, *Survey of Labor Economics*, Harper & Row, New York, 1947, p. 500.

[9] See Lyon *et al.*, *op. cit.*, pp. 623–650.

Table 13–1.   Some of the most common provisions in codes
relating to prices and trade practices

I. PROHIBITIONS	APPROXIMATE PERCENTAGE OF CODES CONTAINING THE PROHIBITIONS
Misrepresentation and deceptive advertising	72
Commercial bribery	71
Defamation of competitors	65
Interference with contracts	62
False marking or branding	49
False invoicing	48
Unwarranted threats of litigation	29
Espionage of competitors	24
Imitation of trademarks or designs	24
Discrimination in price, etc.	22
Sale of one product being in any way contingent upon the sale of another product	19
Style piracy	18

II. REQUIREMENTS	APPROXIMATE PERCENTAGE OF CODES CONTAINING THE VARIOUS REQUIREMENTS
Practices tending to affect minimum price	79
Uniform methods of cost finding	72
Open prices	59
Specified discount and credit terms	43
Specified standards for industry products or services	38
Specified transportation terms	27
Standard forms or terms of contracts	22
Specified forms or terms of, or conditions surrounding the making of, bids and quotations	18

Source: This is a modified version of tables appearing in Leverett S. Lyon, Paul T. Homan, Lewis L. Lorwin, George Terborgh, Charles L. Dearing, and Leon C. Marshall, *The National Recovery Administration: An Analysis and Appraisal*, The Brookings Institution, Washington, D.C., pp. 570–571.

lantic mackerel, lumber and timber, copper, iron and steel, glass containers, cement, and petroleum. (3) Restrictions on production capacity. These included limitations on construction of new plants, limitations on changing from one type of production to another, limitations on changing the location of plants, limitations on reopening plants not operated within a specified time prior to approval of the industry code, and limitations on the opening of new routes or extensions of those already existing. One or more of these types of restrictions were contained in codes relating to various branches of the textile industries, basic materials, and some chemicals. (4) Limitations on inventories. These were included in only a few codes—those for carpets and rugs, cement, petroleum, and carbon black. Their major purpose was to adjust production to sales and to prevent accumulation of large stocks that might lead to price cutting.

The preceding list, although far from complete, suggests the wide range of methods used under the codes. It also indicates why Schumpeter was justified in comparing them with German cartels. The various practices relative to prices were similar to those used by German price cartels to maintain and increase prices. And the restrictions on output, productive capacity, and inventories were similar to those of the German production cartels. However, the codes did not result from importation of a foreign ideology; they were almost an inevitable result of trade associations and relaxation of the antitrust laws.

Wholesale prices of all commodities other than farm products and foods rose by an average of 12 percent between June and December 1933 and thereafter tended to level off. There can be little doubt that the codes played an important role in raising these prices during the latter half of 1933. However, compliance with the price provisions of the codes was from the beginning considerably less than perfect, and it deteriorated with the passage of time. For this growing noncompiance there were many reasons. One was the complexity of the price structure within an industry. Huge numbers of individual prices were involved because of many different products, different types and sizes of each product, numerous classes of buyers, and so on. To detect price violations was very difficult, especially where there were many producers in the industry. Another reason for noncompliance was the profitability of violations for individual sellers, especially if their price-cutting was not matched by others. With large amounts of excess capacity, an increase in sales volume was much desired. Some felt justified in violating because they considered the price provisions of codes to be unfair. For example, uniform minimum prices were established for all brands of a tire of a given size and quality. Makers of lesser known brands complained that their inability to quote lower prices reduced unfairly their ability to compete with makers of the better known brands. Such complaints were widespread.

Another major reason for growing noncompliance was the inadequacy of enforcement procedures. Violators could be prosecuted in the courts, and some were. However, Roosevelt and NRA officials were very reluctant to take cases to court, and they strongly preferred to rely upon other methods of enforcement by the code authorities. This was only partly because of the philosophy of self-regulation by industry itself; it was also because of increasingly critical attitudes toward the NRA and rising doubts about its constitutionality.

By the spring of 1935, the NRA was in disarray and widely criticized. Labor disputes were widespread. Frictions had developed among members of many industries. Noncompliance was growing. "Monopolistic practices" under the codes were under attack. And the constitutionality of the NRA was being questioned in the courts. Many opposed extension of the NIRA beyond June 1935, and even some of those who favored extension admitted that reforms were necessary. The issue was settled on May 27, 1935, when the Supreme Court, in the Schechter Case, declared the NRA to be unconstitutional.[10] It was ruled invalid because the relation between industries covered by the codes and interstate commerce was remote, and also because the NIRA itself was an excessive delegation of legislative power without provision of adequate standards for its use.

Although the NRA was dead, some of its functions were transferred to other government agencies. The most important of these were in the field of labor and in the oil and bituminous coal industries.

■ LABOR LEGISLATION   The National Labor Relations Act was approved in May 1935. In effect, it extended the provisions of Section 7a of the NIRA; proscribed certain unfair labor practices by employers; and created a nonpartisan board, the National Labor Relations Board (NLRB), to administer the Act. The NLRB was given two principal classes of duties: (1) to aid in the free selection of employee representative agencies by holding elections or otherwise determining the choice of the majority of the workers in an appropriate bargaining unit; and (2) to prevent unfair labor practices by employers and to see that employers bargained in good faith.

The NLRB had a busy time during the next few years, partly because of important and controversial changes within the labor movement itself. It was at the 1935 convention of the American Federation of Labor (AFL) that John L. Lewis and the presidents of seven other AFL unions created the Committee for Industrial Organization "for the purpose of encouraging and promoting the organization of the unorganized workers in mass-production and other industries upon an industrial basis." This action, and the emphasis upon industrial unions, inevitably led to sharp conflicts with the remaining members of the AFL, which emphasized craft unions. The unions whose officers were on the Committee for Industrial Organization were expelled from the AFL in 1938. By this time, 32 national unions had become members of the Committee. Shortly thereafter, these unions, together with some state and local organizations, formed the Congress of Industrial Organizations (CIO).

These changes brought very large increases in union memberships. The CIO itself achieved remarkable success in unionizing the mass-producing industries, and it also stimulated the AFL to step up its own organizing efforts. The NLRB had to deal with a wide variety of labor problems: continued attempts of employers to prevent unionization or to influence labor elections; charges that employers were not bargaining in good faith; strikes, picketing, boycotts, and sit-ins; and large numbers of jurisdictional disputes

[10] Schechter v. United States 295 U. S. 495. Schechter had violated a provision of the poultry code by selling sick chickens.

among unions, many of them involving craft versus industrial unions. When Section 7a was inserted in the NIRA, few would have predicted that union membership would rise from only about 3 million to nearly 9 million by 1940.

While the National Labor Relations Act of 1935 continued and extended the provisions of Section 7a of the NIRA relating to unionization and collective bargaining, the Fair Labor Standards Act of 1938, approved on June 25 of that year, continued and markedly extended provisions formerly included in most of the codes of fair competition relating to child labor, maximum hours, and minimum wages. The Act applied to all workers engaged in interstate commerce or in the production of goods for interstate commerce, and its coverage was made very broad by an administrative ruling that an employee was covered if even a small part of the goods on which he worked was moved in interstate commerce or if the employer had reason to believe that any part of the product would be moved across state lines or would become a part of an article that would move in interstate commerce. A few industries, notably farming, were exempted.

The Act prohibited child labor, and it set maximum hours of work and minimum wages for other employees. In general, it provided that the maximum workweek should be 44 hours during the first year, 42 hours during the second year, and 40 hours after October 1940. Minimum wage rates were initially set at 25 cents an hour, but with provision for higher levels, not to exceed 40 cents, for individual industries. These were to be increased from year to year.

■ **PETROLEUM AND BITUMINOUS COAL**   The voiding of the NRA in May 1935 ended the codes of fair competition and the code authorities in the various industries and also terminated the exemption of activities of trade associations from the antitrust laws. However, the government sanctioned programs "to balance production and consumption" in two industries—oil and bituminous coal. In essence, oil production was to be kept in line with demands through cooperative efforts of the federal government and the oil-producing states. A federal agency estimated demands for petroleum, presumably at some "reasonable" price, and the oil-producing states, acting through an interstate compact, allocated production quotas.

After two Acts to raise and maintain the prices of bituminous coal had been declared unconstitutional, the Bituminous Coal Act of 1937 was enacted and later upheld by the courts. This legislation permitted price-fixing agreements in the industry, subject to approval by a federal agency.

■ **CONCLUSIONS**   The NRA and related government programs could be judged on various bases—as measures to promote general economic recovery, as temporary reform measures, and as means to long-term changes in the structure and behavior of the economy. However, Roosevelt stressed most strongly the objective of promoting recovery. Economists' evaluations of the NRA as a recovery device differ widely. For example, the verdict reached by economists at the Brookings Institution was largely adverse.

> In trying to raise the real purchasing power of the nation by boosting costs and prices, the NRA put the cart before the horse. Raising the prices either of labor or of goods is not the way to get a larger volume purchased. Instead the NRA should have sought the maximum enlargement of spending with the minimum increases in costs and prices, thus securing with the augmented expenditure the greatest gain in the number of units of labor and goods taken off the market. Thus increase in spending could have been sought by (1) the removal of the deterrents to the free and prompt utilization of the existing money of the country, and (2) monetary expansion. The NRA accomplished neither of these objectives.
>
> The conclusion indicated by this resumé is that the NRA on the whole retarded recovery. To what extent it was detrimental no one can say with much assurance. The situation has been too complex to warrant any definite conclusions from comparisons of recovery in this and other countries, or of this recovery and previous ones. The verdict must rest, we believe, largely on considerations of the sort outlined in the foregoing discussion. We do not feel justified in stating our judgment more definitely than to say that the retarding effect of the NRA has been substantial.[11]

On the other hand, Schumpeter concluded that on balance both the AAA and the NRA created conditions favorable to recovery, whatever may have been their other effects.

> We easily arrive . . . at the result that, on balance, both of them promoted recovery of the usual type without replacing it by a recovery that would have to be explained on different principles. They certainly paralyzed, and replaced by others, certain parts of the ordinary capitalist machine but, taking the national organism as a whole, in a way and to an extent which was corrective rather than constructive. . . .
>
> Whatever we may think about technique, details, aims professed, or arguments used, the success of the policy in removing a major obstacle from the road of recovery and in reviving shriveled tissues in the economic organism is beyond doubt. . . .
>
> Immediate results for the general business situation were . . . only the stronger because of the range over which this policy was indiscriminately applied—though very unequally enforced—and so were its psychological effects, which *in a situation of this kind* we have a right to consider an important factor—even Blue Eagles do count for something when, objective conditions for revival being given, it is broken morale that is the matter.[12]

Schumpeter's stress on the improvement of business morale cannot be dismissed lightly by anyone who witnessed the marked shift from almost hopeless despair to optimistic hopefulness that accompanied the NRA campaigns during the summer of 1933. It is difficult to believe that this did not increase the willingness of employers to offer more employment

[11] Lyon *et al.*, *op. cit.*, pp. 873–874.
[12] Schumpeter, *op. cit.*, Vol. II, pp. 988, 992, and 993.

and to increase output at that time. However, this fillip to business activity was probably only temporary, for optimism faded as business recovery proved to be slower than expected and as conflicts over the NRA codes developed within industries. After its initial stage, the NRA probably did impede recovery. Code provisions limiting plant use, production, and expansion of capacity could hardly have served to increase total employment and real income, and provisions raising wage rates, costs of production, and prices may well have tended to decrease both the amount of labor and the amount of output demanded. It was unrealistic to expect that the aggregate effects of efforts of individual industries to enhance their own profits by increasing their prices would be to raise total real output and employment.

Ironically, a major long-run effect of this experiment in industrial self-regulation was to encourage unionization of labor and greater federal intervention in labor markets. These changes might have occurred later even in the absence of the NRA, but the latter at least hastened the process. Most businessmen were so disillusioned by the NRA experience that the movement for "industrial self-government under government surveillance" lost its attractiveness.

14

Could It Happen Again?

As one studies the great depression that scourged the Western world during the 1930s, the question inevitably arises: Could it happen again? Could the economies of these nations again slide into such a deep depression and remain so depressed for a decade or more? The answer must surely be, "No, not unless the governments of those nations are plagued by some sort of political deadlock that prevents them from taking the actions that we now know can shorten a depression and induce recovery." Since the great depression, and partly because of that experience, almost revolutionary economic and political changes have occurred—changes in our state of economic understanding, in our attitudes toward the role and responsibility of government, in economic aspirations, and in institutional arrangements. These make it almost inconceivable that depressions will again be allowed to become so deep and so prolonged.

This is not to say that we have solved all the problems of maintaining economic stability and stable growth. Our continuing difficulties in preventing and containing inflation are well known. Another stock market crash of the magnitude of that in October and early November 1929 is by no means inconceivable. Neither regulation of the use of credit for purchasing or carrying securities nor regulation of trading practices by the Securities and Exchange Commission can prevent surges of optimism and pessimism that become reflected in fluctuations of stock prices. Anything that altered expectations downward could bring sharp declines of stock prices even if no stocks were held with borrowed money.

Moreover, four recessions within the first 25 years after World War II remind us that cyclical downturns of employment and output have not been eliminated, and suggest that they probably will not be. An economy so heavily dependent on production of durable capital goods and durable consumer goods is almost inevitably subject to cyclical pressures. Desired spending for private investment purposes does not grow at a steady rate, and consumer spendings for durable goods also fluctuate. In addition, monetary policies and government fiscal policies can themselves be sources of economic fluctuations, and on occasion have been. Our understanding of the magnitudes and timing of their effects is not yet so precise that we could avoid errors in their use, even if the monetary and fiscal authorities would follow the best of economic advice.

Thus, we have no reason to believe that recessions will not continue to occur, and but little basis for confidence that none in the future will be deeper or more prolonged than any of the four that occurred in the first quarter of a century following World War II. However, we do have reason to believe that we now have the knowledge, instruments, and national will to prevent recessions from developing into deep and prolonged depressions. A crucial element is the revolutionary change in our knowledge of macro-economics—of the determinants that influence the behavior of employment, output, and prices. In the early 1930s, it was still possible for not only businessmen and government officials but also many professional economists to believe that depressions were inevitable and inescapable results of maladjustments during the preceding period of prosperity, that recovery could come only after a process of "natural liquidation," and that "artificial measures" to increase spending would only worsen and prolong the depression. While such ideas prevailed, the formulation and adoption of rational and effective recovery policies were virtually impossible.

All such ideas and their implications for policy have been swept away by the Keynesian and post-Keynesian revolution in macroeconomics. Now not only professional economists but also large majorities of businessmen, government officials, and members of the public firmly believe that the appropriate and effective way to remedy underemployment of labor and other productive factors is to increase aggregate money demands for output. Moreover, they believe that effective instruments for inceasing aggregate demands for output are at hand and should be used under such circumstances—expansionary monetary policies, and expansionary government tax and expenditure policies. They may indeed differ on such things as the relative roles of the various instruments and on the magnitude and timing of actions, but not on basic principles.

This growth of economic understanding has swept away some of the rules of thumb that inhibited the adoption of rational and effective recovery measures in the 1930s. One casualty is the rule of an annually balanced budget regardless of general economic conditions. Even conservatives no longer blanch when a recession brings a deficit in the federal budget by decreasing federal revenues and increasing certain federal expenditures, such as unemployment benefits. Instead, they point approvingly to the "automatic stabilizer" or "automatic snubber" effects on the economy. Moreover, if depressive forces appear to be strong, they approve discretionary reductions of tax rates, or increases of government expenditures, or both, even though they recognize that larger government deficits will result. The growth of economic understanding has also had profound effects on monetary policy. Neither Federal Reserve officials nor others can now contend that the proper policy during recession or depression is one of "passive accommodation" and promotion of "orderly liquidation of money and credit." They now believe that under such circumstances a positive policy of monetary expansion can help restore aggregate demands for output, and Federal Reserve officials know that they will be roundly criticized if they fail to take such actions.

These new attitudes also make it far less likely that the use of monetary policy for recovery purposes will be prevented by the objective of defending the gold value of the dollar at any cost. Although many are still willing to countenance some loss of employment and output to prevent a depreciation of the dollar in exchange markets, it is almost inconceivable that such views would prevail in a period of serious depression.

Both the traumatic experience of the great depression and the change in our state of economic understanding have contributed to almost revolutionary changes in concepts concerning the responsibility of the federal government for promoting economic stability. In retrospect, it is not surprising that the Hoover Administration denied responsibility for maintaining economic stability and did so little to combat the depression. Neither Hoover nor others could believe that the depression would become such a catastrophe and last so long. Moreover, in the prevailing state of economic understanding, it was not believed by Hoover or by the public in general that the federal government could do anything effective to halt the depression and hasten recovery. Under such conditions it was politically feasible for a federal Administration to deny responsibility for promoting economic stability at high levels of employment. This is no longer true, now that the people have experienced the hardships of a major depression and have become convinced that government can in fact make major contributions to the promotion of stability.

One evidence of this is the Employment Act of 1946, in which the government explicitly assumed such a responsibility. However, this Act is important primarily for its symbolism. More to the point are the nature of the political consensus and the state of political realities. No candidate who explicitly rejected such responsibilities could achieve election, and no Administration that failed to take positive actions to combat a significant recession could long remain in power. Now it is even politically dangerous for an Administration to run the risk of decreasing even temporarily the rate of economic growth and of raising even slightly the rate of unemployment in order to combat inflation.

Thus, the revolutionary change in our state of economic understanding and the popular consensus that government can and must promote economic stability are essential bases for hopes that recurrence of deep and prolonged depressions such as that of the 1930s can be prevented. However, partly because of these developments and partly for other reasons, there have occurred changes in some institutional arrangements that enhance our power to combat depressions. One has been the great increase in the scope of the economic activities of the federal government, and in the sizes of its receipts and expenditures relative to the nation's GNP. We noted earlier that in 1929, total federal receipts were equal to only 3.6 percent and total federal expenditures were equal to only 2.5 percent of that year's GNP. These low levels of federal taxes and expenditures militated against the potential effectiveness of fiscal policy as an instrument for combating depression. For one thing, the low levels of effective marginal tax rates meant that "automatic stabilizer effects" were very weak. Most of every decrease in national money income was reflected in decreased private incomes after taxes rather than in decreased revenues of the federal government. Also, the low level of federal taxes and spending meant that very large percentage changes would have been required to exert a substantial impact on aggregate demand. For example, a complete abolition of federal taxes would have added only small amounts to private incomes after taxes, and very large percentage increases of federal expenditures would have been required to offset any substantial part of the decline of private investment spending.

By the late 1960s, the situation had changed markedly, with both federal receipts and total federal expenditures having reached levels equal to nearly 25 percent of GNP. The power of fiscal policy to stabilize or destabilize the economy has been greatly enhanced. The higher marginal tax rates have increased the responsiveness of federal tax yields to changes in national income and strengthened automatic stabilizer effects. Also, even small percentage reductions of effective tax rates can add significantly to private incomes after taxes, and comparably small percentage increases of federal expenditures can directly increase significantly both private incomes and demands for output. This ability to secure strong direct effects from relatively small percentage changes in tax rates and government expenditures has enhanced the political feasibility of stabilizing fiscal actions.

Resistance to cumulative depression has also been increased by measures to maintain incomes. Prior to 1936, there was no governmental unemployment insurance program, and only a handful of employees were covered by private plans. Moreover, many of those who became unemployed received no relief from government, and relief payments were generally very small relative to wages lost. Now a large majority of workers are covered by unemployment insurance programs that provide benefits equal to one-third to one-half of wages lost. Also, there is reason to believe that in a serious depression, benefits would be extended beyond the normal period, and that the unemployed not covered by insurance would receive relief far more generous than that in the early 1930s.

The ability of financial institutions to withstand depression has also been enhanced. In the early 1930s, there was no program to insure the liabilities of financial intermediaries. Now, governmental institutions insure the first $15,000 of each account at virtually all commercial banks and most savings and loan associations .There are now also federal programs to insure home mortgages and some other types of private debts. In the early 1930s, there were only two types of federally sponsored institutions—the Federal Intermediate Credit Banks and the Federal Reserve Banks—to lend to private financial intermediaries, and they lent on only a narrow range of assets and to only a fraction of the intermediaries. Now the Home Loan Bank System has been added to lend on urban mortgages, and the Federal Reserve now lends on a wider range of assets. The system needs to be further strengthened by providing access to some "lender of last resort" for every type of financial intermediary. This would probably be done if a serious depression should recur.

Although such measures to decrease the vulnerability of financial institutions are useful, by far the most effective method of protecting financial institutions and the economy as a whole is to employ monetary and fiscal policies to prevent the serious decline of aggregate demands that would generate financial strains.

Thus, the great depression, tragic as it was, left some favorable heritages. It stimulated studies that have greatly increased our understanding of the determinants of the behavior of output and employment and of the instruments that can to be used to regulate—although not yet control precisely—the behavior of aggregate demands. It created a determination that "it must not happen again." And it created new concepts of government responsibility, new economic aspirations, and a new orientation of political forces that make it feasible to prevent deep and prolonged depressions. Of course, it is not inevitable that we shall in fact achieve an almost continuous state of high employment and output. New generations, ignorant of the tragedies of a great depression, may fail to act in time.

Selected Bibliography

I. GENERAL

Bird, Caroline, *The Invisible Scar*, McKay, New York, 1966.

Friedman, Milton, and Schwartz, Anna J., *The Great Contraction, 1929–1933*, Princeton University Press, Princeton, N. J., 1965.

Hoover, Herbert C., *Memoirs: The Great Depression, 1929–1941*, Vol. 3, Macmillan, New York, 1952.

Mitchell, Broadus, *The Depression Decade: From New Era Through the New Deal, 1929–1941*, Holt, Rinehart and Winston, New York, 1947.

Romasco, Albert V., *The Poverty of Abundance; Hoover, the Nation, the Depression*, Oxford University Press, New York, 1965.

Roosevelt, Franklin D., *The Public Papers and Addresses of Franklin D. Roosevelt*, Vols. 1–7, Random House, New York.

Schlesinger, Arthur M., Jr., *The Age of Roosevelt*, 3 vols., Houghton Mifflin, Boston.

Schumpeter, Joseph A., *Business Cycles*, 2 vols., McGraw-Hill, New York, 1939.

Shannon, David A., *The Great Depression*, Prentice-Hall, Englewood Cliffs, N. J., 1960.

U. S. President's Research Committee on Social Trends, *Recent Social Trends in the United States*, 2 vols., McGraw-Hill, New York, 1933.

Wecter, Dixon, *The Age of the Great Depression, 1929–1941*, Macmillan, New York, 1948.

II. UNEMPLOYMENT AND RELIEF

Bakke, E. Wight, *The Unemployed Worker*, Yale University Press, New Haven, Conn., 1940.

Brown, Josephine Chapin, *Public Relief, 1929–1939*, Holt, Rinehart and Winston, New York, 1940.

Burns, Arthur E., and Williams, Edward A., *Federal Work Security and Relief Programs*, WPA Research Monograph No. 24, U. S. Government Printing Office, Washington, D. C., 1941.

Charles, Searle F., *Minister of Relief: Harry Hopkins and the Depression*, Syracuse University Press, Syracuse, N. Y., 1963.

Hopkins, Harry, *Spending to Save*, Norton, New York, 1936.

Howard, Donald S., *The WPA and Federal Relief Policy*, Russell Sage Foundation, New York, 1943.

Ickes, Harold L., *Back to Work; the Story of the PWA*, Macmillan, New York, 1935.

Meriam, Lewis, *Relief and Social Security*, The Brookings Institution, Washington, D. C., 1946.

National Youth Administration, *Final Report of the NYA, Fiscal Years 1936–1943*, Washington, D. C., 1943.

Salmond, John A., *The Civilian Conservation Corps, 1933–1942: A New Deal Case Study*, Duke University Press, Durham, N. C., 1967.

Works Progress Administration, *Analysis of Civil Works Program Statistics*, Washington, D. C., 1939.

Works Progress Administration, *Final Report on the WPA Program*, Washington, D. C., 1946.

Works Progress Administration, *Final Statistical Report of the FERA*, Washington, D. C., 1942.

III. AGRICULTURE AND AGRICULTURAL POLICIES

Benedict, Murray R., *Farm Policies in the United States, 1790–1950*, The Twentieth Century Fund, New York, 1953.

Benedict, Murray R., and Steve, Oscar C., *The Agricultural Commodity Programs: Two Decades of Experience*, The Twentieth Century Fund, New York, 1956.

Blaisdell, Donald C., *Government and Agriculture; the Growth of Federal Farm Aid*, Holt, Rinehart and Winston, New York, 1940.

Fite, Gilbert C., *American Agriculture and Farm Policy Since 1900*, Macmillan, New York, 1964.

Kirkendall, Richard S., *Social Scientists and Farm Policies in the Age of Roosevelt*, University of Missouri Press, Columbia, Mo., 1966.

Martin, Robert F., *Income in Agriculture, 1929–1935*, National Industrial Conference Board, New York, 1936.

Nourse, Edwin G., Davis, Joseph S., and Black, John D., *Three Years of the Agricultural Adjustment Administration*, The Brookings Institution, Washington, D. C., 1937.

Rau, Allan, *Agricultural Policy and Trade Liberalization in the United States, 1934–1956*, Libraire Ninard, Paris, 1957.

Schmidt, Carl T., *American Farmers in the World Crisis*, Oxford University Press, New York, 1941.

IV. DEBTS AND FINANCIAL REHABILITATION

Harris, C. Lowell, *History and Policies of the Home Owner's Loan Corporation*, National Bureau of Economic Research, New York, 1951.

Jones, Jesse H., *Fifty Billion Dollars; My Thirteeen Years with the RFC (1932–1945)*, Macmillan, New York, 1951.

Kimmel, Lewis H., *The Availability of Bank Credit, 1933–1938*, National Industrial Conference Board, New York, 1939.

The Twentieth Century Fund, *Debts and Recovery, 1929–1937*, The Twentieth Century Fund, New York, 1938.

Upham, Cyril B., and Lamke, Edwin, *Closed and Distressed Banks; A Study in Public Administration*, The Brookings Institution, Washington, D. C., 1934.

V. MONETARY AND FISCAL POLICIES

Chandler, Lester V., *American Monetary Policies, 1928–1941*, Harper & Row, New York.

Everett, Allan S., *Henry Morgenthau, The New Deal and Silver; A Story of Pressure Politics*, Kings Brown, New York, 1950.

Friedman, Milton, and Schwartz, Anna J., *A Monetary History of the United States, 1867–1960*, Princeton University Press, Princeton, N. J., 1963.

Hardy, Charles O., *Credit Policies of the Federal Reserve System*, The Brookings Institution, Washington, D. C., 1932.

Johnson, G. Griffith, *The Treasury and Monetary Policy, 1932–1938*, Harvard University Press, Cambridge, Mass., 1939.

Kimmel, Lewis H., *Federal Budget and Fiscal Policy, 1789–1958*, The Brookings Institution, Washington, D. C., 1959.

Maxwell, James A., *Fiscal Policy*, Holt, Rinehart and Winston, New York, 1955.

Nurkse, Ragnar, *International Currency Experience: Lessons of the Inter-War Period*, League of Nations, 1944.

Reeve, Joseph E., *Monetary Reform Movements: A Survey of Recent Plans and Panaceas*, American Council on Public Affairs, Washington, D. C., 1943.

Roose, Kenneth D., *The Economics of Recession and Revival: An Interpretation of 1937–38*, Yale University Press, New Haven, Conn., 1954.

Villard, Henry H., *Deficit Spending and the National Income*, Farrar & Rinehart, New York, 1941.

VI. THE NATIONAL RECOVERY ADMINISTRATION AND RELATED MEASURES

Brooks, Robert R. R., *When Labor Organizes*, Yale University Press, New Haven, Conn., 1937.

Galenson, Walter, *The CIO Challenge to the AFL; A History of the American Labor Movement, 1935–1941*, Harvard University Press, Cambridge, Mass., 1960.

Johnson, Hugh S., *The Blue Eagle from Egg to Earth*, Doubleday, Garden City, L. I., N. Y., 1935.

Lyon, Leverett S., Homan, Paul T., Lorwin, Lewis L., Terborgh, George, Dearing, Charles L., and Marshall, Leon C., *The National Recovery Administration: An Analysis and Appraisal*, The Brookings Institution, Washington, D. C., 1935.

Peterson, Florence, *Survey of Labor Economics*, Harper & Row, New York, 1947.

Richberg, Donald R., *The Rainbow*, Doubleday, Garden City, L. I., N. Y., 1936.

Roos, Charles F., *NRA Economic Planning*, Principia Press, Bloomington, Ind., 1937.

Stein, Emanuel, *et al.*, *Labor and the New Deal*, Appleton-Century-Crofts, New York, 1934.

Sternsher, Bernard, *Rexford Tugwell and the New Deal*, Rutgers University Press, New Brunswick, N. J., 1964.

Whitney, Simon N., *Trade Associations and Industrial Control*, Central Book Co., New York, 1934.

Wilcox, Clair, *Public Policies Toward Business*, Richard D. Irwin, Homewood, Ill., 1955.

Index

251

Financial system (*cont.*)
  in New Deal, 143–160
    See also Banks; Monetary and
      fiscal policies
Fiscal policies, *see* Monetary and fiscal
    policies
Foreign exchange, *see* Exchange rates;
    Gold-exchange system
Foreign investment, net, 133
Foreign loans, 102, 133
Foreign securities, 98–100
Franc, value of, 96, 166, 168
France, gold and exchange reserves,
    96–97
  in international crisis, 103–104, 118
Frazier-Lemke Act, 151 n.
Frazier-Lemke Amendment, National
    Bankruptcy Act, 65

Germany, depression in, 11, 91
  events leading to World War II, 171
  gold standard, 94
  gold standard abandoned, 12, 103
  in international finance, 99
Glass, Carter, 70, 90, 159
Glass-Steagall Act, 89–90, 104–105
GNP, *see* Gross national product
Gold, collateral for Federal Reserve notes,
    118
  debts, gold clauses in, 166
  distribution of, 96–97
  dollar redeemability in, 135
  dollar value, 161, 163–168
  exports of, 166
  "free," scarcity of, 118
  in international crisis, 103–105, 117
  in international finance, 99, 106–107,
    165
  as money, 94, 135–136
    coinage ended, 166–167
  New Deal policies, 164–168
  price of, 167–168
  purchases of, 167, 170–171
  stocks, 1932–1941, 161–162
Gold certificates, 166–167, 175
Gold-exchange system, 94–96, 104, 118
Gold Reserve Act, 164, 167, 174
Gold reserves, 94–97
  sterilization of, 178, 181
    See also Federal Reserve System,
      reserves
Gold standard, 12, 93–94, 96–97, 108–
    109
  abandoned, 12, 102–108, 168, 171
  criticism of, 135

Government, responsibility of, 111–112,
    243–244
Government expenditures, 121–125
  for defense, 130–131, 138
  in GNP, 1929–1933, 21–22, 121–123,
    243–244
    1960s, 244
  local, 121–122, 125, 137–139
  net income-creating, 140
  in New Deal, 136–141
  in 1920, for capital goods, 16
  1929–1932, 121–122, 124–125
  1933–1941, 137–141
  state, 49–50, 121–122, 125, 137–139
Grange, 218
Great Britain, depression in, 91
  gold and exchange reserves, 94–97
  gold standard, 94
  gold standard abandoned, 12, 103–104
  in international crisis, 103–104
  in international finance, 97
  monetary stabilization, 165
  pound, *see* Pound
Gross national income, decrease, 7–9
Gross national product (GNP), definition
    of, 3
  exports and imports in, 100–101
  full-employment level, 138
  government receipts and expenditures
    in, 21–22, 121–123, 243–244
  lost output, 4–5
  money supply and, 184–185
  money value of, and prices, 6–9, 22–24
  potential, 4–5, 129 n., 131
  real, in 1920s, 15
    1929–1933, 20–22
    1929–1941, 2–5
    1932–1941, 128–132
    in World War II, 131–132
Gross private domestic investment,
    1929–1933, 20–22
  1932–1941, 131–132

Harrison, George L., 172–173
Haugen, Gilbert N., 213
Home mortgages, *see* Mortgages
Home Owners Loan Corporation, 148,
    150, 153–155
Hoosac Mills Case, 219
Hoover, Herbert, and depression, 92–93,
    243
  in election of 1932, 133
  Emergency Relief and Reconstruction
    Act signed, 50
  farm program, 211, 222

70 71 72 73 7 6 5 4 3 2 1